TRANSCENDENCE AND HISTORY

ERIC VOEGELIN INSTITUTE SERIES
IN POLITICAL PHILOSOPHY

Other Books in the Series

America and the Political Philosophy of Common Sense
Scott Philip Segrest

A Government of Laws: Political Theory, Religion, and the American Founding
Ellis Sandoz

Hans Jonas: The Integrity of Thinking
David J. Levy

Lonergan and the Philosophy of Historical Existence
Thomas J. McPartland

The Narrow Path of Freedom and Other Essays
Eugene Davidson

Voegelinian Readings of Modern Literature
Edited by Charles R. Embry

TRANSCENDENCE AND HISTORY

THE SEARCH FOR ULTIMACY FROM ANCIENT SOCIETIES TO POSTMODERNITY

Glenn Hughes

UNIVERSITY OF MISSOURI PRESS
COLUMBIA

University of Missouri Press, Columbia, Missouri 65211
Printed and bound in the United States of America

First paperback printing, 2020

Library of Congress Cataloging-in-Publication Data

Hughes, Glenn, 1951–
Transcendence and history : the search for ultimacy from ancient societies to postmodernity / Glenn Hughes.
p. cm. — (Eric Voegelin Institute series in political philosophy)
Includes bibliographical references and index.
ISBN 978-0-8262-1476-8 (hardcover : alk. paper)
ISBN 978-0-8262-2219-0 (paperback : alk. paper)
1. Transcendence (Philosophy)—History. 2. Voegelin, Eric, 1901– 3. Lonergan, Bernard J. F. I. Title. II. Series.
BD362 .H84 2003
111'.6—dc21 2003002537

This paper meets the requirements of the
American National Standard for Permanence of Paper
for Printed Library Materials, Z39.48, 1984.

Designer: Kristie Lee
Typefaces: Minion and Cancellaresca

For permissions, see page 247.

The University of Missouri Press offers its grateful acknowledgment for a generous contribution from the Eric Voegelin Institute in support of the publication of this volume.

This book is dedicated to my father

GLENN HUGHES

playwright, theatrical director, scholar, professor, poet

and to my mother

CLETA HUGHES

who taught me to love what is excellent

This World is not Conclusion.
A Species stands beyond —
Invisible, as Music —
But positive, as Sound —
It beckons, and it baffles —
Philosophy — don't know —
And through a Riddle, at the last —
Sagacity, must go —

—Emily Dickinson

Contents

Acknowledgments

IN HIS PREFACE to *Travels with a Donkey,* Robert Louis Stevenson wrote that "we are all travellers in what John Bunyan calls the wilderness of this world . . . and the best that we find in our travels is an honest friend. . . . They are the end and the reward of life. They keep us worthy of ourselves. . . . Of what shall a man be proud, if he is not proud of his friends?"

Many friends have inspired and assisted me in writing this book. Most marvelous has been the dedicated involvement and enthusiastic support of Pat Brown, who has considered and responded to virtually every idea in it, and improved it at each step of the way. Tom McPartland, the truest of partners in philosophical eros, has been a brilliant guide through the complexities of the thought of Bernard Lonergan and Eric Voegelin. I am happy to thank Paul Caringella for his delightful companionship, advice, and encouragement over many years. David Levy has been a constant source of critical insight and, more important, of confidence in my ability to grapple with such complexities. The wonderful Mary Pope Osborne has inspired me again and again to keep writing.

I have had the excellent fortune to have been able to discuss at length most of the topics in this book with my friend Sebastian Moore, O.S.B., in whose honor the essay that became Chapter 2 was first written. I hope that his open-mindedness and spiritual passion are reflected in these pages. Fred Lawrence, whose invitations to give papers at the Boston College Lonergan Workshop resulted in two of these chapters, has been a gracious friend and collaborator as well as the most inspiring and challenging of teachers. I have benefited greatly from the many opportunities to engage the work of Eric Voegelin provided by Ellis Sandoz, director of the Eric Voegelin Institute at Louisiana State

University, who has been an unfailing source of support in my professional endeavors.

A number of friends have contributed to this work as partners in dialogue, thoughtful readers or listeners, and, at times, providers of solace. They include Paul Kidder and Paulette Kidder, who have patiently accompanied me through all stages of enthusiasm and travail; Julian Bull, whose honest intellect and humor, and intensity of spirit, light the way; Ken Whelan, intellectual gadfly and steadfast friend; and my spiritual brother, David Schuldberg, from whom I take inspiration in startling measure and before whom I gratefully bow.

Chapters or passages have benefited from the expert advice and scholarship of various friends and colleagues. Bob McMahon has been extremely gracious in reading sections and closely commenting upon them. Gene Webb has been the source, over many conversations, of insights and inspiration pertaining to a wide spectrum of the issues addressed here. Michael Franz, fellow Voegelin scholar, was responsible for my writing the material that became Chapters 3 and 4, the germ of the project, for which I am most appreciative. The section on Ernest Becker in Chapter 8 originated in lectures given for the Ernest Becker Foundation at the kind and generous invitation of its director, Neil Elgee. The analysis of Ezra Pound's *Cantos* came about due to an invitation from Jack Trotter. Others providing scholarly assistance include Marie Baird, Tom Bolin, Jim Sauer, Todd Breyfogle, David Walsh, and Steve Shankman.

Finally, there are those whose friendship or assistance nourished the writing of this book in ways less easy to pinpoint, but who nevertheless have been instrumental in its development and completion. They include the ever gracious Robert B. Heilman; Faith Smith; Carl Adler; Brian St. John; Geoff Price; Barry Cooper; Bill Thompson; Mike Morrissey; Sheldon Solomon; Walt Crowley; and my dear friend, poet of the Ish River country, Robert Sund (1929–2001).

Grateful acknowledgment is made to the Earhart Foundation for a substantial grant that made the planning and writing of this book possible, and to the patience of its administrators. I would also like to express especial gratitude to the Ernest Becker Foundation, and to its founder Neil Elgee, for a generous grant in the early going, as well as for moral support.

St. Mary's University has been steadfast and generous in providing me with resources to attend crucial conferences and workshops that contributed to the development of the material in this book, including support during the sabbatical year in which it was begun.

Finally, I would like to express gratitude to Beverly Jarrett, director and editor in chief of the University of Missouri Press, for her longtime and unwavering devotion to the cause; to Jane Lago and Karen Renner of the University of Missouri Press for their kindness and expert assistance; and to Annette Wenda for her fine copyediting.

TRANSCENDENCE AND HISTORY

Introduction

MUCH IN contemporary culture, both popular and intellectual, pushes us to conclude that the physical and temporal universe is the whole of reality. All of the major world religious and wisdom traditions are based, of course, on precisely the opposite conviction: that ultimate reality transcends the finite universe; that to be human is to be implicated in this divine transcendence; that we are always implicitly, and can be explicitly, conscious of this transcendent reality; and that human fulfillment entails the willing embrace and development of our relationship to the eternal and imperishable ground of existence. The Chinese Tao and the Brahman of the Hindu Upanishads are ultimates beyond the world of duality and direct human understanding. So is the Creator-God of Judaism, Christianity, and Islam. Among philosophers, transcendent reality is acknowledged and affirmed in the writings of Confucius, Plato, Aristotle, Plotinus, Shankara, Aquinas, Maimonides, Descartes, Pascal, Locke, Rousseau, Kant, Hegel, Emerson, Kierkegaard, and Jaspers. A truth of transcendent being is an elementary assumption of Newton, Goethe, Jefferson, Thoreau, Tolstoy, Einstein, Gandhi, and Martin Luther King Jr. Yet, in most academic and intellectual circles today, and among many of the cultured and educated, notions of transcendence are dismissed as naive or retrograde, and the avowal of transcendent truth regarded as an implicit disavowal of critical reason and intellectual progress.

Three causes of this widespread modern attitude toward transcendence are easily identified. First, it is a response to the relentless historical recurrence of wars and outrages arising from religious intolerance, based on competing claims to exclusive possession of an absolute sacred truth about a transcendent ultimate meaning and human destiny. Second, it is a consequence of the impact of modern science on popular imagination, and the widespread embrace of the assumption that the empirical method of the natural sciences is the only trustworthy and rational basis for determining if something is real or if a proposition is true. And third, it reflects the growth of historical sensitivity in the modern era, which brings with it the suspicion that, as human understanding is always immersed in a historically particular situation, we can only pretend to speak of a truth that transcends those limitations. It might be useful to look briefly at each of these points.

The rejection of transcendence in contemporary images of reality is partly a reaction to religious absolutism, to claims of privileged access to a divine and universal set of truths, claims that lend themselves to self-aggrandizement through oppression, dehumanization, and even slaughter of those without "the true faith." Who would dispute the reasonableness of the charge? Of all the distortions to which the affirmation of transcendent reality is prone, by far the most harmful is the assumption that, through embracing a particular set of religious doctrines, one has thereby become possessor and guardian of the exclusive and absolute truth about the human situation. The uncertainties and fragility of human life make it tempting to find comfort in such an assumption, but from it flows a vast history of religious persecution, conquest, and destruction in the supposed service of holy and righteous ends. This is a history that mocks, of course, the central teachings in all major religions about the limits of human wisdom and the paramount importance of love and compassion. Nevertheless,

> thus it has been in the history of religions. The faithful among the higher religions have opposed one another again and again, indeed if not engaging in bloody persecution, then despising the followers of other religions as deplorably ignorant persons who must be led with all possible speed to the true church and religion. How many human beings have become the victims of religious wars, how frequent the oppression of other religious consciences, how numerous are the martyrdoms suffered in courageous confession of individual faith![1]

Such is one of the legacies of the claim that there is a transcendent absolute and that we can know of it: the supposition that its truths can be the

1. Friedrich Heiler, "The History of Religions as a Preparation for the Co-operation of Religions," 132–33.

unambiguous and exclusive possession of a community or a religious institution, and that this possession warrants intolerance and brutality toward others.

Our sensitivity to religious arrogance and its consequences is essentially, if not exclusively, modern. We learned it from our seventeenth- and eighteenth-century forebears, especially the Enlightenment thinkers for whom religious warfare, fought against a backdrop of ecclesiastical wealth, power, and privilege, was the incontestably supreme manifestation of minds shrouded in darkness. For Voltaire, for Hume, for Kant, the spread of "enlightenment" meant above all freedom from superstition guiding action in thrall to religious authority. They aimed, by subjecting the superstitions and mystifications embedded in religious tradition to rational analysis and critique, to destroy the very roots of religious intolerance and fanaticism, along with those of political absolutism based on ideas of divine right. Progress in society, they argued, would follow to the degree in which blind belief in authority —religious and otherwise—was replaced by the use of critical and self-reliant reason, a conviction famously summarized in Kant's motto of "the spirit of enlightenment": *sapere aude!* (have courage to use your own reason!). And though Enlightenment critique was directed toward all aspects of personal and social life, one can understand why religion was the focus of its most passionate energies. The champions of progress agreed that the most malign interference with free, self-governing thought is that which claims divine authority and threatens with gestures of eternity.

The Enlightenment, it has often been said, introduced a new faith: faith in the complete self-sufficiency of human reason. However, we should remember that, at first, this confidence in human reason was not considered to be antagonistic to every and all religious sentiment or conviction. Its target was what is *irrational* in religion, such as awed acceptance of rites and practices amounting to belief in magic, passionate embrace of fantastical dogmas, and superstitious belief in miracles or the power of relics. Thinkers such as Voltaire trusted that a critical purging of the irrational elements in religion would produce a sound and rational reverence for divine being, a confidence echoed in the title of Kant's late book, *Religion within the Limits of Reason Alone* (1794). By the time of its appearance, though, Kant's book was no longer in the progressive mainstream of European thought. The momentum of critique had brought most influential thinkers of the later "radical" Enlightenment—such as Holbach, La Mettrie, Condillac, and Condorcet—to a total rejection of religion, accompanied by vigorous promotion of outlooks such as naturalism, atheism, or materialism. For these thinkers—and in this they were far more representative than Voltaire of the intellectual tendencies of the next two centuries—the rejection of religious superstition and mystery entailed a rejection of the very notions of divinity and transcendence. And this position, with its complete repudiation of the divine or supernatural, required that the realm of "nature"—the finite universe, wholly accessible (in principle) to imaginative exploration and scientific understanding—be accepted as the sole reality and complete context of human origins, life, thought, and destiny.

Thus the late Enlightenment (and the Romantic movement that was born of it) completed the critique of religion by eclipsing transcendence altogether and conferring ultimacy on the universe of space and time. The horizon of modernity, one might say, was established through the absolutization of immanence (nontranscendent reality). This transformation of the finite universe into a completeness of reality designated as "Nature" necessarily brought with it a new interpretation of human nature to replace the Christian anthropology that had dominated European thought for more than a millennium. Briefly summarized, the new anthropological vision was shaped around these assertions and assumptions: (1) natural human reason can accurately explain the physical world, as modern science has demonstrated; there is no reason to assume that it will not one day solve, in addition to the social and political problems that face humanity, all of the basic "mysteries" of the universe; (2) human worth and dignity are not dependent on either divine benevolence or a transcendent destiny; rather, worldly existence is its own worthy and ultimate purpose, and the pursuit of perfected happiness in this world is a noble goal; (3) human will and reason are not implicated in a *mysterium iniquitatis,* to which transcendent meaning or redemption holds the key; persons are born with a natural desire, and under proper conditions the potential, to fulfill the human good within worldly existence alone; and (4) the steady improvement of the human condition and its accompanying increase of happiness are inevitable outcomes of an increasingly effective secular rationality, a rationality freed from the idea that history is oriented to a transcendent meaning or purpose.

In this modern anthropological vision, humanly caused evils are finally susceptible to complete rational explanation and gradual correction. Once the roots of such evils are understood to lie, not in the impossibility of actualizing in soul or society the perfections that belong to transcendence, but in the imperfect arrangements and influences of society, or a person's failure to respect the rational moral law present in his or her own consciousness, they can be imagined to be eradicable given sufficient time, analysis, education, and reforming effort. Of course, there are also natural evils, such as disease and early death, and the destruction and misery brought on by natural calamities such as famines, earthquakes, and floods. Nonetheless, these, too, appear to be more and more subject to human control or containment through advances in natural science and technological creativity. And this point brings us to a second cause of modern resistance to notions of transcendence, namely, the impact of modern science.

Enlightenment confidence in reason was inspired in part by the tremendous successes of the modern mathematical sciences during the sixteenth, seventeenth, and eighteenth centuries. During this time, through the discoveries and writings of such thinkers as Copernicus and Galileo, Descartes and Newton, Huygens and Buffon, modern science had revealed the physical world to be knowable as an integration of structures and relations governed by laws that can be clearly understood and expressed through careful observation and exact mathematical measurement. One consequence of these discoveries was an accelerating development of technological inventions made possible by scientific prediction and control. Another, no less significant, consequence was a hugely enhanced conception of the mind's investigative and creative powers. The combined result of these two developments was a growing conviction that human beings would before long become, in Descartes's famous phrase, the "masters and possessors of nature" through scientific knowledge and technological innovation. Furthermore, this conviction served to inculcate the notion, soon installed as an unquestioned truth among many of the educated, that the method of the modern natural sciences should be regarded as the very paradigm of reason and a universal standard of rational cogency. Because widespread embrace of this conviction has profoundly conditioned cultural and intellectual life in the past two centuries, a few further comments on its impact are in order.

Once the modern natural sciences had revealed their stunning explanatory power, it was inevitable that the method of analysis on which they were based would come to be regarded as an exemplary model of how to discover and verify the real and the true. However, the proper objects of this method are exclusively phenomena approached through sensory observation, and what gives the natural sciences their precision, predictability, and control is exact measurement provided by mathematics in the analysis of structures and regularities in the physical universe. Such a mathematics-based method is applicable and successful because physical phenomena—material objects, their measurable relations to each other, their movements, their tendencies of development—are quantifiable. How, though, may this method be applied, or in what way is it relevant, to nonphysical, nonquantifiable realities? How can it be used to investigate the nature of human thought and freedom, or the institutional and cultural meanings human beings create? Are the dazzling achievements of the modern natural sciences reproducible in other areas of human knowing? Modernity has responded to these questions in different ways, but in general has tended to insist on the connection between sense-based measurement and genuine knowledge. Two principal lines of thinking branch out from this insistence.

One line of thinking is to accept the quantifying method of the natural sciences as the established standard of proof and validity, and to regard other areas of inquiry as "scientific" only to the degree that their methods approximate those of the natural sciences. From this tendency derives the attitude prevalent in contemporary social science that serious conclusions must be based on the "objectivity" of measurement. Today's "experimental" psychologists, for example, who embrace this assumption, tend to treat the findings of "humanistic" psychologists (such as Freud, Jung, Maslow, Erikson, Rogers, Alice Miller, and Ernest Becker) with indifference or suspicion, holding to the "hard scientific" line that phenomena are knowable only to the degree that they can be observed and explained through precise measurement. In this view it is conceded that there may well be nonphysical reality, which can be called mind or soul or spirit, but because it cannot be examined by means of sensory observation or quantitatively measured, it is not directly or unambiguously knowable. Beyond this, knowledge of divinity or transcendence is simply impossible, because God, even if real, is by definition beyond observational verification.

The second, more aggressive line of thinking is not only to insist on the dependence of genuine knowledge on quantification-based methods, but also to interpret this relation more narrowly to mean that nothing is real that is not accessible to sense-based observation and verification. This is the attitude that manifests itself in the many varieties of materialism. One finds it in the scientistic assertion that consciousness is only an epiphenomenon of material processes, in the denial of human freedom by hard determinists, and, of course, in the dismissal of transcendent reality as mere superstition.

By the end of the eighteenth century, it is true, there had broken forth a cultural reaction against the proliferation of materialist visions of omnicompetent comprehension of and rational control over human living, a movement that became known as Romanticism. Before the century was out, the Romantic rebellion was insisting on the priority of feeling, beauty, art, and immediate experience over dry facts and impersonal analysis, on the supreme importance to human living of "irrational" experiences (profound emotion and apprehensions of the sublime in art and nature). Its tendency was the opposite of antireligious. It had little more use, though, than did enlightened scoffers at religion for traditional religious authority and its doctrines, dogmas, and carefully prescribed rituals. Romanticism did exalt experiences of the sacred and mysterious, but its explanation of those experiences pointed not to transcendence but to Nature: to the palpable, awe-inspiring world of natural beauty and grandeur that prompts in us mystic sentiment and inarticulate feelings of communion. For the Romantics, too, Nature was all in all. Their defense of the sublime and the holy rested on the beauty and majesty of the natural world and the value of the inner world of personal feeling, and so they too played their part in the absolutization of immanence. Indeed, the Romantic answer to the question of where we must turn to discover essential reality—the ultimate ground of consciousness, the source of meaning and beauty—was the same answer as that of Enlightenment empiricists and materialists: to the "depths" of Nature. Just as for materialists a complete explanation of human experience is to be found in a thorough understanding of underlying organizations of matter, the Romantic view imagines ultimate meaning in terms of a profound union with the deep and mysterious heart of Nature. This shared symbolism of the "depths" of Nature, though it is, of course, only a metaphor, constitutes an imaginal rejection of any account of the human situation that would ground consciousness in a reality radically "beyond" matter or Nature. Considered simply as a metaphor, of course, the symbolism of the "depths" is fully compatible with the fact of transcendent reality. Still, as the chosen modern alternative to traditional religious and philosophical symbols of ultimacy, it has since the eighteenth century effectively served to obscure, and by obscuring to deny, the distinction between transcendence and immanence, fostering the image of immanence (reality conditioned by space and time) as the whole of reality.

That image corresponds to a conception of human existence as fully immersed (or trapped) in historical time. Thus, during the modern period we witness the growth of concern, especially in the nineteenth and twentieth centuries, with the historical conditions of human life and thought. This has become another source of resistance to notions of transcendence. If reality is wholly immanent, and world history is the ultimate context of our human drama, then the affirmation of transcendence is not only mistaken, but also dangerous, for two reasons. First, it deflects attention from historical responsibility by focusing human concern on an illusory "beyond" of meaning, diminishing the value of our knowing the world and sapping our will to struggle to improve it. Marx and Nietzsche both denounce the concept of transcendence for precisely this reason. Second, a human existence radically bound to the world of space-time is one in which ethnic, biological, cultural, and linguistic factors inescapably limit and particularize human thought, so that there could be no access to a "universal" perspective or a genuinely transcendent truth. The very notion of transcendence suggests that such access is possible, though; and so, according to the "hard" historicist argument, by bolstering the absolutist pretensions of those who claim access to a transcendent perspective, the notion of transcendence lends support to arguments for this or that cultural superiority and an accompanying will toward domination. For these combined reasons, then, the affirmation of transcendence has come to be seen as contradictory to a proper regard for the historicity of language and culture as well as to the nurturing of a proper appreciation of tolerance and pluralism.

In sum, moderns are suspicious of the idea of transcendent reality on both moral and epistemological grounds. Morally, it is associated with intolerance, religious fanaticism, self-righteousness, the abuse of authority, and the darkness of malice and unreason. Epistemologically, it is regarded as denoting an object unverifiable by reason or science, in which one could have faith only through naively or willfully ignoring the historical and time-bound condition of human thought and existence. In both respects it is deemed a deceptive promise of stability, falsely suggesting that we can know and speak of eternal verities and values. The general "modern" view is that real knowledge of stable and enduring meanings is restricted to the truths of science. The "postmodern" view, gaining ground, is that even scientific truths are irremediably riddled with cultural and historical bias. Each stance presents itself as an epistemological alternative to dogmatic intolerance. Instability of meaning and knowledge, whether in the entire nonscientific realm or indeed in all of human thought, is seen as "a guarantor of tolerance," as George Steiner notes, while there is seen "in any thirst for absolutes not only an infantile simplicity but the old, cruel demons of dogma."[2]

The contemporary person is confronted with powerful motives and arguments, then, for dismissing the idea of transcendent reality. But an open-minded and openhearted realism requires that these motives and arguments be resisted. The recorded history of human questioning, aspiration, and discovery testifies massively to a native human awareness of participation in a reality that is not intrinsically conditioned by space and time. Thinkers again and again over millennia realize and explain why the idea of a completely self-explanatory and nonmysterious spatiotemporal universe—a purely self-sufficient immanent reality—is a theoretical blunder. In the experience of consciousness human beings respond, as ever, to intimations of transcendent significance and purpose, to awareness of an elemental mystery of ultimate meaning that transcends and completes human living and the universe. This awareness can be suppressed, misinterpreted, devoted to unholy causes—but it cannot be eliminated, because it is native to consciousness. It is the essence of our experience of having emerged from an essentially mysterious ground of being that even the entirety of what is commensurate with finite human understanding—the universe of space and time—cannot account for. Moreover, it is basic to our awareness that we are participating in a unified human drama that transcends geography and century, ethnicity and gender, language and culture.

We spontaneously think of human history as a single story, as a drama of "universal humanity" that embraces peoples of all times and places. Reflection reveals, however, that any such conception relies upon a notion of transcendence, upon implicit affirmation that human beings participate in a transtemporal, transcultural dimension of meaning. If there were no element of human meaning that transcends environmental, biological, psychological, societal, and linguistic circumstances, then those combined circumstances

2. Steiner, *Real Presences,* 199–200.

would completely delimit and define human reality. If that were the case, there would be nothing that unites human groups scattered through space and time into one human community. In fact, though, our spontaneous ability and readiness to conceive of universal humanity testify to—would in fact be impossible without—a universal awareness (however rudimentary or implicit) of human participation in transcendent meaning.

The modern suspicion of and resistance to transcendence has, inevitably, had an impact on how we feel and think about the notion of a unified human story, a notion that comes to us so naturally. The idea of universal humanity itself remains in easy currency in contemporary discourse, but attempts to discuss the *content* of the human drama—to suggest the narrative trajectory of the embracing human story, or its meaningful plot—tend to cause unease, consternation, or downright disapproval. Even the metaphor of the "human drama" may, when pointedly expressed, cause hesitation, because in everyday imagination what many of us feel ourselves to be participants in is not so much a unified drama as a largely accidental tangle of private lives and irreconcilably diverse cultures.

This feeling is sometimes explained in terms of a breakdown of shared myths. If one of the principal functions of myth is to create communal solidarity through shared apprehension of participating in a common human story, then it seems fair to say that the grand Western cultural myths have been rendered mostly ineffective. Our hearts do not assent to them; they are too various, and we are too skeptical of their origins and purposes. The tendency in contemporary life is to believe a number of incompatible claims. Stories from the Jewish and Christian traditions jostle alongside images from Newtonian physics and Cartesian philosophy, and these are joined to Enlightenment visions of progress, Romanticist worship of Nature, Darwinian science, and Freudian psychology to produce a rich but incoherent picture of the human story that can only loosely be called a worldview. Early in the last century, in "The Waste Land" (1922), T. S. Eliot described our situation: our outlook upon the universe and history is upon "a heap of broken images."

This chaotic sense of the human drama has been evoked by preeminent Western artists of the last century. Picasso's fractured portraits, Giacometti's pinched and isolated figurines, Beckett's dramas and novels of desolation, Berg's jarring operas, and the flotsam of quotations gathered in the poetry of Eliot and Pound—just to mention a few famous but hardly outdated examples—testify to our disjointed sense of cosmos and history, if also to the artistic creativity and even exuberance that can discover new worlds in the disintegration of the old.

The artists have done their job magnificently, but at their best they have given us private mythologies. And as solacing as those mythologies might be to those able to appreciate them, they are no substitute for public myths that securely orient a culture in relation to the ultimacies and mysteries of universe and history. What the artist raises to the level of private myth, the rest of us tend to suffer as privations—for each, a primarily personal story, immersed in cultural conformities but styled in isolation, and, if troubled, rendered up to the psychotherapist.

If in everyday culture our guiding image of the human drama is that of an immense aggregate of individual desires and pursuits, so among intellectuals, too, we find the most marketable trends of philosophy and literary criticism entailing an attack on the very idea that all human lives participate in a common story. The conception of an embracing human drama, we are advised by the most influential philosophers and academics, betrays a naive and unjustifiable confidence in metaphysical stability, a rationalist nostalgia for fixed truths, and, whether we realize it or not, a complicity in the ideological buttressing of systems of social domination and oppression. In philosophical circles it has been fashionable for some time to denounce unities of all kinds—unities of meaning, the unity of the self, the unity of history, the unity of reality—in favor of irresolvable pluralities. The so-called deconstruction of metaphysics, of reason, and of the human subject has culminated in philosophical doctrines that presume it possible to inquire seriously into the facts of existence and the events of human history while denying that there is any unifying context to those facts and events.

Nevertheless, despite the pressures of both popular and intellectual culture, despite contemporary feelings of isolation and fragmentation, we continue to surmise, also, that we are actors in a common drama of existence, and so we continue to try to orient ourselves by some vision or another of the whole. Awareness of the unity of human history remains alive. If we lack convincing myths of universe and history, though, how is this felt awareness of mutual involvement in an overarching story to be successfully articulated? Can the illumination and orientation once provided by such myths be recovered? What would such recovery entail?

A response to these questions should begin by distinguishing two different aspects of such a recovery. On the one hand, there is the challenge of intellectual recovery, of discovering or contributing to philosophies that, provoked by contemporary experiences and critiques, reattain an intellectually convincing account of a genuinely universal human drama. On the other hand, there is the quite distinct problem of recovering such orientation in the spontaneities of human living—the problem of the recrudescence of images and symbols that satisfyingly orient people in their daily lives in relation to the ultimacies and mysteries of a universal drama of existence. It is only the first of these, of course, the philosophical challenge, that can be met directly by intellectual labor—and the aims of such labor are the subject matter and justification for the present book, as the argument of the following pages is that just such an intellectual recovery is not only possible but under way as well. The challenges of modernity and postmodernity require new questions, insights, and expressive means in order to convincingly address the question of the unity of human history; however, those challenges have for some time been provoking a worthy response. It is the thesis of this book that this intellectual recovery has been and continues to be dependent upon successfully addressing the problem of transcendence. *This is because the experience of the unity of human history is, at bottom, the experience of a transcendent meaning that embraces all human particularities.* Transcendent meaning is the key, not only to the causes of contemporary hesitation about whether we can legitimately speak of a drama of universal humanity, but also to the recovery of reasonable confidence that such a drama exists.

This book is an effort in the philosophical clarification and retrieval of the notion of transcendence. It begins with a look at the postmodern resistance to transcendence, and at the vulnerability of that resistance to thoughtful appreciation of the experiences from which historical symbols of transcendence have arisen. Then, because we are indeed historical creatures, it continues by taking up the question of history in relation to the notion of transcendence. It does this by asking, among other questions: When and how did human beings begin to explicitly discover, explore, and express the problem of transcendent reality? How have those discoveries themselves served to shape history (for better and worse)? Finally, what has clarification of transcendent meaning suggested or revealed about the meaning or purpose of history? These questions will bring us to a consideration of certain functions of myth, art, and poetry, and then, in the final chapters, to a reflection on the hints and promises of the divine that we find both in the natural world and in the solitude of individual consciousness.

The scale and profundity of the topics demand the most streamlined of treatments; therefore, the book is not a long one. It will have served its purpose if it manages to clarify some ways in which transcendent meaning constitutes an inescapable, if extremely problematic, truth—a truth that lies, for far too many, eclipsed and betrayed in the current atmosphere of thought and opinion.

1

THE PROBLEM OF TRANSCENDENCE

> It is enough to recognize what is obvious to any mind: that all the goods of this world, past, present, and future, real or imaginary, are finite and limited and radically incapable of satisfying the desire that perpetually burns within us for an infinite and perfect good.
>
> —Simone Weil, "Some Reflections on the Love of God"

FOR SOME TIME now contemporary culture has been described as postmodern, and our age as that of postmodernity. The prevailing outlook of postmodern culture has been summed up by the French philosopher Jean-François Lyotard: "Simplifying to the extreme, I define *postmodern,*" he states, "as incredulity toward metanarratives."[1] That is, the most striking characteristic of contemporary life in the West is the suspicion, in some cases hostile suspicion, of accounts of history or human experience that claim to speak from a transcendent point of view, from a position that transcends individual or culture-specific perspectives. Any convincing account of the universal human drama, of course, *must* have the character of a metanarrative, because it must represent all humans of all times as a single community, participating in a reality that, transcending all specific places and times, binds the meaning of each to the meaning of all. Any such account presupposes some dimension of shared human experience that transcends biological, psychological, and cultural circumstance—a dimension of reality, humanly experienced,

1. Lyotard, "The Postmodern Condition," 74.

that is not intrinsically conditioned by the contingencies of space and time. Only human participation in a dimension of meaning that is nonparticular, nonfinite—a realm of transcendent meaning—justifies any metanarratives about humanity. The contemporary incredulity toward metanarratives, then, manifests a rejection of the notion of transcendent meaning. Indeed, if we consider intellectual antecedents of the postmodern outlook, we can see that historically it culminates a centuries-long attack waged against notions of transcendent reality. A skeptical attitude toward transcendence is at the heart of postmodern self-interpretation.

The contemporary suspicion of transcendent reality has many causes. As noted in the Introduction, the major general causes include, first, the frustration and revulsion provoked by centuries of religious warfare on the part of claimants to privileged possession of truths about transcendent divine being and transcendent human destiny. A second, and crucial, cause has been the understanding of nature introduced with the modern mathematical sciences, which inspired hopes, initially among the few and then among the many, that all of reality might one day be explained within a system of rational science. During the eighteenth century, growing confidence in the modern scientific method of reason as exclusive arbiter of what is true and real led to an assault by Enlightenment thinkers on what they considered to be the harmful and retrograde forces of unreason in society, focused in particular on the institutional voices of religion that demanded that reason be set aside when faced with Church authority and the mysteries of faith. That assault gradually broadened into a widespread intolerance of any purportedly mysterious truth, or any truth declared to be beyond the grasp of scientific reason. Third, in a parallel development during the eighteenth and nineteenth centuries, the growth of historical consciousness resulted in increased sensitivity to the culture-bound character of human understanding, to the limitations of personal perspective and social horizon, a sensitivity that gradually undermined religious and philosophical declarations of access to unchanging, transcendent truths. Together these developments have cooperated to cast suspicion on any claims to human knowledge of a transcendent reality. Though they are only three of the sources of such suspicion, they are three of the most important, and mentioning them serves to indicate some of the problems faced by any critical effort to recover the legitimacy of the notion of transcendence.

Along with the suspicions spread by religious fanaticism and warfare, scientism, and historicism, a fourth obstacle to such a recovery is the language traditionally associated with transcendence. The primary Western symbols used to express and communicate human intimations of transcendence have lost much of their power to convince or to console. They have become devitalized, stale, opaque. Nietzsche was an accurate barometer of language when he announced that "God is dead." The words *spirit* and *spirituality* in popular speech and writing have become imprecise to the point of irrelevance. As the philosopher Eric Voegelin would say, *symbols* regarding transcendence tend, in the course of their use and diffusion, to become cut off from the *experiences* of transcendence that originally engendered them, from personal acts of insight that reveal transcendent meaning, and so increasingly lose the power to communicate, or to evoke, such experiences and insights. What is most crucial, Voegelin argues, in the contemporary effort to recover the legitimacy of the notion of transcendence is an analysis that effectively delves beneath the language-symbols pertaining to transcendence to the fundamental *experiences* of human desire and insight that have given rise to those symbols.[2]

Voegelin's approach is not unique. The desire to "return to experience" to grasp the living truths buried beneath the stale phrases and propositional dogmas of philosophical or religious orthodoxies has motivated more than a few major twentieth-century thinkers concerned with the truth of transcendence. Perhaps the most influential recovery efforts have been those undertaken by comparative religionists and historians of religion, such as Rudolf Otto and Mircea Eliade, through their examinations of elements basic to the sense of the sacred and their comparisons of wide varieties of religious experience, ancient and modern, Eastern and Western.[3] A handful of twentieth-century philosophers, too, have made critical recognition or rehabilitation of experiences of transcendent meaning a principal focus of their work, among them Gabriel Marcel, Karl Jaspers, Martin Buber, and Emmanuel Levinas. In the following pages I will mainly be relying, however, on the writings of two less widely known twentieth-century philosophers, Eric Voegelin and

2. On Voegelin's approach to the problem of transcendence by way of his methodological distinction between the experiences that generate symbols and the potential for such symbols to become detached from the actual meanings of those experiences, see esp. his essays "Immortality: Experience and Symbol" (1967), "Equivalences of Experience and Symbolization in History" (1970), and "The Gospel and Culture" (1971), all in *Published Essays, 1966–1985*.

3. Otto's groundbreaking work *Das Heilige* was published in 1917, and translated into English in 1923 as *The Idea of the Holy*. The two most concise introductions to Eliade's studies are *The Myth of the Eternal Return; or, Cosmos and History* and *The Sacred and the Profane: The Nature of Religions*.

Bernard Lonergan, as guides in my investigation into problems concerning transcendence.

Voegelin, best known as a political philosopher and as author of *The New Science of Politics* (1952) and the five-volume *Order and History* (1956–1987), the latter a philosophical study of human existence in society from ancient to modern times, has treated the problem of transcendence with rare breadth and sophistication, in accordance with his conviction that it constitutes "the decisive problem of philosophy."[4] Bernard Lonergan is a philosopher and Catholic theologian whose achievement rests on an analysis of both the structure of human cognition and the explanatory power of an accurate philosophical exposition of that structure, an analysis presented most fully in his two major works, *Insight: A Study of Human Understanding* (1956) and *Method in Theology* (1972). Though Lonergan devotes fewer pages than does Voegelin to the topic of transcendence, he approaches and illuminates it from a similar perspective. Both philosophers, emphasizing that a human being is first and foremost a *questioner,* analyze and develop the implications of the human capacity *to out-question the finite and the knowable* and thereby to encounter transcendent meaning. Lonergan's detailed explanatory account of the scope and structure of human thinking nicely complements Voegelin's historically oriented "meditative exegeses" of the experiences that gave rise, across the world, to religious and philosophical symbols of transcendence. Their combined insights on these matters will, together, provide much of the thematic and philosophical guidance in this and subsequent chapters.

Experiences of Transcendence

For the notion of transcendence to be examined on the basis of experience, one feature of human experience in general must first be clarified. The basic dynamic principle of human consciousness, Lonergan and Voegelin agree, is *the desire to understand.* In his analysis of cognition, Lonergan takes pains to emphasize that human consciousness is a *process:* it has an intrinsically dynamic character, because its essential nature is to search for meaning.

4. Peter Emberley and Barry Cooper, eds. and trans., *Faith and Political Philosophy: The Correspondence between Leo Strauss and Eric Voegelin, 1934–1964,* 34. For an extended study of Voegelin's approach to the problem of transcendence in terms of the experience of mystery, see Glenn Hughes, *Mystery and Myth in the Philosophy of Eric Voegelin.*

Questioning—as wonder, as curiosity, as concern—is what prompts our engagement with experience and propels human development through all types of discovery, assimilation, affirmation, evaluation, and decision. Lonergan asserts that there is a primordial urge to inquire into our experiences, an urge that precedes and gives rise to all specific questions, an urge that may be described as "the root question, the fundamental question," "the pure question" that carries us from sense experience through the play of imagination to understanding and all the uses of understanding.[5] It is the phenomenon famously referred to by Aristotle in the first sentence of his *Metaphysics:* "All human beings, by nature, desire to know."

The human desire to know is, as the phrase itself indicates, a disposition both emotional and intellectual. As *desire* it is affective, an attraction, a longing. As a longing for *insight,* for the illumination provided by understanding, it is an intellectual phenomenon. Its goals are cognitive, for it seeks to perceive and to know that which it perceives. Its goals are also intrinsically moral or value-related, because with time it unfolds into considerations of what to do, of how to act, in light of what is thought to be useful or good or valuable. Finally, the root question, as the underlying desire for understanding, is only and ever partially appeasable—for from questioning comes knowledge, but knowledge is always the source of yet further questions. In fact, Lonergan explains, the scope of human questioning is unrestricted, both in a practical and in a formal sense. Practically, no matter how much we have learned, there are always further questions inviting further discoveries. Formally, the root question is unlimited in the range of its concern: it seeks to know whatever might be known, which is to say, everything. The innate, ultimate objective of the "pure" question is nothing less than knowledge of *being,* of all that is, with nothing left over. Thus, it is an *unrestricted questioning,* oriented cognitively to the goal of unrestricted knowledge and morally to the goal of an unrestricted good—goals that, needless to say, are unrealizable within the temporal and finite structure of human existence, but that nevertheless continually draw us, however vaguely apprehended (and however frequently ignored or resisted), as the fulfillment of human intending and longing.

In harmony with what we might call this Socratic principle, then, Lonergan asserts, as does Voegelin, that *fidelity to the spirit of inquiry* is the elementary normative standard for gauging human genuineness or authenticity. If to be

5. Lonergan, *Understanding and Being,* 139; *Insight: A Study of Human Understanding,* 34.

human is to be a questioner, one is authentically human to the degree that one remains open to further questions, where one's accumulation of understanding functions constantly as a springboard for renewed inquiry with an open mind and open heart. Voegelin encapsulates this principle by stating that every human being is, most essentially, what may be called "the Question": an open-ended search for meaning that aims finally at understanding the ground or ultimate meaning of reality.[6] One of the consequences of being faithful to this spirit of inquiry, both philosophers agree, is that in the long run notions of transcendent reality—and the insight that there must be such a reality—inevitably arise. The main features of their agreement on this point may be summarized as follows.

As human beings, we desire to know. Especially, though, we want to know about ourselves, and about our situation in reality: who we are, where we came from, what we are involved in, what we are intended for, what we may and may not aspire to, what we might become, create, arrive at. We are concerned, in short, about the meaning of our existences, our parts in the human drama. However, the purpose of one's own participation in the human drama could be known fully only by knowing the meaning of the drama as a whole—through comprehending the ultimate truths pertaining to the whys and wherefores of human existence and history. For each of us, then, our questioning is, whether we like it or not, and whether we acknowledge it or not, a desire to understand the ultimate meanings that would explain for each of us the significance of our participation in the cosmic process.

A person's search for ultimates, however, when pursued with sufficient honesty and discernment, leads to the realization that human curiosity about the whys and wherefores of existence could never be adequately answered on the basis of knowledge about the finite universe. This is because *the entire universe of objects and relations in space and time is not a complete or sufficient explanation of its own existence.* All finite reality is contingent, or dependent, reality, that is, its existence presupposes prior causes, and contingent reality in its entirety ultimately presupposes a nondependent—a necessary—reality as the intelligible basis or ground of its existence. Why is this so? Because an infinite series of dependent causes does not answer the question, "Why does the universe exist?" It instead extends the question indefinitely without hope of rational resolution. The universe is not rationally complete, is not

6. Voegelin, *The Ecumenic Age,* 388–410.

graspable as fully intelligible, unless the series of dependent causes comes to rest in a cause that itself does not rationally require a prior cause. To be fully intelligible, then, the finite universe must finally rest upon an ultimate cause or "ground" that is not dependent but self-sufficient, not contingent but necessary. To state the matter summarily: if reality as a whole, including our participation in it, is to be fully intelligible—*and our unrestricted desire to understand the meaning of our own questioning operates on that assumption*—then the contingent, finite universe that is not self-sufficient must have its ultimate origin in, be somehow "emergent" from, a necessary, nonfinite reality that *is* self-sufficient and self-explanatory.

Human consciousness, then, is an unrestricted seeking of its own intelligibility as a component of reality; in the course of its search, it discovers the rational requirement of a nonfinite and self-sufficient ground of reality; and if this ground did not exist, then its own structure and direction—as a questioning that seeks a completeness of intelligibility—would be pointless, meaningless.

The search of human reason for ultimates has led repeatedly, therefore, to the affirmation of a nonfinite, noncontingent ground of reality. However, if questioning brings us to such an affirmation, it also brings us to the recognition that we are incapable of direct or substantive insight into this ground of reality. For while the reality under consideration is nonfinite and unconditioned, or "absolute," our imagination and understanding are, we are well aware, finite and limited. Therefore, the finite reality of the universe that we experience and understand leads us, if we remain true to the intrinsic implications and demands of rational inquiry—if we remain true, that is, to the Question that we are—to the apprehension of an ultimate reality that we understand to lie beyond our direct or complete understanding. This reality is *transcendent reality,* or *transcendence* in the strict sense, because it transcends the conditions of space and time (as nonfinite and necessary), and also transcends our direct or substantive understanding. We *do* understand that it must exist if the finite universe is to be completely intelligible, but in itself, in its content, it is a mystery to us, the mystery of ultimate origins and final meanings, the mystery of the ground of being.[7]

7. For a full exposition of the sequence of insights abbreviated in these last three paragraphs, see Lonergan, "General Transcendent Knowledge," chap. 19 in *Insight,* 657–708.

The idea of transcendent being or meaning has frequently been objected to on the basis of the assumption that only sense data, or data conditioned by space and time, can be affirmed to be real. This is an objection that Lonergan, in particular, has addressed and disarmed with impressive clarity. We should note the essential features of his argument.

The assumption that only sense data can be known to be real, Lonergan explains, is philosophically untenable, because a consistent account of human cognition requires affirming that the only coherent criteria for determining what is real are the criteria of *intelligent grasp and reasonable affirmation.* Put simply: the real, or being, is what is verifiable, and what is verifiable must be intelligible, but intelligible data need not be material data, "need not be imaginable entities moving through imaginable processes in an imaginable space-time"—as modern physicists have come to recognize. Second, as being is always intelligible, by extrapolation, *complete* being—the whole of reality—must be *completely* intelligible. Third, as we have already noted, the complete intelligibility of being requires that there be a self-sufficient, self-explanatory, necessary ground or origin of being that is absolutely unconditioned, or transcendent.[8]

On the basis of these and other clarifications, Lonergan in chapter 19 of *Insight* shows that it is eminently reasonable to affirm that transcendent meaning is real. In doing so he explains how this reasonable affirmation has both invited and informed the development of all *valid* arguments for transcendent being—better known in Western philosophical traditions as "arguments for the existence of God." Still, granting the validity of such arguments, Lonergan's overall analysis as well as that of Voegelin would urge us to bear in mind three crucial points about them.

First, valid formal arguments affirming transcendent being or "God" do not suggest, indeed they discredit, any claim to direct knowledge of what transcendent being is. Only by imperfect analogy from human experience do we apply to it such characteristics as "cause," "perfection," "ground," or "Creator." As reality understood to lie beyond substantive human understanding, transcendent being is a mystery, which may be called "God." Second, formal arguments, as found, for example, in the *Summa Theologiae* of Thomas

8. Lonergan, *Insight,* 15. For the basic points in Lonergan's elaboration of the validity of insights into transcendent being, see chaps. 1, 9, 12, and 19 in *Insight.*

Aquinas or in Lonergan's *Insight,* are the *consequence of*—not a means to—the discovery of transcendence. Transcendence is always first *experienced* as the mystery sought for and encountered in a person's loving quest for unrestricted meaning and goodness; it is only subsequent methodical reflection on the experience of transcendence that produces formal arguments. So, third, as Karl Jaspers has written, we should realize that such arguments do not function "as real proofs," that they are not "means to refute our doubt." Their purpose, Jaspers explains, is only to rationally fulfill "the clarity [we] carry in [ourselves]" regarding our experiences of transcendence, to "clarify and strengthen our awareness" of the transcendent reality that reveals itself "as a cipher." Lonergan and Voegelin would firmly agree with Jaspers's warning: "The arguments fool us if they become known results that take the place of *existential ascertainment.* . . . The only strength of the arguments lies in their *existentially fulfilled* content."[9]

Like Lonergan, Voegelin usually describes the rational unfolding of the experience of transcendent mystery in a way that emphasizes the unrestrictedness of human questioning. "[Human] questioning," he explains in a typical passage, "has reached intelligibly its end when the hierarchy of being is exhausted while the *intentio animi* [the seeking of the soul] reaches further out toward its Beyond."[10] In other words, at the limit of its search for meaning, the human question about *ultimate* meaning out-questions the knowable to find its answer in the discovery of a reality "beyond" the finite and contingent, a reality known to be finally humanly unknowable. This is the point, Voegelin indicates, at which one personally, self-appropriatingly, discovers oneself to be "the Question," because it is to find that the core of one's existence is a desire to understand that which is both the most real reality and also not fully comprehensible under the conditions of human existence.

Here it should be emphasized again that the human search for an understanding of ultimacies of self and reality is an affective as well as an intellectual process. It is as much an emotional longing or yearning as it is an intellectual seeking. This fact is crucial to a proper understanding of the questioning that has led human beings again and again to the apprehension and conception of transcendent reality. Our search for ultimacy always begins as a restless

9. Jaspers, *Philosophy,* 3:175–78 (emphasis added).

10. Voegelin, "The Beginning and the Beyond: A Meditation on Truth," in *What Is History? And Other Late Unpublished Writings,* 175–76.

yearning that arises from awareness of our ignorance about what is most important, a yearning encouraged by whatever symbols grip our imaginations and induce quickening apprehensions of the fact that ultimate truths are both real and beyond our ken. We are led to the experience and conception of transcendent being only by trusting in this experiential "undertow," as Lonergan calls it, that stirs our hearts with intimations of ultimate mystery. In fact, the human search for meaning finds the mystery of its goal only through a kind of love: through caring about and trusting in our own longing for ultimate meaning to the point that the unrestricted scope of our questioning is answered by an experience of encounter or communion—however understood—with an unrestricted mystery beyond human knowing, and through being willing to accept that mystery even as it fails to appease our desire for final answers through any direct or substantive understanding. So the experienced discovery of transcendence, as the limit to our yearning for ultimate meaning, is in one sense the homecoming of our desire to know, but at the same time no homecoming at all, because what has been discovered is a realm of meaning whose presence to conscious experience is at the same time the revelation of its essential being as lying beyond any possible human understanding. As Voegelin states the matter, with typical concision: "There is no answer to the Question other than the Mystery as it becomes luminous in the acts of questioning."[11]

Three further important facts about the experience of transcendence should also be noted. First, it is an experience that is assimilable, capable of being incorporated into one's self-interpretation, only by remaining faithful to the open-ended spirit of inquiry. The discovery of transcendence is the discovery of a *mystery* of ultimate meanings; therefore, it is a discovery that leaves our deepest questions fully alive as questions, indeed more intensely alive than ever, resonant as they now are with awareness of the Mystery. In other words, the experience of transcendence is a *validation of questioning openness itself as the means of being responsibly related to ultimate reality.* In a person's ascent to transcendence, Josef Pieper has written, "the horizon of the question becomes the horizon of reality as a whole."[12] And it is only the person who has made such an ascent for himself or herself, and who thereby has verified his or her

11. Lonergan, *Method in Theology,* 103–10, 113; Voegelin, *The Ecumenic Age,* 404.
12. Pieper, "The Philosophical Act," 128.

very self to be constituted as the Question, who is able to embrace the fact of transcendence.

Second, the experience of transcendence is the experience of a "deepest" or ultimate reality in which we *participate.* Transcendent meaning is not something outside of ourselves that we are trying to discover or figure out. It is the deepest identity of human existence, the "ground" of conscious existence. We do not have to search to find out *if* there is such a ground; the ground of existence is a *given* of our experience, because we are aware that we are not self-caused, yet exist within a reality that, rationally, must have an ultimate ground or cause. Conscious existence, as Voegelin says, "is an event within reality, and man's consciousness is quite conscious of being constituted by the reality of which it is conscious."[13] What we *do* have to search for is *adequate understanding* of just what this ground is—and this ground of our participating existences is what is revealed, through the search, to have the character of transcendence. The fact that transcendence is experienced as the deepest being of existence itself, and not as something external to consciousness, is a point that will require frequent reiteration in the chapters that follow, because it is a common error to imagine that symbols of transcendence refer to some kind of place, or thing, some "second world" somewhere, or some kind of super being beyond even the farthest stars. The "beyond" of transcendence is not physical or spatial. Transcendent being is not something on the other side of a spatial dividing line, not something of concern to NASA. It is not a thing but (as Lonergan puts it) a *realm of meaning*—the realm that constitutes the ultimate answers to our deepest questions about ourselves and reality.[14] It is the realm of meaning that mysteriously completes all the meanings in which we know ourselves to participate.

Third, when the transcendent mystery that is the implicit or explicit concern of every human being is focused upon in personal experience, it may not be—and usually is not—described by the word *transcendence,* or understood precisely as such. Most of us remain acquainted with it as a vaguely surmised "beyond" to our humanly possible understanding of things, a "beyond" revealed in recurrent apprehensions of what Lonergan calls reality's "undefined

13. Voegelin, "Remembrance of Things Past," in *Published Essays, 1966–1985,* 312.

14. On transcendence as a realm of meaning, see Lonergan, *Method in Theology,* 81–85, 120, 265–66. We will discuss in Chapter 8 transcendence as one of four fundamental realms of meaning identified by Lonergan.

surplus of significance and momentousness."[15] Our most basic connection to transcendent mystery is through the hope, love, anxiety—perhaps even terror—that is engendered by images or symbols that evoke in us, often in quite idiosyncratic ways, the "undefined surplus" of transcendent meaning. For the vast majority of human beings in history, these images and symbols have been those at the heart of specific religious and philosophical traditions. To continue this introductory look at experiences of transcendence, then, it will be helpful to discuss briefly a few traditional symbols of transcendence.

Symbols of Transcendence

A number of the most familiar symbols of transcendence from the world's religions and philosophies first appeared, or received a crucial refinement of meaning, during the period that Karl Jaspers named the "Axial Period" of human history, roughly 800 B.C.E. to 200 B.C.E.[16] In various cultures during this period, the quest for ultimate meaning led to experiential and conceptual breakthroughs in which the ground of human existence and the universe became explicitly recognized and symbolized as a reality beyond the conditions of space and time, and consequently unknowable in its essence by human beings. Let us consider four such symbols—bearing in mind, of course, that we are rudely plucking them from richly elaborated traditions of thought and worship.

In classical Chinese culture, the primordial origin of the universe and the basis of its meaning is described in the text of the *Tao Te Ching* (attributed to the sage Lao-tzu, or Laozi, ca. sixth century B.C.E.) as a reality beyond limits and language. This ultimate reality, we are told, may be called the Tao (the "Way"), but the word is presented as no more than a handy metaphor. The reality itself is beyond naming and direct human understanding.

> The tao that can be told
> is not the eternal Tao.

15. Lonergan, *Insight,* 556.

16. Jaspers, *The Origin and Goal of History,* 1–21. For Voegelin's use, critique, and development of Jaspers's idea of the Axial Period, see *The World of the Polis,* 86–90; and *The Ecumenic Age,* 47–51, 380–85.

The name that can be named
is not the eternal Name.

The text explains that although the entire universe arises from and constantly returns to the Tao, and although the Tao is immanent in all of nature and constitutes the true essence of all things, the Tao itself is not like elements in nature, and not genuinely describable, or even thinkable, existing as it does beyond all form:

There was something formless and perfect
before the universe was born.
It is serene. Empty.
Solitary. Unchanging.
Infinite. Eternally present.
It is the mother of the universe.
For lack of a better name,
I call it the Tao.[17]

A notion similar to the Tao appears during roughly this same period in India. In Hindu culture, in the tradition deriving from the late Vedic scriptures known as the Upanishads (developed ca. 800–200 B.C.E.), what is called Brahman is described as the one transcendent reality underlying and constituting the true being of all physical reality, all finiteness, all individuality. The Upanishads elaborate a systematic search for both the ultimate principle of the universe and the truest identity of every human self—these being, it is concluded, one and the same. The essence of the universe is a supreme and absolute reality without finite characteristics, here named Brahman, and the essence of the human self, designated Atman, is affirmed to be identical with it. The mystery that is both the core of the questioning self and the basis of the universe is a reality

. . . beyond name and form,
Beyond the senses, inexhaustible,

17. Stephen Mitchell, trans., *Tao Te Ching,* chaps. 1, 25. The most venerable tradition holds Lao-tzu to be a slightly older contemporary of Confucius (551–479 B.C.E.), but scholars disagree about placing him or the composition of the *Tao Te Ching* this early, some arguing for the fourth or even third century B.C.E. Indeed, as with Homer, there is disagreement about whether Lao-tzu (a name commonly translated as "Old Sage") was even a historical figure. See Wing-Tsit Chan, ed. and trans., *A Source Book in Chinese Philosophy,* 136–39.

> Without beginning, without end, beyond
> Time, space, and causality, eternal,
> Immutable.[18]

In the Vedantic tradition deriving from these texts (especially that associated with Shankara, ninth century C.E.), the finite universe is called maya, and maya is described as the manifesting or showing-forth to perceptual consciousness of the one reality of Brahman in the forms of space, time, and causal relations. The height of wisdom, however, is to recognize reality for what it truly is, the transcendent oneness of Brahman.

Continuing westward, during the first millennium B.C.E. we find the God of the Hebrews, Yahweh, proclaimed to be the sole divinity and fashioner of the universe, a divinity not to be identified with any aspect of the physical world or worshiped like the nature gods or fertility gods of other "idolatrous" nations. This transcendent God is eventually understood, in the Jewish-Christian-Islamic orbit of traditions, to have created the universe out of nothing *(ex nihilo)*. All finite reality is regarded as a manifestation of God's unlimited freedom, a freedom in which human beings, alone among creatures, have been created to participate. Made thus in the image of absolute divine freedom, the limited free consciousness of human beings, through its questioning search for meaning and direction, allows for those experiences of transcendence that reveal the absolutely spiritual origin of human and worldly existence.

For a final example we turn to ancient Greece. In classical Greek culture, between the sixth and fourth centuries B.C.E., we find the emergence of distinctively *philosophical* symbols of transcendence, first in the writings of pre-Socratic philosophers such as Heraclitus, Parmenides, and Xenophanes, and then in more developed fashion in the works of Plato, Aristotle, and the Hellenistic schools. In Plato's *Republic*, for example, at the climactic center of the grand dialogue on justice, when Socrates has at last been persuaded by the other participants to reveal his notion of ultimate reality, we are given a careful articulation of transcendent being. Everything that can be known and everything that has being, Socrates proposes to his companions, comes into being because of "the Good" *(agathon)*. However, he asserts, as the engendering source of all that has being (or "is"), we must conclude that the *agathon* itself "isn't being but is still beyond being, exceeding it in dignity

18. Eknath Easwaran, trans. and ed., *The Upanishads*, 89–90.

and power."[19] The intentionally paradoxical notion of a reality that is said to *be* "beyond being" conveys to the reader at once an idea of transcendent reality and the crucial accompanying insight that such a reality lies beyond language and can be alluded to only through expressions that indicate their own inadequacy. ("The tao that can be told / is not the eternal Tao.")

"The Tao," "Brahman," "God," "the Good": whatever it is named, the naming refers to a finally unnameable fact, to a reality whose essential being is known to be humanly unknowable but that nevertheless is our ultimate origin and that contains us. Each symbol represents both the truth of transcendence and the truth of its ineffability, and each is meant to awaken in its recipients a responsive insight, a personal intimation and recognition of the nameless, timeless, spaceless, formless mystery that is the most real of all realities.

But symbols, of course, do not carry within themselves the insights from which they arose. It is possible to hear the text, the word, yet to mistake or fail to grasp the meaning. One must have made one's own ascent through one's own search for ultimate meanings to the extent of having acknowledged—or at least to the extent of being ready to acknowledge—the "beyond" of the ground of reality, in order for such symbols to resonate with their proper meaning and to not be misinterpreted or even be dismissed as meaningless. When such symbols fail to function as carriers or catalysts of truth experienced and recognized, and when this failure is rampant in a community that has inherited or been introduced to these symbols as authoritative, they will be only so many dead letters at the center of a religious or philosophical tradition. This is a point made frequently by Voegelin in his analyses of symbols of transcendence. We should bear in mind, he states, that

> when the experience engendering the symbols ceases to be a presence located in the man who has it, the reality from which the symbols derive their meaning has disappeared. The symbols in the sense of a spoken or written word, it is true, are left as traces in the world of sense perception, but their meaning can be understood only if they evoke, and through evocation reconstitute, the engendering reality in the listener or reader.[20]

The increasingly widespread failure of traditional symbols to do precisely this—to evocatively reconstitute the experienced reality of transcendence—

19. *The Republic of Plato* 189 (509b).
20. Voegelin, "Immortality: Experience and Symbol," in *Published Essays, 1966–1985*, 52–53.

is, Voegelin states emphatically, one of the defining characteristics of modern Western culture. Though many people still profess religious belief and participate in rituals of worship, the language of transcendence has increasingly become ineffective and opaque. That is, it has largely ceased to prompt imaginative and affective openness to the Mystery of transcendent meaning, to illuminate the fact that every human existence is a Question oriented to the Mystery, or to serve as a convincing articulation of personal partnership in a common drama of humanity. This failure, Voegelin and Lonergan would agree, is a crucial element in our present crisis of culture, a crisis whose most brilliant analysts, such as Kierkegaard, Dostoyevsky, Nietzsche, and Heidegger, have alike (though with differing interpretations of its meaning) described as a crisis of disorientation resulting from a loss of felt participation in transcendent meaning.

Recovery of Transcendence

Thus, Voegelin and Lonergan are among those who would argue that, whatever else it might entail, a successful response to the contemporary crisis of culture must involve a recovery of the truth of transcendence—both a philosophical recovery, to which they have made their respective contributions, and a renewal of spontaneously felt and acknowledged participation in transcendent meaning at the level of everyday living. A recovery of transcendence is essential to moving beyond the alienations and confusions of our epoch because, as Lonergan puts it, human beings are by nature oriented into transcendent mystery, and therefore human existence that is balanced, integrated, and joyful will always require convincing symbolic articulations of the human drama that incorporate the fact of transcendent meaning. Without images and visions that spontaneously speak to our sense of the ultimate oneness of humanity and history, either through philosophical symbols or through what Jaspers calls the "cipher language" of religious myth, we will remain (in Walker Percy's phrase) lost in the cosmos. Moreover, both Voegelin and Lonergan insist that such a recovery is not promoted, but is rather delayed, by reactionary insistence that hallowed symbols and myths should not be challenged, or by summonses, however eloquent, to retreat from history into a fortress of unquestioned dogma. The recovery of an informing and healing awareness of human participation in transcendence, and the broader social effects of such a recovery, can arise only by acknowledging the widespread modern inefficacy of traditional symbols, which then may alert one to the real task at hand—that task being, as Voegelin declares, to successfully return "from symbols that have lost their meaning to the experiences that constitute meaning."[21] In other words, the elementary task is to assist human beings in the contemporary world in regaining access to the types of experiences of personal illumination that engendered the various traditional symbols of transcendence in the first place.

As has been indicated, their positions on this and related issues place Voegelin and Lonergan at some distance from the current philosophical mainstream (though for this reason to label either of them as "conservative" or "classicist" would be misleading).[22] At present, philosophical discussion remains dominated by the deep suspicion of transcendence mentioned earlier, and by distrust of all "metanarratives" in which human participation in transcendent meaning is explicitly or implicitly affirmed. Contemporary philosophers associated with influential "poststructuralist" or "deconstructive" schools of thought, such as Jean-François Lyotard, Jacques Derrida, Michel Foucault, and Richard Rorty, make the unwarrantedness of affirmations of transcendent reality a cornerstone of their interpretations of the

21. Voegelin, *The Ecumenic Age,* 107.

22. Both Voegelin and Lonergan repudiate the reactionary conservatism that tries to downplay modernity's emphasis on human historicity and to sidestep its pluralist implications. Voegelin fiercely objected to the conservative label, and was contemptuous of attempts to associate his philosophical analyses with conservative intellectual or political movements. See Michael Franz, "Brothers under the Skin: Voegelin on the Common Experiential Wellsprings of Spiritual Order and Disorder," 139–40, 157–58 n. 5. Again, both Voegelin and Lonergan are outspoken in their rejection of antihistorical, "classicist" notions of philosophy or culture. The classicist position, Lonergan explains, is that one particular set of cultural achievements should be regarded as normative and universal. Thus, the classicist "is no pluralist. He . . . [is] deeply convinced that circumstances are somehow accidental and that, beyond them, there is some substance or kernel or root that fits in with classicist assumptions of stability, fixity, immutability." However, classicism's "claim to be the one culture of mankind can no longer be entertained," Lonergan asserts, and above all "what ended classicist assumptions was critical history." Modern culture is informed by "a thorough grasp of man's historicity" and the cumulative product of empirical human studies, and quite properly it "conceives itself empirically and concretely." A responsible contemporary philosophy is therefore one that—like the philosophy of Lonergan or Voegelin—"recognizes cultural variation, difference, development, breakdown, that investigates each of the many cultures of mankind, that studies their histories, that seeks to understand what the classicist would write off as strange or uncultivated or barbaric. . . . If it can discern common and invariant structures in human operations, it refuses to take flight from the particular to the universal, and it endeavors to meet the challenge of knowing people in all their diversity and mutability." Lonergan, *Method in Theology,* 301, 302, 326; "The Future of Thomism," in *A Second Collection,* 52; "The Future of Christianity," in ibid., 161.

human search for meaning. Each of them dismisses as illegitimate the idea of a stable foundation or ground of meaning beyond finite contingencies, historical situatedness, and the shifting significations or allusions of language. Rorty, for instance, presents himself as an "ironist," which he describes as "the sort of person who faces up to the contingency of his or her most central beliefs and desires—someone sufficiently historicist and nominalist to have abandoned the idea that those central beliefs and desires refer back to something beyond the reach of time and chance." That this abandonment of transcendent reality is also a denial of every notion of divinity is made explicit: Rorty urges "that we try to get to the point where we no longer worship *anything*, where we treat *nothing* as a quasi divinity, where we treat *everything*—our language, our conscience, our community—as a product of time and chance." Rorty is, as Voegelin would say, presenting human existence as a "state of groundlessness," where the search for meaning has no origin or insurance beyond contingency.[23]

Jacques Derrida, likewise, rejects all notions of a ground of meaning. His "interpretation of interpretation"—his view of the human search for meaning—is, he says, more authentic for being "no longer turned toward the origin." The actual experience of conscious existence, he asserts, is that of a foundationless "play" among ever unstable meanings; therefore, he urges, we should try "to pass beyond man," beyond the human seeker who throughout history "has dreamed of full presence, the reassuring foundation, the origin and end of play." For Derrida, "full presence" has, of course, theological signification, referring to the Western conception of a transcendent fullness of divine presence. This is the foundation or ground that must be removed, in his view, from an accurate interpretation of the human situation in reality, and along with it any firm assurance that the meanings we discover or achieve or create in existence finally mean anything at all—because, as George Steiner has remarked, "[t]he meaning of meaning is a transcendent postulate."[24]

Such philosophers of groundlessness, as I shall call them, understand well that the removal of transcendent meaning from our understanding of reality tends to induce a sense of disorientation in human existence. We should nevertheless endure this and adapt to it, they would argue, not only for the

23. Rorty, *Contingency, Irony, and Solidarity,* xv, 22 (italics in original); Voegelin, "Anxiety and Reason," in *What Is History?* 83.

24. Derrida, *Writing and Difference,* 292; Steiner, *Real Presences,* 216.

sake of honesty but also for ethical reasons, because religious or metaphysical assertions of a ground of being are invariably tied to systems of thought that, they assert, harmfully attempt to homogenize differences of culture and language, to hinder or prohibit new ways of thinking, and to impose upon all people one set of final answers about the meaning of human existence and the goals of history. To borrow (and simplify) Lyotard's useful term once more, affirmations of transcendence are linked to metanarratives, and all metanarratives are, in their view, oppressively totalistic. That is, every metanarrative presents itself as the one true account of the story of reality, but, these philosophers claim, no such account can be embraced without inhibiting, delegitimating, degrading, or silencing alternative worldviews and cultural self-interpretations.

Of religious metanarratives this is presumed to be self-evident. Religious absolutism, with its worldwide (and ongoing) history of persecution, destruction, and conquest, is the preeminently familiar target of modern intellectual critique. However, the philosophers of groundlessness point out that there are modern abstract-philosophical and secular metanarratives as well, seductively clothed in the antireligious garb of rational enlightenment. Kant and Hegel, for example, each tell the story of universal humanity's inevitable march of progress toward the ever greater exercise of reason and freedom in human affairs (which for Hegel is also the dialectical unfolding of Spirit, and as such the "inner truth" of Christianity). Still, such a story can be accepted as authoritative, Rorty and Derrida would say, only if one dismisses alternative (especially non-European) cultural or historical self-interpretations. Grand philosophies of existence and history like those of Kant and Hegel, therefore, ought to be regarded as examples of philosophical imperialism, their claims to universality resting on the invalidation of alternative visions of the purposes of human life in time.

The philosophers of groundlessness view Kant and Hegel as still speaking for transcendence in the strict sense, but in a rational-philosophical rather than a religious way, in a language, that is, suited to the temper of the Enlightenment's worship of secular reason and rational science. Kant and Hegel realize, they argue, that the modern sciences themselves throw no light on the tragic or comic meaning of the drama of existence and are necessarily silent about ultimate meaning; so, accepting the Enlightenment's rejection of religious myth, the story of universal humanity in their work takes the form of an overarching rational-philosophical metanarrative that ratifies and contextualizes the modern sciences. However, these accounts of the story of humanity, the philosophers of groundlessness point out, are clearly still animated by the totalizing spirit of religious metanarratives.

By the time we reach the mid-nineteenth-century metanarrative of Karl Marx, transcendence has been explicitly repudiated: the drama of existence has become radically world-immanent. Unlike Kant and Hegel, Marx altogether rejects the fact of transcendent or divine being. However, his metanarrative still assumes, one might say, the privilege of a transcendent point of view, allowing his version of philosophical materialism to be as totalistic in character as any religious absolutism. This totalizing ambition can be turned aside and rendered harmless, declare the philosophers of groundlessness, only by denying legitimacy to any foundational conception: any universalist conception of human nature, any account of the direction (much less the "necessary laws") of world history, any notions of human access to a realm of meaning beyond contingency and transience.

But—these philosophers have been asked—with all metanarratives rejected, what is one to do with the human search for ultimate meaning? What is the proper focus of our sense of an encompassing context for the drama of history? What of our need for guiding myths?

The philosophers of groundlessness answer that our inherent sense of drama and play, and our need for myth and story, is in fact *liberated* through the rejection of all metanarratives along with all types of totalizing thought. In deposing the tyranny of such systems of answers, they assert, we for the first time grant real validity to an actual, vital *plurality* of linguistic worlds, cultural contexts, historical situations, biological facts, and psychological horizons. This, they proclaim, is an important step in the promotion of human freedom and solidarity. "Let us wage war on totality [and] activate the differences," declares Lyotard. For what purpose? In order to promote what Rorty calls "an endless, proliferating realization of Freedom." Thus they declare their protective recognition of an *irreducible* plurality of cultural and linguistic contexts of meaning, a recognition that, to be effective, must remain on guard against all universalizing conceptual or symbolic *resolutions* of that plurality—that is, against any ascription of an ultimate intelligibility or coherence to reality. So, in their view, a protective recognition of plurality must constantly affirm (as Steiner puts it) "the illegitimacy of the intelligible, as it was grounded in a transcendent dimension or category."[25]

25. Lyotard, *The Postmodern Condition: A Report on Knowledge,* 82; Rorty, *Contingency, Irony, and Solidarity,* xvi; Steiner, *Real Presences,* 116.

It is evident from all of this that the philosophers of groundlessness are attempting to protect and nurture a lively sense of meaningful participation in the drama of human existence. In direct contrast to Voegelin and Lonergan, though, they hold that this can be accomplished only through the *elimination* of any affirmation of transcendent meaning, and thereby of the full intelligibility of reality—through *turning away* from any presumption of a universal human story.

Voegelin and Lonergan would argue in response that although there is a great deal to agree with in the cultural critique mounted by the philosophers of groundlessness—in particular, the ethical concern manifested in their defense of pluralism, and the denunciations of systems of answers that claim final, substantive knowledge about the meaning of history—it is nevertheless a critique built on three crucial oversights.

The first of these oversights pertains to the nature of rational consciousness. The dynamic principle of human consciousness, Voegelin and Lonergan would point out, is the Question. This Question, this desire to understand, is aimed ultimately at knowledge of and communion with the true ground of being. Now, first, this true ground of being is not something that can ever be effectively dismissed as a proper object in the search for meaning, because it is universally *experienced,* as the "something" from which each questioner has emerged and which constitutes his or her deepest identity. Second, because human questioning is *unrestricted,* it belongs to its very nature to desire to grasp the *complete* intelligibility of the contingently existing universe of which it is a part. Third, because the contingent universe is not completely intelligible without the supposition of a necessary (noncontingent) ground, human rational inquiry is itself meaningful only on the supposition that such a ground is real. Thus, the ground experienced as the questioner's very source and identity is *inevitably and rationally* sought as the necessary reality from which contingent consciousness has emerged. Human consciousness is *by nature,* therefore, contingent existence in search of the necessary, transcendent ground its very existence presupposes. Human existence is *in its essence* the "experienced tension between contingency and necessity."[26] So the philosophical attempt to remove a necessary, transcendent ground of existence

26. Voegelin, "Quod Deus Dicitur," in *Published Essays, 1966–1985,* 379. This phrase appears in Voegelin's brief exposition of Thomas Aquinas's treatment in the *Summa Theologiae* (1.2.3) of the question of God's existence; here the essence of the Thomasic analysis, Voegelin states, is that there "is no divinity other than the necessity in tension with the contingency experienced

from human self-interpretation, to reduce all experience to "sheer contingency," implicitly denies meaning to the unrestrictedness of human questioning, and is consequently doomed to discreditation by the fundamental character of human experience and thought itself.

The second key oversight is that the critique assumes, wrongly, that any affirmation of transcendent being implies a totalistic claim—that the affirmation of a realm of transcendent meaning is incompatible with a tolerant concern for otherness and with recognition of the historicity and contingencies of the human situation. However, this is to misinterpret both experiences of transcendence and the proper meaning of symbolic affirmations of transcendence, which, as we shall have occasion to discuss, are in fact quite harmonious not only with the rejection of totalistic attitudes and the promotion of a sense of solidarity with human beings of all times, places, and cultures, but also with recognition of the complete contingency of the finite universe.

Third, as a result of these first two oversights, the respect for mystery so evident in the writings of the philosophers of groundlessness—their acknowledgment of elemental and permanent unknowns in our search for meaning—gets *misdirected* away from transcendence. In their interpretations of the human condition, the ambiguities and unknowns that properly pertain to transcendent meaning are injected or folded back into the experience and knowledge of mundane reality. Practical and psychological judgments, interpretations of historical events, solutions to the problems of everyday living, even scientific explanations, are portrayed as the thrust of mythic imagination and intention: in their view, all knowledge is finally no more than a kind of creative play among permanently unstable meanings. Adopting this attitude may certainly induce a quickened sense of participating in a surprising and open-ended drama, but at the cost of renouncing a most significant and hard-won achievement in the human struggle for adequate self-understanding. That hard-won achievement is, first, the clear and explicit recognition that the basis of human mysteries is a transcendent realm of meaning, and, second, the careful differentiation of this realm from the finite realms of meaning accessible to direct human understanding.

---

in the noetic [rational-critical] question" (379). Shortly afterward in the same essay, he points out that Descartes's analysis of the question of God's existence in the *Third Meditation* and *Principles of Philosophy* is similar: for Descartes, "[t]here is no doubting contingency without the tension toward the necessity which makes the doubt evident as such" (380).

Because of these oversights, philosophies of groundlessness will always remain vulnerable to critical pressure arising from the religious and philosophical traditions in which the realm of transcendent meaning has been explicitly identified and symbolized. No philosophical interpretation of our human condition, however brilliant and sincere, that ignores or denies these discernments and symbolizations will finally succeed in its effort to eclipse them and reduce the fullness of reality to groundless contingency. Such reductionisms will always in the long run "invite their own reversal," to use Lonergan's phrase, because in linguistic and cultural horizons long informed by sophisticated symbolizations of experiences of transcendence, the need for common recognition of a common story rooted in the actually experienced transcendent ground will always continue to be felt, and the human search for meaning will sooner or later rejuvenate traditional symbols, or create new symbols, for the authentic articulation of that recognition.

What will such a reversal look like in contemporary philosophical culture? It will have to unite the postmodernist rejection of totalizing systems of thought with the acknowledgment that transcendent meaning is a fact, but not a fact that implies that human beings can legitimately claim knowledge of a complete and systematic explanation of all reality. It would respect that transcendence means *mystery:* that what is truly transcendent can never be substantively known by human consciousness. Second, it will have to critically emphasize the distinction between, on the one hand, the many types and domains of human knowledge of finite reality and, on the other hand, stories, myths, or visions of the Whole that orient us in relation to transcendence through the articulation of a common drama. Third, it will have to appreciate that the human orientation to transcendence through stories of the Whole *must* be pluralistic and "multicultural," because while there is only one realm of transcendence, a drama of the Whole can be convincing to a person only if it succeeds in integrating the particulars of local experience and history into a comprehensive narrative. Different societies and cultures will inevitably understand themselves through different stories of the Whole.

In other words, the very notion of such a recovery presumes metanarratives that not only are not exclusivist but *require* the embrace of the full range of human otherness as well. While any metanarrative remains a story comprehensive *in scope,* by its affirmation of the Mystery at the center of all human self-understanding, a responsible metanarrative is both a repudiation of every system of final answers and also open to a diversity of cultural stories of the Whole that explores and affirms transcendent meaning. Thus, a postmodern reversal of the eclipse of transcendence will see the emergence of a fully responsible, transcendence-oriented pluralism—a pluralism open and responsive, that is, to the full scope of the Question.

Finally, it is only through such a pluralistic recovery of transcendence that we will move beyond the two distorted views of *history* that dominate contemporary thought. One of these is the view that a totalizing system of final answers about history is available to humans. This view is distorted both because it ignores history's open-endedness and because it sidesteps the mystery of transcendent meaning. The other dominant view is the "postmodern" understanding of history as the ongoing expansion of human freedom and tolerance through increasing recognition that existence is nothing other than a "free play" of meanings within a purely contingent universe. As already indicated, this view is distorted because accounts of history arising from philosophies of groundlessness and their rhetoric of sheer contingency are, in the last analysis, if not nihilistic, at least experientially and rationally self-defeating. In the end, only a human history grounded in a mystery of transcendence can be a genuinely and ultimately meaningful story, a drama to which one may give one's full assent while simultaneously recognizing the diversity of human cultures, respecting the unknown future uses of human freedom, and embracing the oneness of the human community. The following chapters will explore such an understanding of human history.

2

THE TERROR OF HISTORY

History, Stephen said, is a nightmare from which I am trying to awake.

—JAMES JOYCE, *ULYSSES*

HISTORY, to be precise about the term, is not everything that has ever happened, but the remembered and recorded past, the past judged worthy of reflection and narration. A "history" is a story comprising, not all events, but significant events. The weight of significance is something to be determined by the person trying to make sense of the flow of events, and the result is a tale, a story worth narrating, a pattern of the significant and essential.

History is therefore a somewhat complex phenomenon, in that two components are required for its constitution: the occurrence of the significant events themselves, and the subsequent recognizing and telling of them. For this reason, when we speak of a "history" we might be referring to (1) a course of events, (2) the recorded narrative of those events, or (3) the combination of the two. Not only must there be a tale worth telling, but the tale must be drawn out or deciphered from the flux of events, and must be told, heard, and remembered, for history to exist.[1]

What makes events memorable? In general, we could say that memorable events are those that have the most explanatory, or revelatory, power. A biographer eliminates the dross, the insignificant, from a life story, in order to expose the essential identity—the essential development, self-understanding, decisions, actions, and influences—of a person. When Jean-Paul Sartre in his

1. On this "double constitution" of history and its epistemological implications, see Voegelin, "What Is History?" in *What Is History?* 10–13.

autobiography recollects that youthful occasion on which, after performing some mischief, he suddenly and painfully felt himself "seen by God," and reacted by flying into a rage "against so crude an indiscretion" as divine omniscience and by severing from that point all relations with God, we do not wonder why he includes the episode in his memoirs.[2] He does not tell us, nor does he probably remember, what he ate for breakfast that morning; it is irrelevant to the formation of his character, and thus to his desire to understand and explain himself. The same principle, the desire to understand the essential, guides the writing of the story of a political or cultural movement, or the history of a nation or civilization. World history, too, is a narrative chosen in the hope or confidence that it is precisely these recollected events that will most help us comprehend ourselves and our human situation.

There is disagreement, of course, about which data have the highest explanatory value for telling the comprehensive human story. A world historian of Marxist persuasion, for example, will insist that material and economic conditions together with economically determined social relations provide the most fundamental data for making sense of human history, on the principle that these elements are constitutive of the human "essence."[3] By contrast, a Jewish or Christian portrayal of world history will be organized ultimately around shifting patterns of human response to divine presence (as understood within these respective traditions), as the key factors in making sense of the human story. Disagreements arise because events recommend themselves as most pertinent to human history in direct relation to certain assumptions about the ultimate nature of reality. Every historian or philosopher of history identifies or presumes a ground of meaning, a bedrock of meaning, that consists of the reality or realities he or she is convinced are the most fundamental and enduring. For the Marxist historian, human meaning is ultimately to be determined in terms of material conditions and economic relations (these

2. Sartre, *The Words,* 102.

3. "[At] each stage [of history] there is found a material result: a sum of productive forces, an historically created relation of individuals to nature and to one another, which is handed down to each generation from its predecessor; a mass of productive forces, capital funds and conditions, which, on the one hand, is indeed modified by the new generation, but also on the other prescribes for it its conditions of life and gives it a definite development, a special character. . . . This sum of productive forces, capital funds and social forms of intercourse, which every individual and generation finds in existence as something given, is the real basis of what the philosophers have conceived as 'substance' and 'essence of man' " (Karl Marx and Friedrich Engels, *The German Ideology,* 59).

function as the ground of meaning); for the Jewish or Christian historian, human meaning is ultimately to be determined in relation to God (God is the ground of meaning).

However, professional historians and biographers are not the only people who construct histories. We all do, to the extent that we fashion into narrative wholes the stories of our own lives for telling to ourselves and to others. Our personal stories, we realize, are embedded in ever broader contexts of meaning that include family histories, national histories, and civilizational histories, all of which we interpret in some fashion; these ever more embracing histories are in the end embraced by the overarching drama of humankind. We have noted in the Introduction that despite a breakdown of shared myths together with contemporary rationales for an irreconcilably fragmented human drama, an experiential sense of the unity of human history remains alive. So it is that most everyone has at least some interpretation, however vague, of the overarching human drama as the ultimate backdrop of meaning within which his or her personal search for meaning takes place. Moreover, whatever a person's interpretation of the drama of history might entail, it reflects, as does that of any philosopher of history, assumptions about the ultimate nature of reality. In other words, every mature person's self-understanding reflects some interpretation of the drama of human history, and this interpretation in turn reflects assumptions about the ground of meaning.

It will be revealing, then, to approach the question of human history by way of the constant human concern with the ground of meaning. Such an approach will help to make clear how the modern eclipse of transcendence discussed in the Introduction has, by misdirecting the search for the necessary and transcendent ground of meaning toward contingent being, given rise both to disastrously influential visions of historical determinism and to experiences of history as a monotonous sequence of strictly mundane and equally valueless moments, in each case exposing contemporaries to what Mircea Eliade calls "the terror of history."

The Search for the Ground in Cosmological Existence and the Discovery of Transcendence

Because it belongs to the very nature of human consciousness to be (to repeat Eric Voegelin's phrase) an "experienced tension between contingency and necessity," the human search for the ground of reality has always been a search for some necessary mode of being. The ground sought for is being or truth that is stable and enduring; only reality that *must* be the way it is, that is intrinsically beyond change and thus unalterable, is an absolute guarantee of stability of meaning. An example of such reality is the God of ancient Hebrew faith: "The grass withers, the flower fades, but the word of our God remains for ever" (Isa. 40:8). The God Yahweh promises an eternal law and justice that are not subject to change, as are mere created things: "The heavens will vanish like smoke, the earth wear out like a garment . . . but my salvation shall last for ever and my justice have no end" (51:6). The enduringness of this same God and his salvific justice is further revealed, for Christians, through the epiphany of Jesus the Christ, who in witnessing to that justice declares in the Gospel of Matthew: "Heaven and earth will pass away, but my words will never pass away" (Matt. 24:35). Thus the anonymous author of the Letter to the Hebrews writes confidently to his Christian brethren: "We have been given possession of an unshakeable kingdom" (Heb. 12:28).[4]

The transcendent ground of meaning need not, of course, be symbolized as a personal divinity. For instance, in the Chinese conception of the Tao, as already noted, we find affirmation of an impersonal reality that is both a necessary and unshakable law and the measure for grasping the true meaning of all things and all actions. Because necessary reality is that which is never otherwise, the Tao is not subject to change as are finite things:

> There was something formless and perfect
> before the universe was born.
> It is serene. Empty.
> Solitary. Unchanging. . . .
>
> Man follows the earth.
> Earth follows the universe.
> The universe follows the Tao.
> The Tao follows only itself.[5]

East and West, early and late in human history, the ground of being is conceived of as permanent and noncontingent—a necessary reality with which

4. Translations are from *The Jerusalem Bible.*
5. Mitchell, *Tao Te Ching,* chap. 25.

humans seek to establish a firm and truthful relation as the final arbiter of personal and historical meaning.

It has been indicated in the Introduction why the search for a necessary ground of being is ubiquitous in human culture. The search is impelled by the natural human desire to understand as fully as possible the reality in the midst of which we find ourselves, a desire resonant with the awareness that our own personal existences are derived, dependent on something other, contingent. As René Descartes put it, we are conscious of occupying some sort of "middle ground" between "supreme being and non-being": we do not have the power either to create ourselves or to ensure our existence, and we participate in the temporal order whose law is that of coming-to-be and passing-away.[6] Human existence is fragile, a precarious emergence out of nonexistence, hovering over the abyss of nonexistence to which it may return at any time. Part of the normal response to our awareness of this situation is anxiety: we feel an anxious concern to diminish the threat of precariousness, to seek a connection to what is more lasting in reality, to secure a more firm foothold in being.[7] Thus, the search for that which exists of necessity is scarcely a disinterested intellectual exercise. On the contrary, it is endowed with massive emotional value, impelled partly by our anxiety over our own precarious existences, but impelled also, we should remember, by our trustful and hopeful yearning for ultimate meaning, whose most satisfying expression is unrestricted love of the mystery of unrestricted being.

As our references to the Hebrew and Christian God and to the Chinese Tao have suggested, the search for insight into necessary being and our human relation to it has for most of humanity not been experienced as a vain undertaking. A permanent and necessary order of reality has been identified, symbolized, analyzed, and made the focus of meditation and contemplation, worship and prayer. We should be aware, though, that the Western God and the Chinese Tao are sophisticated symbols of transcendent reality that made their appearance relatively late on the human scene. They are two expressions

6. Descartes, *Meditations on First Philosophy,* Meditation Four, 79.

7. For the classic philosophical texts on anxiety (angst), see Søren Kierkegaard, *The Concept of Anxiety;* and Martin Heidegger, *Being and Time,* esp. 225–35. For an analysis of the relationship between anxiety and the search for the ground to which the present chapter is much indebted and which deserves a place among the basic philosophical texts on anxiety, see Voegelin, "Anxiety and Reason," in *What Is History?*

of that profound transition in human self-understanding wherein the transcendence of the ground became *explicitly* distinguished and thus *conceptually sharply separated* from worldly, spatiotemporal reality. In cultures not yet touched by this explicit identification of transcendence, the whole of reality including the sacred or divine ground was experienced without this sharp distinction between world and transcendence. In all early cultures, reality in its completeness was experienced and understood in a more interpenetrating fashion, as an interwoven unity of order, which may be designated by the word *cosmos* (from the Greek *kosmos,* meaning "an ordered whole"). In such cultures, the ground of reality was, we might say, imaginatively and conceptually still interfused with what we would call the natural world. In "cosmological" cultures, therefore, the search for necessary and permanent being found the goal of its search not in a transcendent divinity or principle, as this had not yet been sharply and clearly "differentiated," as Voegelin puts it, but rather in the forces and rhythms of cosmic order, whose energy, lastingness, and regularities were understood to evidence sacred power and intention.[8] The "undifferentiated" consciousness of cosmological cultures will be revisited in expanding detail in the following chapters. For now what needs to be understood is that in such consciousness, the necessary ground of being, not yet radically divorced from spatiotemporal being by critical thought, found adequate representation in an exotic multiplicity of imaginable and semi-imaginable divine beings, in stories of the relationships and conflicts of divine beings with each other, and in accounts of their creative actions with and upon the palpable world of experience. The connection with permanent reality, then, for members of cosmological societies, was the connection with "intracosmic" gods who were, inevitably, closely identified with what we would call the "forces of nature." Furthermore, the ritual, sacred activities that secured and maintained that connection were the central scenes in the drama of cosmological human existence.

8. For an introduction to the cosmological perception of reality, see Voegelin, *Israel and Revelation,* 39–84. Voegelin regards the explicit discovery or "differentiation" of transcendence in various world cultures, and the ensuing transitions from what he calls "compact" (or cosmological) to "differentiated" styles of self-understanding, to have constituted the single most important and problematic development in the history of the human search for meaning. For a summarizing account of his treatment of the subject, which dominates his writings on consciousness and underpins the organizational plan of much of *Order and History,* see "The Question of the Ground," chap. 2 in *Mystery and Myth,* by G. Hughes, 41–69.

Mircea Eliade has explained in persuasive detail how the essential goal of religious activities in archaic societies, which was to forge a connection with the power and enduringness of sacred reality, involved the repeated *annihilation of time* through ritual participation in the archetypal actions of divine personages that established the world and its features "in the beginning." These divine personages and events were understood to be *true* reality, *real* reality: efficacious, necessary, perfect, and immune from the deteriorating effects of time. Human existence, however, is lived in time, or in "history," defined in this context by Eliade as "a succession of events that are irreversible, unforeseeable, possessed of autonomous value." From our present perspective, one of the most striking characteristics of the cosmological outlook is its refusal to place a value on history so defined. It is an attitude typified, indeed, by an intense desire to abolish historical time, to periodically annul it and thus experience time as "starting over."[9]

Why was this desire so intense, and how was it possible to experience the abolition or cancellation of historical time? First, the desire to annul time springs from the view that because "merely historical" or temporary things or events have no enduring or self-sufficient being, they have no *intrinsic* value. As finite and temporary realities they are not *really* real; they exist or happen, but because they are transient they are saturated with nonexistence and so with meaninglessness. Life in "historical time," therefore—life in its character as a succession of unique and irreversible events—is not as such meaningful; it becomes significant only through its involvement in, its connection with, the unchanging, archetypal, true reality of divine being. From within this perspective, the desire to transcend the merely historical or temporal would be especially acute where suffering is concerned, because suffering that is merely "historical" and unconnected with sacred being and purpose would be experienced as arbitrary and pointless. As Eliade emphasizes, it is possible for human beings (whether of cosmological or later cultures) to tolerate sufferings such as those inflicted by disease, natural disaster, or the cruelties of warfare so long as they have a meaning that raises them above the level of pure arbitrariness, as long as they are not absurd. Purely "historical" suffering,

9. Eliade, *Myth of Return*, 95. The present chapter is indebted for its title and one of its guiding themes to Eliade's detailed analysis in *Myth of Return* of what he calls "the terror of history," which is also the title of its fourth and final chapter.

however—suffering unrelated to any transtemporal meaning—is terrifying, and for many unbearable.[10]

Second, the annulment of the effects of historical time could be experienced as a genuine occurrence because cosmological consciousness identified the ground of reality—what exists originally and of necessity—with the powers and rhythms of what we would call the natural universe. That is, the eternal ground of meaning was conceived in such a way that it was not *radically* distinguished from spatiotemporal entities and events, and consequently the things and events of everyday life could, through appropriate ritual, be followed by the searching and participating imagination to a point of seamless merging with divine archetypes, and thus mundane reality could be experienced as dissolving into primordial, sacred reality. A return to pristine origins, for both society and world, could therefore be experienced as fact. Through the efficacy of *rituals of a renewing return to the sacred,* historical time with its threat of meaninglessness and its accumulation of imperfect action, guilt, and suffering could be experienced as periodically annihilated and as beginning anew.[11]

It is a commonplace in historical studies to assert that as a consequence of these cyclical experiences involving the periodic annihilation and renewal of historical time, cosmological cultures had no genuine experience of "history" in the larger sense of an overarching and ongoing linear progression of unique human events. History, we are frequently told, was (in the West) a discovery of the ancient Hebrews, through their experiences of an explicitly transcendent God, in relation to which human events for the first time took on the character of a unique series of unfolding situations, the story of a one-time Creation and its career in time. While this view reflects a solid core of insight concerning the decisiveness of the Hebrew experience of transcendence and its accompanying radical insistence on the significance of historical particularity, it is also partly misleading, because it oversimplifies the cosmological experience. While the cosmological understanding of existence was indeed dominated by cyclical experiences of time, unrepeatable linear time was not simply excluded from cosmological awareness and self-interpretation. After all, it is the disquieting awareness of linear or "historical" time that constitutes

10. Ibid., 95–102.

11. See Eliade, *The Sacred and the Profane,* 69–80.

the motivating cause of cosmological efforts to abolish time through rituals of renewal. However, unrepeatable linear time also, in many cosmological societies, received symbolic articulation and acknowledgment. Voegelin has established this through his analysis of the phenomenon he calls "historiogenesis," a feature of cultural self-interpretation readily discernible in cosmological cultures of the ancient Near East.

Historiogenesis is a mythopoeic speculation on ultimate beginnings. As cosmogony is a mytho-speculation on the origins of the cosmos, and theogony on the origins of the gods, and anthropogony on the origins of humankind, so historiogenesis speculates on the ultimate beginnings of the presently experienced social order. It functions in the same way as does all myth: it explains how a phenomenon—in this case the speculator's society—came into existence in an ultimate sense. It does this by telling the story of this society beginning at an absolute point of divine-cosmic origins, proceeding through mythical and legendary events that merge into the known events of recent history, and concluding with the establishment of the society in which the author is writing, now firmly revealed in its inevitability.[12]

An example of historiogenesis can be seen in the Sumerian King List (ca. 2050 B.C.E.). The list identifies a continuous line of Sumerian kings and dynasties beginning with a divinely creative origin—"When kingship was lowered from heaven, kingship was first in Eridu"—and culminating in the author's present (which was a period of imperial restoration). Research has shown that, in fact, the imperial territory of Sumer included numerous city-states with parallel royal dynasties, one of which would temporarily gain imperial ascendancy over the others. In the King List, though, the parallel histories and dynasties are placed in temporal succession, straightened to a

12. Voegelin makes it clear that historiogenesis is not universally found in cosmological societies: "As a matter of fact, wherever it can be dated, historiogenesis proves to develop later than the speculations on the other realms of being [the gods, the world, and human being]; and in some cosmological societies it does not develop at all" ("Anxiety and Reason," in *What Is History?* 55). Nevertheless, its presence in those cosmological cultures in which it is found confirms that the concern with irreversible time, and thus with "history," is not entirely absent from cosmological societies. Even more fruitfully, Voegelin finds historiogenetic speculation to be "virtually omnipresent" in all later developed societies, East and West, from ancient Israel, China, and India up to and including the modern West (56). It thus appears to be a symbolic form of considerable importance for the understanding of historical self-interpretation. For Voegelin's analysis, see "Historiogenesis," chap. 1 in *The Ecumenic Age*, 108–66. The essay "Anxiety and Reason," published posthumously in *What Is History?* (1990), is an earlier version of this chapter.

unilinear stream of history that firmly and directly links the present society to the divine origin. "The relevant course of events," Voegelin states, "descends ineluctably from the cosmic origin down to the present of the authors whose society is the only one that matters." The present society is thus legitimated and sanctified as the inevitable goal of history.[13]

There is no getting around the fact that unrepeatable and ongoing linear time is the object of interest here. Historiogenesis, with its rigid documentation of the inevitability of the step-by-step process leading from cosmic beginnings to the current social order, is a "ruthless construction of unilinear history." Cosmological experiences of time, then, can be regarded as having been somewhat more complex than is often assumed by scholars. The cyclical experience of time, and of time's periodic abolition and renewal, can dominate a perspective that also, however, accommodates some recognition of unrepeatable linear time, the historical time in which "opportunities are lost forever and defeat is final."[14]

However, it may be asked: is such an accommodation truly possible? It would seem to be a psychological impossibility to experience natural or social time as starting anew while simultaneously recognizing time's linear continuity. In reply, it may be argued that such an accommodation only seems impossible to us because we have so completely lost the cosmological perspective, which in part is characterized by the absence of certain conceptual distinctions. Most crucially, there is as yet no explicit conceptual idea of a transcendent ground of reality, and so correspondingly no explicit conception of an immanent, worldly, *temporal* reality radically distinct from the sacred. Reality is still the unity of the cosmos: the space and time of the finite universe are still saturated with the timelessness of divine presence. With respect to the "compact" cosmological experience of time, then, we might say that the *experience* of (worldly) unrepeatable time did not yet have enough distinct meaning to challenge the *experience* of the cyclical dissolution of time in the ever present sacred, that is, that the experience of ongoing linear time was enough of a concern to prompt the creation of such speculative forms as historiogenesis where these appear, without as yet posing a conceptual threat to the validity of cosmological experiences, in religious ritual, of the cyclical abolition and

13. Voegelin, *The Ecumenic Age,* 115. On the Sumerian King List, see 114–18, 134–36. The classic text is Thorkild Jacobsen, *The Sumerian King List* (1939).

14. Voegelin, "Anxiety and Reason," in *What Is History?* 55.

renewal of time through its immersion in the sacred. There would be *a sense* of time as ongoing, but also an *ultimately more important sense* of time as repeatedly beginning anew. This appears to be the only explanation compatible with the harmonious coexistence in cosmological cultures of historiogenetic speculation together with a rich body of rituals and symbols the primary purpose of which is the annulment and rebirth of "historical" time.

Moreover, a single and fully understandable motive can be discerned behind both the ritual return to timeless, archetypal being *and* the indulgence in historiogenetic speculation. That motive is the desire to overcome the precariousness of existence and its attendant anxiety. We have noted how cosmological religious rituals, by connecting participants with enduring and necessary being, overcame the threat of meaninglessness associated with merely temporal, contingent existence. In a related way, the firm linking of the present state of society through historiogenetic accounts to the original divine ordering of reality, in a manner indicating that no other course of events was possible, removed the index of contingency from social existence, and conferred upon it the sanction of necessity and the aura of predestination. Both symbolic forms, then, assuaged the anxiety that arises from an awareness that the meaning of particular, contingent existence depends on its relation to a self-sufficient and necessary ground of meaning. Both defused the threat of "mere" historicality—the threat, that is, of existence in time divorced from enduring, exemplary, timeless being.

The cosmological achievements in ordering human existence into a proper relation to necessary being were therefore successful—up to a point. That point was the revelation of the transcendence of the ground of being. In ancient Israel, in Hellas, in the cultures of ancient China and India, there occurred breakthrough discoveries that established the ground of reality as lying beyond the orders of space and time. In Israel Yahweh revealed himself to Moses as the "I AM WHAT I AM," separate from all created things, and to later prophetic understanding as the God of all the nations. In Greece poets and philosophers discerned with increasing clarity the transcendent universality of the first principle of reality, culminating in Plato's conception of a "being beyond being" and Aristotle's "unmoved mover." In India the Upanishadic texts on Brahman and the teachings of the Buddha, and in China the Confucian and Taoist insights, affirmed that the ground of reality is not to be identified with anything "intracosmic" but rather with a mysterious nonthing "behind," "underlying," or "beyond" all natural things.

The revolutionary impact of these discoveries, as they spread through their own and then surrounding cultures, can hardly be overestimated. The solace-providing myths and rituals that secured attunement with ultimate reality for cosmological societies eventually shattered or dissolved under the pressure of symbols of transcendent reality. A massive reordering of human existence was initiated that involved assimilating the fact and implications of these revelations and restructuring social, political, and religious life in accordance with their truth.

A first, brutal consequence of this differentiation of transcendence was that it made prominent and emphatic not only the essential unknowability of the ground of reality but also its relative inaccessibility. A certain sense of the palpable closeness of the divine, of human consubstantiality with the divine, had been lost. The ground had receded to a "beyond" of space and time and of the finite conditions of imagination, leaving humans with a heightened awareness of the precarious contingency of temporal existence and a correspondingly heightened anxiety about securing the meaning of that existence. The new dispensation ushered in by the explicit differentiation of transcendence was characterized above all by "existential uncertainty" about the fragile status of the human relationship to the ground of meaning.[15]

A second consequence pertained to understanding the relationship between the temporal world and timeless being. As the case of Israel shows most clearly, when the ground ceases to be identified with the natural world—when the "cosmos" conceptually splits asunder into (1) a world of spatiotemporal or immanent nature and (2) a transcendent beyond of nature (a Creator-God, in Hebrew and Christian thought)—then the finite (or created) world is indeed released into "history" in a pregnant sense. That is, objects and events of the physical world can no longer *be* archetypal in an immediacy of participatory identity; rather, they must be understood as only *related* to the timeless ground, in a permanent tension of relatedness. However, this places them solidly under the index of temporal and individual objects and events, so that the course of human events becomes a historical sequence of unique situations.[16]

15. Ibid., 69–70.

16. Voegelin, "What Is History?" in *What Is History?* 21–23, 35–36. This consequence of worldly things and persons being understood as unique and temporal in a profound way, and as existing in a "tension of relatedness" to transcendent reality, equally pertains to those cultures,

A third consequence was that direct access to necessary and transtemporal meaning could now be found only through internal processes of the soul. Once the ground has been conceptually divorced from the physical universe, there can be no experience of *direct* access to transcendence except through the interior element in human being that is capable of discerning and responding to transcendence. In the Hebrew and Christian traditions, this element is the "spirit"; the Greek philosophers identify it as psyche (soul) and, more precisely, nous (intellect, reason); the teaching in the Upanishads stresses the recognition of Atman (the true self) in its oneness with Brahman (the transcendent principle). Thus, the search for the ground was forced to turn inward, and to develop those subtle powers of self-reflective discernment that lead one to truth only by exposing one also to the many dangers of spiritual self-deception. And not the least significant obstacle to such a search is the need to develop the emotional capacity to embrace its permanent uncertainties.

In the new dispensation, then, access to the timeless was still possible, but only under the conditions of what Christians call "faith": the effort to order one's existence through a hopeful and loving relation to an essentially mysterious ground of reality that, in relation to the natural world, is a "no-thing," nothing. Under these conditions, the experiences of ritual renewal and regeneration are still accessible, though, of course, only in the realm of interiority, and so only on the level of the individual person, not on that of nature, or of society en masse. A clear example of this is the Christian experience of personal regeneration through ritual participation in the birth, passion, death, and resurrection of Christ, which allows the believer to transcend "mere" history and its threat of pointless action and meaningless suffering and which sanctifies historical reality by infusing it with divine participation.[17] The

---

such as the later Hindu, in which the physical universe is conceived as a thing that will be born and reborn in infinite succession, and to philosophies, such as certain branches of post-Aristotelian thought, in which history is imagined to be a finite thing whose persons and events will periodically recur, repeating themselves down to the smallest detail. The transcendent timelessness of the ground must have already been conceptually removed from the finite and physical realm for the cosmos to be considered a "thing" that can be successively reborn, or for history to be thought of as a "thing" that can occur over and over. See Voegelin, *The Ecumenic Age*, 128–33, 393–95. We will return to this topic in the following chapter.

17. Eliade, *Myth of Return*, 129–30.

Hindu teachings on *moksha* ("liberation") and the Buddhist paths to "enlightenment" likewise promise an escape from time, through appropriate self-discipline, attentiveness, right-mindedness, and spiritual struggle. The anxiety over contingent existence, heightened now through explicit recognition of the sharp distinction between particularity and the divine ground, need not remain unassuaged; the anxious soul can adjust itself, through "faith," to proper performance of its role as a temporal existence in whom a conscious relation to transcendent meaning is capable of being realized. It is still possible for history to be resolved in timeless reality, but only in the invisible silence of the soul.[18]

"Faith," so understood, has a limited appeal. Most people, it has turned out, are incapable of embracing its high demands, particularly its permanent uncertainties, so memorably characterized by Søren Kierkegaard: "Faith is precisely the contradiction between the infinite passion of the individual's inwardness and the objective uncertainty. . . . If I wish to preserve myself in faith I must constantly be intent upon holding fast the objective uncertainty, so as to remain out upon the deep, over seventy thousand fathoms of water, still preserving my faith."[19] Another demand arises from the transformation of world time into a historical unfolding of unique situations. If all world

18. There are, of course, important differences between Western and Eastern religious views on access to transcendent timelessness and salvation from time. The most important of these derive from the Western view of the universe as created *ex nihilo* by a personal God, while classic Confucian, Taoist, Buddhist, and Upanishadic teachings portray the universe as a beginningless and endless process arising from an impersonal divine mystery (though Hinduism and Buddhism embrace rich traditions in which the transcendent ground is personified, and Western mystical theologies acknowledge an unknowable ground of being beyond all analogies of personification). These differences lead to a difference in the value placed on the finite world. In the West, as the creation *ex nihilo* of a personal God, the imperfect world with its inevitable suffering is emphatically sacred and good, while in Eastern thought there is a tendency to devalue the world and the suffering existence naturally entails. Importantly, it also leads to different experiences of history. In the West, the concept of a Creator-God who creates the world *ex nihilo* separates the ground so radically from finite being, while simultaneously establishing it as the work of free and loving divine intention, that world history enjoys a high degree of autonomous value. In comparison, the Eastern concern with history is mild: the "nearness" of transcendence, as it were, limits the value of history. In this connection, Voegelin speaks of the rather "muted mode of differentiation" and the "muted" historical consciousness present in Eastern traditions (*The Ecumenic Age*, 356, 394).

19. Kierkegaard, *Concluding Unscientific Postscript*, 182. The "objective uncertainty" here referred to concerns the very Western problem of the mystery of God, but it can equally be applied to the question of the mystery of the Tao, or Brahman, or nirvana.

events constitute a singular unfolding in relation to a transcendent ground, then each individual life is also a sequence of unique moments in which the willingness and ability to attune oneself to transcendent meaning take on decisive importance. Religious life no longer has the "general" character, as Eliade puts it, of periodic dissolution into archetypal meaning for the purpose of ensuring the overall functioning of the divine economy. Now religious demands are personal, isolated, irreversible. The pressure of such responsibility is too great for most people to endure.[20] The alternative, though, to adjusting to at least some of the demands of faith, in a culture where cosmological myths and rituals have been rendered inefficacious and the intracosmic gods unbelievable due to the advancing influence of symbols of transcendence, is the relinquishing of access to timeless reality and the experiencing of existence as wholly contained within the time of "mere" history, that is, the time of history unredeemed by absorption into and resolution in the eternal present of necessary being and its self-sufficient meaning. This, too, is existentially daunting, perhaps in a strict sense psychologically impossible.

What in fact has emerged for most people in cultures East and West are ways of living that succeed in fending off the anxiety of historical contingency while not fully embracing the adventure of faith. These include nurturing a partial faith, which acknowledges to some degree the transcendence of the ground of meaning and the implications of transcendence, while nevertheless continuing to some degree to invest temporal objects and events with sacred power or the value of necessity (including all forms of belief in "magic," in strict intracosmic karma, and in "fate"); transferring to representative religious institutions the absolute authority corresponding to the perfection of the ground, thereby rendering the ground comfortably "visible"; and tolerating history by anticipating the end of time, taking refuge from the uncertainties and sufferings of existence in the thought of the *eschaton,* the last things and the end of world, which annuls history from the future, anticipatorily.[21]

20. Eliade, *Myth of Return,* 108–10. Voegelin highlights the difficulties of faith as one of the psychological consequences of the discovery of transcendence: "[The] thread of faith, on which hangs all certainty regarding divine, transcendent being, is indeed very thin. Man is given nothing tangible. The substance and proof of the unseen are ascertained through nothing but faith, which man must obtain by the strength of his soul. . . . Not all men are capable of such spiritual stamina; most need institutional help, and even this is not always sufficient" (*Science, Politics, and Gnosticism: Two Essays,* in *Modernity without Restraint: The Political Religions; The New Science of Politics; and Science, Politics, and Gnosticism,* 310).

21. On eschatological hope as an antihistorical attitude, see Eliade, *Myth of Return,* 111–12.

In the major Western religious traditions, the discovery of transcendence established God as the ground of meaning and the backdrop of history, the ultimate reality in relation to which events have historical significance. In Jewish, Christian, and Islamic cultures, history is a story told by God—or, rather, cotold by God and humanity, humanity shaping the story of history through its sharing in the privileges of divine freedom and creativity. Accordingly, the core of historical meaning is understood to be constituted by what takes place in human-divine interchange, in human response to divine initiative, in the dialogue between God and human creature repeatedly provoked by God's manifestations of divine truth and will. History, then, in these traditions, is in its deepest meaning the history of theophany—of divine presence, appearance, invitation, provocation, and impact.[22]

Regarding historical (or differentiated) existence in the context of Western traditions following from the discovery of divine transcendence, two consequences of special importance should be emphasized. First, from this perspective the entire universe is a contingent affair: none of it is being that *had* to be, none of its events has an intrinsic necessity, and so the meaningfulness of personal action and suffering in the world are not guaranteed through ritual alone but only affirmed in the tension and uncertainties of faith. Second, because each personal existence is unique, a one-time appearance in a one-time story, every person carries an individual burden of responsibility for successful action in history—for either attuning personal life with the truths of transcendent meaning or dissipating it in a flourish of irrelevancies. Together these consequences make up the frightening aspect of humanity's release from cosmological into historical existence, which can be characterized as the conscious exercise of unique and contingent existence. They are what lead people to try to avoid historical existence—through, for example, attempted reintroductions of intracosmic notions of the sacred, or through adherence to a rigid belief in "fate" or "destiny," or through hope for an imminent end to history, or through the practice of techniques for being released from this world into a better one—all of them efforts to escape from history. This explains why, typically, the demands of historical existence are able to be graciously affirmed and assimilated into action only so long as those traditions (religious, literary, political, philosophical, or educational) remain effectual that orient human living in conscious relation to transcendence.

22. Ibid., 102–12; Voegelin, *The Ecumenic Age,* 289–90, 317.

The Modern Eclipse of Transcendence and the Problem of World-Immanent History

As discussed in the Introduction, the most recent act in the drama of the Western historical imagination involves a wide-scale dwindling of confidence in transcendent reality. Images and symbols of divine transcendence have become, for increasing numbers of people, ciphers that fail to communicate a genuinely intelligible or felt sense of truth. (Friedrich Nietzsche explains, in *The Joyful Wisdom*, that the phrase "God is dead" is to be understood as meaning that "the belief in the Christian God has ceased to be believable.")[23] Some of the many and complex reasons for this have already been mentioned. They include the rise of the modern mathematical sciences, and the impact on popular imagination of the use of their methods as an ultimate measure of truth and reality; the failure of Jewish, Christian, and Islamic theologies of history to respond adequately to changing political and economic circumstances involving global commerce and exploration, the emergence of nation-states, and the rise of industrial technologies; the defensive hardening of religious doctrines concerning transcendence into various voices of fundamentalist assertion that respond to the challenge of secular worldviews only with increasingly inexplicable commands; and, not least, with the philosophical "turn to the subject" and the growth of modern historical consciousness, a steadily intensifying awareness of the human role in the constitution of meaning. The outcome has been a decreasing ability or willingness to understand history as a story that begins and ends in God; consequently, modernity has been characterized by a vigorous search for a genuinely believable ground of meaning and historical significance.

The past couple of centuries in the West have produced a wide variety of fresh answers to the question about the ground. In the climate of Enlightenment thought, a rapidly expanding faith in the modern scientific method as the sole arbiter for determining what is true and real, together with a fading of belief in transcendent reality, led the search for the ground to structures of the physical world and the laws that govern their motions and developments. Various forms of philosophical materialism and determinism (the ground of meaning is matter and the laws that govern matter) made their appearance.

23. Walter Kaufmann, ed. and trans., *The Portable Nietzsche*, 447. The title of Nietzsche's work, *Die Fröliche Wissenschaft*, is also translated as *The Gay Science*.

More sophisticated types of determinism emerged that take the human subject as agent more fully into account: the ground of meaning lies in the laws that govern the human use of material circumstances, that is, in the forces of productive relations (Marx); or the ground of (human) meaning lies in sources of psychic energy that, operating below the level of consciousness, guide the direction of human thinking and action with the inexorability of physical laws (Freud). What such answers have in common is their imputation of the ground to some world-immanent aspect or aspects of being. From the point of view of the religions and philosophies of transcendence, they are forms of reductionism, in that they attempt to reduce transcendent meaning to purely worldly meaning. They are efforts at the radical immanentization of reality.[24]

These reductionisms necessitate new answers about where history is headed. A purely world-immanent historical process must have a purely world-immanent goal. There appear secular doctrines of progress, of the relentless improvement of the human condition, perhaps to culminate in a perfected state of fully enlightened human relations and permanent peace (Kant), undergirded by the miracles of technology. Alternately some, like Freud, see history as a battlefield between the forces of life and civilization, on the one hand, and those of destructive human urges, on the other, a scenario that relocates the traditional apocalyptic struggle for spiritual salvation to the natural and social world. Or, history is organized like a drama into a sequence of discrete acts—ancient, medieval, modern, postmodern—that, if

24. As Voegelin has stated the matter: "What has happened to the transcendent ground in [this] connection? It has become, let us say, immanentized. We still have, of course, the quest of the ground, we want to know where things come from. But since God (in revelatory language) or transcendent divine being (in philosophical language) is prohibited for agnostics, they must put their ground elsewhere. And now we can see, beginning about the middle of the eighteenth century, in the Enlightenment, a whole series of misplacements of the ground. The transcendent ground is misplaced somewhere in an immanent hierarchy of being. . . . There is a whole gamut of possibilities of misplacing the ultimate ground: from human reason down to such phenomena as the Nordic race and—in between—the *libido,* the productive relations, economic or political rationality, and so on. . . . If you reflect on the whole series . . . you will find that there is a *limit* to such misplacements of the ground; you can misplace the ground only in more or less identifiable, distinguishable areas of immanent existence: human reason or animal urges or economic or political urges or the *libido* or sex relations or the color of the skin, and so on. But you can go only through: reason, psyche, body, inorganic matter. We can observe, for the last two hundred years, that every possible locale where one could misplace the ground has been exhausted" ("In Search of the Ground," in *Conversations with Eric Voegelin,* 13–16).

not leading to some permanent finale of perfection, still establishes a set of evolutionary categories for classifying its world-immanent mutations. What is clear in all this speculation is the heightened concern with temporal history itself, along with a readiness to invest the immediate present with the highest degree of historical significance. The philosophies of history that burst upon the scene in the eighteenth and nineteenth centuries, such as those of Condorcet, Kant, Comte, Hegel, and Marx, invariably assume, in one fashion or another, that the essential meaning of history lies in the improvements of progress, and that the justification of earlier stages of history is to be found in later (especially contemporary) achievements. Insofar as they assert as well that history had no alternative but to arrive at the present state of things, with the high point of advance being the author's own society, we again come across the comforting conceits of historiogenetic speculation—a type of speculation that, as Voegelin comments, "displays a curious tenacity of survival."[25]

The modern fascination with ironclad laws governing the course of history and with visions of relentless progress toward perfection is not difficult to fathom. It comes above all from the desire to find necessity operating in history. As the vision of transcendence fades, the awareness grows that if God or timeless being is no more than an illusion, the meaning of the historical enterprise is no sure thing. History becomes a story told by fragile human beings in precarious circumstances on a stage that could—by nuclear weapons or other means of devastation—be wiped clean with nothing remaining. The search for necessary laws governing history may be diagnosed as the search for a historical meaning that transcends human intention and action, that will relieve individuals of ultimate responsibility, provide a measure of forgiveness, and reestablish a sense of permanent meaning to human existence in time. It is, of course, a doomed search, for it is yet another reductionism. It unsuccessfully attempts to impose necessity—revealed by the spiritual and philosophical discoveries of the Axial Period to belong only to the timeless and self-sufficient being of transcendence—onto a world history whose intrinsic contingency remains, if unhappily, all too assuredly felt.

The modern secular philosophies of history, then, are not satisfactory solutions to the anxiety of contingent existence, which can be adequately assuaged

25. Voegelin, *The Ecumenic Age,* 117. For an overview of modern progressivist philosophies of history, and an account of their derivation and their deviation from the Hebrew-Christian understanding of history, see Karl Löwith, *Meaning in History.*

only by experiences of timeless being. Mircea Eliade has again put the matter succinctly: all points of view that reduce historical meaning to purely worldly conditions are not only frustrating but finally terrifying, because by removing timeless meaning from those conditions they "empty them of all exemplary meaning," and what results is a "terrible banalization of history," because physical, worldly, historical being is intrinsically *perishable* being.[26] Human actions are reduced, in effect, to temporary maneuverings in the void. Most distressingly, there is no protection against the threat of meaningless suffering. Calamities of misfortune, disease, oppression, and cruelty—not to mention the collective victimization resulting from totalitarian warfare and policies of mass intimidation, incarceration, deportation, and genocide—must be considered brute accidents of history, no more than mistakes or happenstance.

From the victim's perspective, this is hardly supportable. Here we can identify one of the sources—one of many, to be sure, but certainly a significant source—of the explosion of political terrorism on the part of secular revolutionaries during the past century and a half. For the secular revolutionary, if suffering is not felt to be redeemed through its participation in exemplary, divine meaning, then history must be forced, on pain of meaninglessness, to yield an outcome that justifies that suffering. History must be made to achieve a just solution, and the debts of suffering and injustice must be paid in history; only the victims, fighting for their due through violent action, can ensure this result. If political reality is proving stubbornly resistant to being shaped in accordance with envisioned justice, there is at least recourse to the democracy of fear, regardless of any politically realizable goal; through arbitrary acts of terrorism the victims of the terror of history can reduce representative others to their own state, and thus achieve historical parity. The terrorist psychology of secular revolutionaries is quite intelligible as a response to being cornered by the terror of history.[27]

Of course, most people who suffer from the terror of history, even excessively, do not become terrorists. They find other ways to cope with the threat of meaninglessness. As Henry David Thoreau noted, many an existence is

26. Eliade, *No Souvenirs: Journal, 1957–1969*, 55.

27. It might be argued that religiously motivated terrorism, too, springs indirectly from the terror of history, insofar as it erupts from an anxious need to verify God's love for history's victims through visible defeats inflicted upon their "enemies" in the here and now.

lived in "quiet desperation." Others seek out evidence of a fateful necessity ordering the patterns of their lives. In *Four Quartets,* T. S. Eliot presents a catalog of popular antidotes to the burden of historical contingency:

> To communicate with Mars, converse with spirits,
> To report the behaviour of the sea monster,
> Describe the horoscope, haruspicate or scry,
> Observe disease in signatures, evoke
> Biography from the wrinkles of the palm
> And tragedy from fingers; release omens
> By sortilege, or tea leaves, riddle the inevitable
> With playing cards, fiddle with pentagrams
> Or barbituric acids, or dissect
> The recurrent image into pre-conscious terrors—
> To explore the womb, or tomb, or dreams: all these are usual
> Pastimes and drugs, and features of the press:
> And always will be, some of them especially
> When there is distress of nations and perplexity
> Whether on the shores of Asia, or in the Edgware Road.

They are "pastimes and drugs," and not solutions to the question of personal and historical meaning, because they seek answers within the dimension of time, of imaginable past and future, whereas redemption from the terror of history can be found only where the human search for meaning encounters its transcendent ground, at "The point of intersection of the timeless / With time. . . ." We might add to Eliot's list the pastimes of terrorists and neighborhood gangs, the drugs of television and shopping, and the perennial belief that a New Age, with all its consoling perfections, is upon us at last.[28]

Another coping mechanism has been found by the postmodern philosophers of groundlessness and their professional followers, who have decided to

28. Eliot, "The Dry Salvages," in *Four Quartets,* 135–36. In 1930 Austrian Robert Musil, in his novel *The Man without Qualities,* described those who in every age are ready to proclaim "the pernicious nonsense known as the New Age": "This sort of people had in all ages regarded themselves as constituting the New Age. . . . In these people there lived, in the queerest way, the conviction that it was their mission to bring order into the world. . . . It shook them, it blew like a gust through their heads. . . . Ulrich had once, for the fun of it, asked them for exact statements of what they meant. They had looked at him disapprovingly and called his demand a mechanistic view of life, and skepticism, asserting that the most complicated things of all could only be solved in the simplest way, so that the new age, once it had sloughed off the present, would look quite simple" (184, 190–91).

make the most of the death of God and the absence of necessity by announcing, like Richard Rorty, the apotheosis of contingency. Trained to think things through and to eschew outmoded solutions, they are consistent enough to realize that without transcendent meaning, there can be no "ground" of historical relevance at all. It has become, therefore, intellectually au courant to insist that a historian's criteria for selecting pertinent materials are irredeemably subjective and arbitrary—that situating conditions, including unconscious motivations and biases, social and linguistic structures and instabilities, all the factors that make up the completely contingent personal and cultural perspective of a historiographer, render his or her construction of historical narratives unique and contestable at best, self-serving and reactionary at worst. The logical conclusion is that all principles of selection for telling a history, all "backgrounds of meaning," are equally valid—or, with respect to the desideratum of a "true" account of significant events, equally invalid.

It can be exciting to deny that there is any ultimately stable meaning within the scope of human experience. Exciting in the short run, anyway. A more profound experience of the idea leads to more problematic feelings. If it is really true that there is no human connection whatsoever with timeless meaning, then no event can be more meaningful than any other; to thus reduce all events to equal status and every storyteller's perspective to equal arbitrariness is then tantamount to reducing experience to meaninglessness. This is another reason that the idea of groundlessness, as a counter in philosophical and academic games, has little real purchasing power. People continue to search (and search with success) for the genuinely timeless ground of personal and human history in part because the mood evoked by a serious adoption of—rather than mere intellectual flirtation with—the idea of groundlessness is existential despair, a despair evident in those who genuinely suffer, existentially or politically, from the terror of sheer contingency. Eloquent voices of that despair are to be found scattered throughout Western literature of the nineteenth and (especially) twentieth centuries, with none, perhaps, more fluent than those of the characters in the works of Samuel Beckett. With anguished precision they speak of purely historical time as an interminable piling up of valueless moments, each as pointless as the next:

> Have you not done tormenting me with your accursed time! It's abominable! When! When! One day, is that not enough for you, one day he went dumb, one day I went blind, one day we'll go deaf, one day we were born,

> one day we shall die, the same day, the same second, is that not enough for you?
>
> Moment upon moment, pattering down, like the millet grains of . . . that old Greek, and all life long you wait for that to mount up to a life. Ah let's get it over![29]

As Beckett and other artists who speak for innumerable victims of the terror of history attest, the principal symptom of full and honest exposure to sheer contingency is despair.

History as a Process Grounded in Transcendence

In the course of this chapter the term *history* has undergone more than one change of meaning. At the start, it was defined as (1) a record of memorable events with explanatory power, events whose significance is determined in relation to some ground of meaning, however this ground may be conceived. Later, in the context of our discussion of cosmological culture and its eventual dissolution through the explicit identification and symbolization of transcendence, the term *history* was used to designate (2) the experience of temporal existence as a succession of unique persons and events, sharply distinguished from the timeless dimension of reality (which becomes, when the timeless dimension is rejected as an illusion, the experience of "mere" history). And finally, history has been described as (3) a pattern of human events unfolding in relation to a transcendent ground, as human beings search for and undergo transformations in relation to timeless meaning.

It will be noted that in the popular mind, as well as in the writings of most historiographers, world history is understood in the sense of (2) above. That is, even if a permanent ground of meaning is assumed, history is thought of simply as the total world-immanent course of events. However, we have seen that it is this conception of world history, or rather this *experience* of history, that can provoke terror once the timelessness of transcendent meaning ceases to be believable. It is the image of human reality as "mere" spatiotemporal existence that prompts the building of existential and intellectual escape routes, not all of them harmless, from the burden of sheer contingency. It will be noted further that history in the sense of (3) is a version of the general

29. Beckett, *Waiting for Godot*, 57B; *Endgame*, 70.

definition of history with which we began (1)—a refinement, in fact, reflecting the discovery that necessary, timeless reality must have the character of transcendence. For reflecting on world history, then, we will say that history (3) is the most philosophically sound conception of the process of human history, informed as it is by the fullest range of philosophical and spiritual insights into the transcendent nature of the ground of meaning.

At the level of personal experience, it is again history in this sense, history as a pattern of human events unfolding in relation to a transcendent ground, that offers the sole responsible remedy for the terror of history. That is, in the modern world, anxiety over the implicit nothingness of purely contingent personal existence and world history can be genuinely allayed only through consciously gaining access to timelessness through experiences of transcendence, through insights and emotions that connect us with a nontemporal sense of identity. Thus the recurrent appeal for many, even in a strenuously secular culture, of injunctions to "put on the mind of Christ" or to "find one's original Buddha-nature" or in any equivalent way to ground personality in the transcendently real. "[M]an probably cannot rejoice over the gifts of existence," notes Eliade, "if he does not take them as signs that have come from the beyond," for only then can one "build a structure and read a message in the formless flux of things and the monotonous flow of historical facts."[30] This can be accomplished only through personally suffering openness to the mystery of transcendence—an openness that is always existentially challenging, but that is especially hindered, in our times, by the opacity of traditional symbols of transcendence, by modern secular conceits of a purely world-immanent history leading to a purely world-immanent goal, and by postmodern declarations that sheer contingency is all there is. Only through openness to the mystery of transcendence can historical existence in the end be found to be not a nightmare, but a meaningful adventure, perhaps even a blessing.

What, then, would the process of world history look like, so to speak, with its transcendent ground taken properly into account? To answer this we will turn to *The Ecumenic Age*, the fourth volume of Eric Voegelin's five-volume *Order and History*, which stands as the high point of his efforts to articulate and apply the principles of a philosophy of history that would do justice both to contemporary scholarship in all relevant fields and to the fact of a transcendent ground of human existence.

30. Eliade, *No Souvenirs: Journal, 1957–1969*, 85, 94.

3

HISTORY AND TRANSCENDENCE

> It seems, as one becomes older,
> That the past has another pattern, and ceases to be a mere
> sequence—
> Or even development . . .
> . . . for history is a pattern
> Of timeless moments.
>
> —T. S. ELIOT, *FOUR QUARTETS*

THE ECUMENIC AGE (1974), though it was to be followed by the slim, posthumously published *In Search of Order* (1987) as the fifth and final volume of *Order and History,* nevertheless constitutes Voegelin's crowning attempt to develop a philosophy of history adequate to the complexities of human existence, and particularly to the complexities of the human relation to transcendence. It continues and amplifies the first three volumes of the study (*Israel and Revelation, The World of the Polis,* and *Plato and Aristotle,* published 1956–1957), but in his introduction to *The Ecumenic Age,* Voegelin intentionally sets the book apart from the earlier volumes, explaining how its structure and content reflect a revised, more profoundly discerning approach to the history of human experience. The reader is assured that the guiding principle of the project has remained the same: to analyze the principal types of human existence in society through careful examination of how human beings have experienced and symbolized the order of reality from the time of the ancient Near Eastern civilizations to the present. However, the original plan of the series was to present major developments in chronological sequence, on the assumption that the "order of history" is, *most fundamentally,* a linear pattern of historical succession. This assumption Voegelin came to question and finally to reject on the basis of his reflections on documents and materials. In the introduction to *The Ecumenic Age*, the reader is advised that meaning in history—that is, the meaning of how the most significant varieties of human insights into the order of reality are related to each other—is insufficiently conveyed, if not falsified, by presenting that meaning as a linear sequence or "course" of development. The "order of history," Voegelin states, is more complicated than simply the order of a line of development through time. It is a more complex order that he now describes—no doubt to the confusion of many a reader—as a "web of meaning with a plurality of nodal points."[1] What does the phrase mean?

The image of a "web of meaning" is meant to convey that the intelligible order of history is made up not merely of *a line of development through time*, but of many "lines of meaning," as Voegelin calls them. The commonplace image of history as development along a time line has, to be sure, a sound truth at its core: there really are lines of "meaningful advance" in the human understanding of, and attempts to realize, existential and social order in reality. These constitute what might be called diachronic lines of meaning. Also, though, significant developments occur contemporaneously in different and unconnected civilizations. Thus, there are lateral patterns of meaning in history pertaining to the development of societies parallel in time: synchronic lines of meaning, also basic to the "order of history." Finally—and most important with regard to the revised treatment of history in *The Ecumenic Age*—there is a line of meaning that, in Voegelin's words, "runs from time into eternity," as human beings consciously relate the meanings of the order of things to a timeless, ultimate origin of order. This line of meaning, too, is integral to the story that humans discover and tell about their ongoing participation in reality and its order. The order of history is therefore a crisscrossing "web" of lines of meaning that run (1) forward in time, (2) across spatially distant societies simultaneously, and (3) from every society's time to a timeless ground of meaning underlying all societies at all times. To further complicate matters, because human beings in their search for order and self-understanding reach back to the insights of earlier societies, the order of history includes (4) lines of meaning that run "backward" from specific times into various times past. Consequently, the philosopher of history—Voegelin—who wishes

1. Voegelin, *The Ecumenic Age*, 106.

to penetrate to an understanding of the intelligible structures of meaning that constitute "history" must conduct an analysis that itself moves "backward and forward and sideways, in order to follow empirically the patterns of meaning as they [reveal] themselves in the self-interpretation of persons and societies in history," exploring a historical "web of meaning" that, unlike one nice, neat time line, defies convenient imaginal representation.[2]

This accounts for the organization of the analysis found in *The Ecumenic Age* that, in examining events of the period stretching approximately from the rise of the Persian Empire to the fall of the Roman Empire (roughly 600 B.C.E. to 500 C.E.), treats discoveries, thinkers, cultures, and political and military developments in a theme-driven, nonchronological manner, following linked problems and insights, often recurrently, to "nodal points" of concentrated (and complicated) significance. However, for the diligent reader there emerges, gradually, that configuration of patterns of historical meaning that is the "ecumenic age" itself, a period characterized by highly distinctive, interrelated developments in the organization and self-interpretation of societies—developments that, as we follow the argument, are revealed to be crucial to the understanding of later historical epochs. True no doubt to Voegelin's intentions, one consequence of accompanying him on his profound, reflective immersion into the "ecumenic age" and its problems is that the reader's sense of residing at one end of a historical time line—snug in the present, surveying the past—dissolves, replaced by a sense of the intimacy, the intricate interconnectedness, of all the historical varieties of human participation in reality. Examining with Voegelin this middle period of history, one discovers that every historical existence, including one's own, is existence in the middle of a "web of meaning."

Of the many factors that led Voegelin to his abandonment of the original conception for the later volumes of *Order and History* and to the revised approach to philosophy of history in *The Ecumenic Age*, among the most significant was a deepened appreciation of the implications of there being a line of meaning in human existence "that runs from time into eternity." Resulting partly from his intensive work during preceding decades on a theory of consciousness, his profounder recognition of how this line of meaning figures in the "order of history" was key to his being impelled, finally, to reject the portrayal of history as a developmental "course." His intention to give this

2. Ibid., 47, 106.

line of meaning its full due is reflected everywhere in *The Ecumenic Age;* it is one of the book's principal unifying factors. Isolating and examining this factor so important in its composition will allow us to explore how historical meaning demands to be conceived when one remains fully open to the fact and mystery of transcendence.

Between Time and Eternity

Incorporated into the language and arguments of *The Ecumenic Age* is a view of human existence that derives from Voegelin's long and painstaking work on a theory of consciousness during years preceding and overlapping its composition. The direct fruits of those labors on consciousness had already appeared in the German-language *Anamnesis* (1966) and in various essays, but to the reader familiar only with the analyses and terminology of the first three volumes of *Order and History,* the new way of treating human nature in *The Ecumenic Age* was startling and demanded some adjustment.[3] One of the more vivid indicators of the transformation was Voegelin's now recurrent use of the term *In-Between,* or *Metaxy,* to characterize human existence. Much depends, for the cogency and plausibility of the book's analyses, on Voegelin's account of the "in-between" character of consciousness, particularly with regard to consciousness being situated "in-between" human and divine modes of being, a "site" where divine presence meets human response. Let us turn briefly to the principles underlying this characterization, which provide the justification for Voegelin writing of a line of meaning in human experience "that runs from time into eternity."

The image of a "line" running from time into eternity is a metaphor, of course, representing an invisible relation between dimensions of meaning experienced in human consciousness. This relation between dimensions of meaning is experienced *exclusively* in the data of consciousness—though it is not always adverted to or explicitly understood—and is explicated by Voegelin as follows. On the one hand, consciousness finds itself embedded

3. Voegelin, *Anamnesis: Zur Theorie der Geschichte und Politik.* An English-language edition appearing in 1978 as *Anamnesis* differed in content from the German original; two new chapters were added, and a number of the original essays were omitted. In 2002 an English translation of the full original text became available as *Anamnesis: On the Theory of History and Politics.* All further references to essays in *Anamnesis* will be to the 2002 edition.

in and conditioned by a "biophysical existence" in "the time of the external world," and engaged in seeking the meanings of things and events in a temporal and finite process of hard-won understanding. On the other hand, as a "flowing presence" of awareness and attention that transcends the constantly shifting particulars of sensory perception, it finds also within itself the intimation of a fullness of meaning beyond the vicissitudes of change.[4] In consciousness, the illumination of a finite dimension of meaning is always accompanied and contextualized by a dimension of meaning sensed or understood to be ultimate and imperishable. This latter dimension of meaning, one symbol for which is "eternity," has throughout history been conceived as a "divine" mode of lasting, superior to and providing an ultimate context of meaning for all time-bound things.

The factor that sustains consciousness in its multidimensional concern with meaning is *questioning.* The dynamic core of human consciousness, for Voegelin, is our "omnidimensional 'desire to know' " that unfolds in the uncountable variety of human interests, and whose essence, as a search for meaning, is a desire to understand the origin and ground of meaning itself. Human beings are impelled by the intrinsic propulsion of questioning to wonder about the ultimate cause and meaning of things, the "ground of being" as Voegelin calls it. However, this ultimate fullness of meaning, dimly intuited by consciousness from its first slow efforts, is recognized in the course of human discovery to be something beyond both time and time-bound comprehension. Questing consciousness, by natural propensity, seeks out and discovers "eternity," and in doing so, it becomes a bond connecting, in one tension of concern, (1) the meanings of things and events apparent in time and (2) their ultimate meaning in the context of a divine "lasting out-of-time."[5]

This divine ground that functions as the ultimate goal of the search for meaning must be understood as *present in the questioning process* from the start, in addition to being its vaguely intimated object of discovery. The divine ground is present because it is the very substance, the deepest identity, of human consciousness itself, which after all is a questing process that is not self-created but finds itself *given* to itself. Human consciousness—to repeat

4. Voegelin, *The Ecumenic Age,* 376; on "flowing presence," see Voegelin, "Eternal Being in Time," in *Anamnesis,* 328–30.

5. Voegelin, *The Ecumenic Age,* 301, 375.

Voegelin's concise phrase quoted earlier—"is quite conscious of being constituted by the reality of which it is conscious."[6] Consciousness is an emergence from the very ground of reality that is simultaneously the goal of its questioning concern.

Two consequences of particular importance follow from this last point. First, the divine "lasting out-of-time" is at all times the "moving partner" in the search for meaning, the first principle of activity as well as the ultimate goal of the process. Second, each individual consciousness may be viewed, so to speak, from two basic angles: from the perspective of the human participant as a person or subject whose biophysical existence, located in space and time, constitutes the center of the searching process, or in terms of the process of reality from which this particular consciousness has emerged and to which, in a sense, it ultimately belongs, within which it constitutes an irruption of awareness of meaning—a site, not *the* center, where the "cosmic process becomes luminous for its meaning."[7]

To sum up: divine presence is a coconstitutive element in what Voegelin calls "the structure of experiencing consciousness"; human consciousness is always an existence "in tension toward divine reality"; and consciousness is a divine-human "in-between." It is this understanding of the structure of human existence that Voegelin applies to the analysis of history in *The Ecumenic Age.*[8]

The major consequence of this application is that *history itself* is presented as a divine-human "in-between," which, again, can be viewed from two angles. From the human side of the equation, history is the process of the human search for order—personal, social, political, aesthetic, natural, and cosmic—amid, and in response to, the vast manifold of intelligibilities that constitute

6. Voegelin, "Remembrance of Things Past," in *Published Essays, 1966–1985,* 312. "Remembrance of Things Past" was written to provide an introductory chapter for the 1978 American edition of *Anamnesis.*

7. Voegelin, *The Ecumenic Age,* 247, 252. On the divine ground as the "moving partner" in the search for meaning, see also Voegelin, "Reason: The Classic Experience," 271–73; and "The Gospel and Culture," 182–88, both in *Published Essays, 1966–1985;* and "Beginning and Beyond," in *What Is History?* 173–80.

8. Voegelin, *The Ecumenic Age,* 49–50. For the most direct accounts of Voegelin's analysis of human existence as a divine-human "in-between," see the essays "Eternal Being in Time" (1964) and "What Is Political Reality?" (1966), both in *Anamnesis;* and the essays "Immortality: Experience and Symbol" (1967), "Equivalences of Experience and Symbolization in History" (1970), and "The Gospel and Culture" (1971), all in *Published Essays, 1966–1985.*

reality, whose ground is the divine source of all meaning and order. Of course, there have been "advances" in this searching process, by far the most notable among them being, in Voegelin's view, the complex of occasions in various societies during the "ecumenic age" when the search for order underwent a crucial transformation as thinkers discovered that the divine source of order is a reality incommensurate with the limitations and contingencies of the world conditioned by space and time, that is, when the *transcendence* of the divine ground became explicitly understood, carefully identified, and pondered *as such*. This discovery, the discovery of the nonworldly, genuine "eternity" of divine transcendence, dramatically affected the process of the human search for order in a number of ways. For one thing, it introduced the conceptual separation of reality into a "world" and a "beyond." It was now possible to regard reality as a whole to be made up of (1) an "immanent" dimension, the "world" of spatiotemporally conditioned things that come into being and perish, and (2) a "transcendent" dimension, the divine "beyond," imperishable and nonimaginable. The problem of properly understanding the order of a reality composed of immanent and transcendent dimensions, and of properly understanding the history of human participation in such a reality, now entered the field of human concern. For another thing, the discovery of transcendence revealed the organ of discovery, consciousness itself, to be something founded in the immanent world but also ultimately constituted by and responsive to the transcendent ground of its own and all reality. It revealed the "in-between" character of consciousness, its character as "the site where immanence and transcendence meet" with itself being "neither immanent nor transcendent." Thus, the problem of the fact and destiny of this "in-between" reality of human consciousness began its reshaping of the self-interpretations of persons and societies.[9]

That reshaping began with the creation or adaptation of language symbols for the purpose of communicating the more advanced truth of the new insights, language symbols that spread first within and then beyond the cultures of the discoveries. The consciousness that had discovered itself to be a divine-human something, an in-between or intermediate type of reality, attempted to indicate its own nature through symbols that included the Israelite and Christian term *pneuma* (Greek translation of the Hebrew *ruach*), signifying the "spirit" that is both human and divine; the Platonic-

9. Voegelin, *The Ecumenic Age*, 398.

Aristotelian symbol nous, signifying the "intellect" that is both human and divine; the Upanishadic Atman-Brahman formulation, where the individual's true "self" is identified with the mysterious ground of all being; and finally, less famously, Plato's term *metaxy,* signifying the "in-between" of the spiritual reality "halfway between god and man" where the truth seeker moves halfway between knowledge and ignorance (*Symposium* 202a–203a), a symbol Voegelin found analytically precise enough, and untrammeled by misinterpretation enough, to introduce into his own characterization of human consciousness and the human condition.[10]

History as a divine-human "in-between," however, can also be considered from the side of the "moving partner," the permanent divine presence. From this angle, all of history "is transacted in a permanent present as the ongoing drama of theophany [that is, divine manifestation]." In other words, divine presence is complete and one throughout all of history (the "permanent present"), but the *manifestations,* or *revelations,* of this presence in human consciousness undergo significant transformations in the direction of increasing discernment of truth concerning the divine ground (the "ongoing drama" of divine appearance, "theophany"). History may therefore be described as the unfolding drama of divine revelations and their impact on human living (the understanding of the divine ground providing the supervening context for personal and social self-interpretations), or, to put it another way, as the unfolding story of divine presence informing human activity in the world, "the history of incarnation in the realm of things."[11]

History therefore has just as curious an ontological status as human consciousness. On the one hand, it consists of significant events occurring in the

10. In ibid., 244–46, Voegelin refers to passages both in Plato's *Symposium* and in his *Philebus* where the symbol *metaxy* plays an important role. In the *Symposium,* love (eros) is described as a spiritual power *(daimonion)* "halfway between *[metaxy]* god and man" (202e), and the philosophical search for truth ("love of wisdom") is indicated to be spiritual eros moving in the realm "midway between ignorance and wisdom" (203e–204b). In the *Philebus* (16c–17a), cosmic existence is given an ontological-mathematical description as intermediate between *(metaxy)* the One *(hen)* and unlimited number *(apeiron).* Voegelin argues that Plato's recognition of his own questing consciousness as something "in-between" human and divine, time and timelessness, led him to conceive of all cosmic reality as similarly structured: "Once the truth of man's existence had been understood as the In-Between reality of [rationally questioning] consciousness, the truth of the process [of reality] as a whole could be restated as the existence of *all* things in the In-Between of the [divine] One and the Apeiron" (245). See *Symposium,* 555–56.

11. Voegelin, *The Ecumenic Age,* 290.

world's societies over the course of time, as the struggle for meaningful living yields the inspiring and appalling drama of human practical and political successes and breakdowns, the development and transformation of social institutions, discoveries of new technologies and their impact, and so on; also, though, because all of these events occur in a permanent divine presence of timeless meaning, their meanings are both within and beyond time, always at the intersection of time and timelessness. "Although historical events are founded in the external world and have calendar dates," Voegelin states, "they also partake of the divine lasting out-of-time. The historical dimension of humanity is neither world-time nor eternity but the flux of presence in the Metaxy."[12]

This last phrase, "the flux of presence in the Metaxy," and its variants ("the flux of divine presence," "the divine-human flux of presence") are employed throughout *The Ecumenic Age* to identify consciousness, and thus history, as a continual crossroads of eternity and time in the unfolding story of divine movement and human response. What Voegelin calls "the line that runs from time into eternity" is therefore a constant in historical meaning, and the human participant in history can become aware of this fact because in consciousness there is always an awareness of "eternity," of timeless divine presence, though the type or quality of that awareness varies with the historical stages or conditions of the search for the ground.

With this last qualification we arrive at one of the principal themes of *The Ecumenic Age*, which concerns the specific historical variants of the awareness and articulation of "eternity." The most important factor in this variability of awareness has been, in Voegelin's view, the explicit discovery of the transcendence of the divine ground: the conscious "differentiation" (as he puts it) of transcendence and immanence, which first brought the fact of an eternal meaning beyond the perishable world into conceptual focus. Societies as yet unaffected by this differentiation, societies whose interpretations of reality were still "cosmological" in that the unity of the cosmos had not yet conceptually been sharply split into an immanent world and a transcendent beyond, had their own characteristic ways of experiencing and symbolizing the eternal

12. Ibid., 375. Again we find a corresponding formula in Eliot's *Four Quartets,* where, in conformity with the description (in "The Dry Salvages") of conscious existence as the "intersection of the timeless / With time," history is described (in the subsequent poem, "Little Gidding") as a "pattern / Of timeless moments" (136, 144).

dimension of meaning, as we have seen. Then, when the discovery of transcendence did take place, it took different forms in different cultural settings, calling on different resources of tradition and language. Finally, Voegelin explains, in some societies the discovery of transcendence was not as penetrating, not as successful or profound in clarifying the structural relations of meaning that unite transcendent and immanent reality. Thus, Voegelin describes a spectrum of culturally distinctive forms of symbolizing divine eternity in relation to worldly events, writing of a cosmological predifferentiated "compact" understanding, which then gives way in certain cultures to a "differentiated" understanding of the eternal divine ground, with the latter manifesting itself both in "incomplete" and in "radical" differentiations.[13] For our purposes, it will be helpful now to consider a few of the principal forms along that spectrum, starting with another look at cosmological consciousness, briefly treated in the previous chapter, and concluding with Voegelin's account of the most radical—or "complete"—differentiations of eternal reality and their accompanying insights into the process of world history.

The Differentiation of Time and Eternity

In cosmological societies human consciousness is governed by what Voegelin calls "the primary experience of the cosmos," the experience of reality in its interwoven (undifferentiated) wholeness. In these societies there is not yet any thought of a sole Creator-God radically beyond the world, and neither any thought as yet of a world constituted of merely "natural" things, because for cosmological consciousness divine power and the world of sensory and imaginable things are still fundamentally apprehended as a unified whole. The cosmos of the primary experience is, as Voegelin says, "the whole, *to pan,* of an earth below and a heaven above—of celestial bodies and their movements; of seasonal changes; of fertility rhythms in plant and animal life; of human life, birth and death; and above all . . . it is a cosmos full of gods."[14] The ultimate ground and meaning of things are not yet conceived as strictly

13. "The differentiation of the one truth of existence, thus, is broken in a spectrum of spiritual eruptions, each bearing the mark of the ethnic culture in which it occurs" (Voegelin, *The Ecumenic Age,* 372). On the range of less complete to more complete differentiations, see 388–404.

14. Ibid., 118.

"beyond" but rather as interfused with the visible and palpable universe of things; a bit more precisely, there is no conception yet of an "interfusion" of worldly and divine reality, because these have not yet been decisively and strictly distinguished from each other. Rather, the whole of reality is perceived as an interconnected cosmos of things, including those things from which order and meaning originate, "the gods."

So in cosmological consciousness the timeless in a strict sense, the *transcendence* of divine reality, is not yet explicitly conceived, not yet distinguished and named. Still, it is apprehended in a certain fashion. The awareness of a presence of meaning beyond temporal change *informs* the experience of cosmic order and its symbolization, and it does so because that presence and a sense of it are coextensive with questioning consciousness itself. The Question—as Voegelin calls the core of human consciousness, which is ultimately a quest concerning the ground of meaning—always carries with it some intimation, however inexplicit, of transcendence, whose mystery is the ultimate horizon and term of its search. "The Question," claims Voegelin, "is complete even in the cosmological style of truth"; "man's questioning experience of reality is structurally always complete as far back as our historical sources go."[15] Given the presence and intimation of divine transcendence in cosmological consciousness, then, how is it actually experienced and symbolized?

In cosmological consciousness the transcendence of divine reality is not grasped as such but represented by the most lasting "things," which are the gods and the embracing universe. These divine things carry the burden of ultimate meaning, as the imagined sources of meaning and order. However, insofar as they are imagined after the manner of finite, existent things, they cannot be conceived as strictly eternal; the lasting of even the most powerful and lasting things is not quite a "divine lasting out-of-time." The fact of timelessness proper can be discovered only by conceiving of something absolutely unconditioned by finite, thingly "existence"—by conceiving of the divine as "reality in the mode of nonexistence," to use Voegelin's provocative formula. Since the conceptual discovery of reality "in the mode of nonexistence," of transcendent reality, has not yet taken place in cosmological understanding, within the cosmological outlook one may describe a "compression of existence and nonexistence into intracosmic things," a compression that

15. Ibid., 400–401.

restricts the search for the divine to the realm of spatiotemporal imagination. Thus, the cosmological search for the ground moves always among an array of imaginable and semi-imaginable cosmic "things" that includes the gods, without being able to "come to rest on a firm basis outside itself" in a timeless reality beyond the vicissitudes of change.[16]

It must be emphasized that, for Voegelin, the *experience* of timeless reality is present in cosmological consciousness, even if the explicit acknowledgment or critical clarification of such a reality has not yet occurred. The experience of divine timelessness, Voegelin states, is present to all human beings in the fundamental awareness of having come into existence "out of nothing," out of "nonexistence." This is an awareness no less basic to cosmological than to differentiated consciousness.[17] Nonetheless, until the divine ground gets conceived as a kind of "reality in the mode of nonexistence," the "nothing" from which existence has emerged cannot be conceived in its true character as a fullness of divine transcendence, and the experience of "existence out of nothing" must be expressed in terms of existence emerging out of the at least quasi-imaginable actions of gods or primordial, archetypal events. Therefore, while it indeed experiences timeless divine presence, because cosmological consciousness is not yet able to distinguish the "nonexistence" of divine transcendence from "nonexistence" in the sense of nothingness, eternity in the strict sense must remain for it hidden in nothingness, and its search for ultimate reality may reach only so far as to depict the eternal in terms of divine things and the divine lastingness of existing things.

As has already been pointed out in the previous chapter, this has crucial repercussions for the cosmological attitude toward time and history. In the cosmological imagination, if things exist and last in existence, they do so because originally the gods made and ordered them and because repeated divine acts sustain them; thus, the search for ultimacy centers on the originating acts of "coming-into-being" through which divine power has established and

16. Ibid., 122, 126. On the transcendent divine ground as "reality in the mode of nonexistence," see 122–28 and "Immortality: Experience and Symbol," in *Published Essays, 1966–1985,* 52–54.

17. "The 'own ground' of the primary experience, the ground it has in common with all differentiated experiences of the same reality that will challenge it, turns out to be the fundamental tension of all reality experienced: the tension of existence out of nonexistence. . . . Existence out of nothing is indeed the fundamental experience of reality in early societies just as much as in later ones" (Voegelin, *The Ecumenic Age,* 122–23).

continues to establish the cosmos and its order. Myths that orient cosmological societies tell of these events; corresponding rituals seek to remember and reenact them in order to invite and ensure the divine ordering action that cosmic existence requires and to bring social and personal existence into harmonious oneness and solidarity with the true and original order of things. This gives cosmological thought what Mircea Eliade calls its "antihistorical" orientation: finding ultimate meaning in the actions of divine forces in a "time of the beginnings," it indulges regularly in the experiential annulment and rebirth of linear time, aiming through appropriate ritual both to participate in the original divine acts and to "restore being to the ordered splendor that is lethally flowing away with the flow of time."[18]

We may sum up the issue thus: without the conception of a divine lasting beyond the world, divine timelessness must be compressed into the flow of time in the mythic notion of a "time of the beginnings," while the time that passes must be periodically "abolished" in order for society to remain in communion with divine power. The notion of a divine ordering of things in a "time of the beginnings," therefore, is the closest approximation cosmological thought achieves to the understanding of transcendent timelessness in a strict sense.

It is precisely because it is only an approximation to genuine insight into transcendence that cosmological thought is inherently unstable. The Question about the ground of meaning carries latent within it a capacity to outquestion the finite, the temporal and the imaginable, to become dissatisfied with intracosmic answers to its question about the ultimate cause of existing things, to discover that the only answers that satisfy the scope of its questioning and its intimations of imperishable meaning are those that identify a "nonexistent" transcendent ground. "[T]he Question will not rest until the ground beyond the intracosmic grounds offered by [cosmological] myth is found," a ground that is the explicit mystery of a reality unconditioned by space and time, beyond all finite things. In the cosmological answers to the question of the ground, the mystery of explicit transcendence remains veiled due to the divine mystery still being too closely identified with existing things. However, the mystery inexorably draws questioning toward the explicit recognition of transcendence: the transcendence of divine presence,

18. Ibid., 123.

felt in the experience of "existence out of nothing" and implicit in the unrestrictedness of human questioning, presses with an inner exigency toward its own acknowledgment. When, therefore, the things of the universe have at last been recognized to be insufficient explanations of their own existence, and the divine source of meaning has been discovered to be too timeless and spaceless to be any variety of existing thing, the cosmos "differentiates" into the two dimensions of transcendent and immanent reality.[19]

With this discovery, the problem of human response to timeless divine presence enters a new phase. The divine ground, manifestly present in the vast and intricate order of the universe and in the movements of human searching, has been found to be so incommensurate with these that a blurring of distinctions between divine ground and finite reality is no longer possible. Rather, the divine ground is understood to rest beyond every conceivable thing *and even every conceivable experience* of the divine dimension of things. Ultimately, notes Voegelin, the divine ground is understood to be the "nonpresent Beyond of all divine presence."[20] This revelation of the "nonexistence" of ultimate divine meaning undermines the truth of the cosmological myths, throws a shadow of imperfection and incompleteness over worldly existence, and introduces the new challenges of (1) understanding the relationship of worldly existence to a strictly transcendent ground and (2) deciphering the human situation and human destiny in light of that relationship.

About the responses to this revelation and its challenges there are two initial points to be made. First, the revelation is not indigenous to every society. The discovery of transcendence does not occur in every culture, but in some few where, at least partly due to sufficient civilizational development, the conditions for it are ripe. The historian cannot avoid the fact that "some social and cultural situations appear to be more favorable to differentiating responses than others." Second, the differentiations of transcendence do not all occur with the same degree of thoroughness or intensity, and consequently lead to a variety of explanations of the relation between worldly existence and transcendent ground. Not just aberrantly but mostly, according to Voegelin, they consist of "incomplete differentiations," where divine transcendence is not

19. Ibid., 127–28, 392.

20. Ibid., 297. In traditional Western religious language, the same point may be stated as (in John D. Caputo's phrasing): "The action of God in the production of the [universe] does not exhaust or wholly display the Being of God" ("Being and the Mystery of the Person," 104).

distinguished from divine presence in the world with sufficient thoroughness for all the implications such a distinction might carry to reveal themselves. The most complete differentiations, he states, were those of the cultures of Israel and Hellas, while around "the islands of Israel and Hellas extends the sea of other societies with their rich manifold of approximations and intermediate forms, of tentative breakthroughs and compromises."[21] In Voegelin's analysis it was in fact the Israelite breakthrough that provided the conditions for the most radical differentiation of all, that of Jesus and his followers, including Saint Paul, who, in responding to the epiphany of Jesus, gave foundational articulation to what became a tradition of Christian insight into the twin problems of (1) a reality divided into a world and its divine beyond and (2) a human existence "in-between" them.

In *The Ecumenic Age,* Voegelin focuses on the "radical" differentiations of transcendence in the Judeo-Christian and Greek traditions, which he refers to respectively as the "pneumatic" and "noetic" differentiations. "Pneumatic" differentiation—from the Greek *pneuma,* translating the Hebrew *ruach,* "spirit"—refers to the spiritual experiences and discoveries of the prophetic tradition stretching from Hebrew beginnings through the Christian developments. "Noetic" differentiation—from the Greek *nous,* "reason" or "intellect" —refers to the rational-critical insights of philosophy, and more specifically to the component in those insights pertaining to the increasingly nuanced discernment of transcendent being. This spiritual component of Greek philosophizing is typically overlooked or underemphasized. In fact, the testimonies of the philosophers themselves, the writings of pre-Socratics such as Parmenides, Heraclitus, and Xenophanes as well as those of Plato and Aristotle, make this spiritual component abundantly clear. The concept of reason (nous) first emerges from reflection on the structure of questioning consciousness itself as a search for the divine origin *(arche).* Only by passionately seeking the ground of reality and discerning it to be transcendent divine Nous (Intellect) did human nous discover itself to be the organ that can understand and create order in reality. Thus, "reason" as the structure of human consciousness came to be illuminated precisely through philosophical reflection on the ultimate concern of human questioning, and Greek philosophy should be recognized as having been grounded in experiences of divine transcendence.

21. Voegelin, *The Ecumenic Age,* 354, 377.

In his analysis in *The Ecumenic Age* of the two "radical" differentiations, the pneumatic and the noetic, Voegelin gives especially close attention to the insights of Saint Paul and of Plato, examining their respective visions of world, human existence, and divine reality for both commonalities and differences. He argues, finally, that the "Pauline vision of the resurrected," representing and articulating the degree of differentiation of transcendence occasioned by Jesus' experience of divine presence, carries the understanding of the differentiation between world and transcendent ground to a high point of completeness. Before turning to Voegelin's treatment of this culmination of the differentiating processes, however, it will be useful to look briefly at some of his comments on the phenomena of incomplete differentiation, on what he calls "partial" breakthroughs out of the cosmological perspective.

As the Question about the ground begins to suspect the "nonexistence," the radical nonthingness, of divine ultimacy, it may critically concern itself with identifying one ultimate divine source from which all things derive, extrapolating from events recounted by the cosmological myths a series of causes terminating in a highest god, or first principle of origination. The Greek poet Hesiod's *Theogony* (ca. 700 B.C.E.) is an account of this sort, a speculation that clearly reflects the operation of critical reason, but reason not yet critical of mythic imagery itself. In this "speculation that remains subordinate to the cosmological myth," Voegelin says, "[m]ythopoesis and noesis [critical reason] combine into a formative unit that holds an intermediate position between cosmological compactness and noetic [critical-rational, or philosophical] differentiation."[22] This "mytho-speculative" type of answer to the Question is pushing toward, but has not yet discovered, transcendence.

At a further stage of the search for the ground, divine ultimacy is discovered to be something more self-sufficient and more perfect than any existent or imaginable thing, even a "highest god." An explicit notion of transcendence reveals itself, and the question about primordial beginnings at last decisively detaches the aim of its intention from the realm of existing things. To exemplify this type of moment in the search for the ground, Voegelin in *The Ecumenic Age* recounts a dialogue about ultimate causation from the *Brihadaranyaka Upanishad,* in which the questioner follows a chain of causal dependence among existing things to the point where an ineffable mystery beyond human comprehension comes into view, revealing "the border where

22. Ibid., 113.

the realm of [mythic] symbols is exhausted."[23] Here the Question has uncovered the mystery of transcendent reality, distinguishing the "nonexistent" ground from all existing things. Nevertheless, how existing things are finally related to their "nonexistent" ground does not receive a definitive answer simply with this distinction being reached. The question as to just what kind of status existing things have in their separateness from the transcendent ground may be answered in a variety of ways.

For example, in Hindu thought (as in certain strands of post-Aristotelian philosophy) the conceptual removal of the divine ground from the finite realm allows *the cosmos itself* to be conceived as a distinct, unified "thing"—a "thing" that, as in the Hindu view of the living things that populate the cosmos, may be reborn indefinitely. In this Hindu perception, ultimate reality, having disappeared into what Voegelin calls in this context the "void" of transcendence, leaves the causes and effects of existing things—including the "cosmos"—to imaginatively unfold into an infinite regression and an infinite succession. The prospect of endless rebirth, then, focuses Hindu thought upon the goal of *moksha,* "liberation" from the cycles of existence into union with the transcendent beyond, with "true" reality.[24] For Voegelin, these conceptions reflect an "incompleteness" in the Hindu differentiation. The problem centers on the image of a "thingly" cosmos born and reborn through infinite epochs. This "hypostasis of the cosmos," Voegelin argues, is philosophically illegitimate. The cosmos can be conceived as a "thing" only if the finite universe is (1) fallaciously abstracted from time and space, which are its very mode of being and then (2) imaginatively placed as an "object" back into time and space. At the same time, the intrinsic *indefiniteness* of time and space must be misconceived as the self-sufficiency of an *infinitely* enduring medium in which the cosmos as "object" can be "reborn" over and over. In these conceptions, (1) the finite realm, (2) its spatiotemporal conditions, and (3) their divine ground have all been reified, imagined as "things" detached from each other. Most important, finite reality in general has been imaginatively segregated in such a way that its *participation* in the divine ground

23. Ibid., 393; for the full context of Voegelin's discussion of this component of the *Brihadaranyaka Upanishad,* see 389–95.

24. The doctrines of rebirth (or reincarnation) and of *moksha* (liberation) from rebirth are thus linked with the explicit conceptual differentiation of transcendent and immanent realms. This is why, as R. C. Zaehner points out, the doctrine of reincarnation is absent from the earlier Vedic writings and first appears in the Upanishads (*Hinduism,* 57–60).

remains in crucial ways unclarified, resulting in, finally, the "fallacious infinity of a cosmic process that has split off from the void."[25]

These hypostatizations are also connected, Voegelin notes, with the failure of a genuinely *historical* notion of human participation in divine transcendence to emerge in Hindu culture. "History" is a world process moving toward an envisioned goal, but in the Hindu conception the world process runs on indefinitely. The most "striking manifestation" of this absence of a truly historical conception of existence, according to Voegelin, is "the nonappearance of historiography in Hindu culture." For these and related reasons, he explains, the Hindu breakthrough into differentiated consciousness is a breakthrough that "does not quite reach its goal"—a goal that ought to be measured, he argues, by noetic (Hellenic philosophical) and especially pneumatic (Judeo-Christian) standards of differentiated insights into the problem of the relationship between transcendence and immanence.[26]

Through Voegelin's analysis, the crucial element allowing for these more complete differentiations appears to be a more intense experience of the absolute being, absolute freedom, and absolute creativity of the divine ground, with the Judeo-Christian experiences advancing beyond even the Greek in these respects. In both spheres, experiences of this type brought the ontological gap between the immanent world and the divine "beyond" to such a degree of emphasis, and inaugurated such a radical reorientation of consciousness, that they gave rise to what Voegelin calls "epochal" consciousness, that is, the awareness of a decisive and irreversible advance in the understanding of reality and the human situation. In these cultures, the break with the "compact" cosmological perspective was such as to set the new truths of differentiated insights into divine reality into sharp conflict with the traditional myths and cosmological portrayals of the ground. This is in contrast with Hindu culture, where differentiated truths such as those articulated in the Upanishads were absorbed into the older Vedic tradition as simply another and complementary way of expressing the one unchanging truth of human-divine relations also expressed in the inherited compact (cosmological) forms of symbolization. In the Judeo-Christian and Greek cultures, the new truths

25. Voegelin, *The Ecumenic Age*, 130–31, 394, 402–3. This last phrase appears in Voegelin's discussion of Buddhist thought, but he links the Hindu and Buddhist traditions on this issue; elsewhere he refers to Hinduism's "fallacious infinite of cosmological speculation" (394).

26. Ibid., 393–95.

were experienced as revelatory advances discrediting former ways of life and devotion. In these cultures, the discovery of transcendence was understood as a successful human response to an appeal from the "true" divine reality of transcendent being, and the human "turning" to loving participation in this divine Beyond as a transformative step on the part of human beings into a truer mode of participation in reality. Thus, the Judeo-Christian and Greek differentiations were experienced as "theophanic events" that drew their human participants into a consciousness of "epochal advance"; that is, because they were experienced as new divine revelations dramatically changing and advancing human self-understanding, they provoked a sense of discontinuous epochs of Before (the revelations) and After (the revelations), and thus endowed society and world with *historical direction.*

According to Voegelin, the most radical differentiation—and consequently the most profound insights into both the nature of divine transcendence and the structure of historical meaning—arose in "the Judaeo-Christian environment with its millennial Israelite background of differentiating consciousness."[27] Voegelin's treatment in *The Ecumenic Age* of the Christian climax of this differentiating process focuses on the Gospel of John and, more fully, on the writings of Saint Paul. By summarizing a few of his conclusions regarding the "Pauline vision" we will be able to indicate how this "pneumatic" breakthrough that *did* reach its goal—exegetically assisted, over the course of time, by the language and refined tools of critical analysis developed through the complementary "noetic" breakthrough of Greek philosophy—established notions of time, eternity, history, and human existence that have come to dominate Western thought.

In Saint Paul's writings, the God revealed through the person of Jesus is an absolute eternal Creator who freely and lovingly made the finite universe, and who, through the experience of the resurrected Christ, promises eternal life as the goal of worldly existence. Divine reality is presented as an absolutely free and loving God absolutely beyond the world he absolutely created. The purpose of human existence is the opportunity to participate, by way of trusting response to God's appeal, in the divine reality that is beyond perishing. For Saint Paul, transcendent divine presence has become incarnate in order that existence, responding to that incarnate presence, may be transfigured

27. Ibid., 57.

from a state of perishable to imperishable being. The incarnation of the divine Beyond is for the sake of drawing creation, through human acceptance and faith, toward itself; and the historical process of prophetic revelation culminating in Jesus also points toward a conclusion of history in a completed process of transfiguration. That is, divine reality transfigures the reality of this world, through incarnation and through human responsive engagement in the transfiguring process, so that creation may return to the imperishable glory of the God who made it, to the eternal divine being beyond all temporal structures and disturbances. Or, in Voegelin's concentrated phrase: "The history of theophanic incarnation [has become] transparent for its meaning as a movement toward the Beyond of theophany and incarnation."[28]

The Pauline vision, then, is one of temporal, created reality engaged in a "transfiguring exodus"—to use Voegelin's combination of philosophical and biblical phrasing—toward a final and ultimate transfiguration. A completed transfiguration is, in the logic of Saint Paul's account, the only coherent conclusion to the story of a world freely created by an all-powerful and all-loving God; thus, he speaks confidently of the *eschaton,* or "last days," long anticipated by Israelite prophets, whose events will sanctify and justify the trials of existence, and will complete the "return to the imperishable state of creation intended by divine creativity." The eschatological component in Saint Paul's account of reality, Voegelin argues, conforms precisely to his radical differentiation of the transcendent divine nature, which emphasizes "the freedom and love of divine creativity":

> Paul differentiated the truth of existence . . . so far that the transcosmic God and his Agape [love] were revealed as the mover in the theophanic events that constitute meaning in history. . . . Paul, furthermore, differentiated fully the experience of the directional movement by articulating its goal, its *teleion,* as the state of *aphtharsia* [imperishing] beyond man's involvement in [time and perishing]. . . . The movement, in order to have meaning, must come to an end. . . . [In] the pneumatic theophany of Paul, with divine creativity differentiated, an eschatology is required to complete the meaning of the movement. The Pauline myth indeed pursues the drama of the movement to its conclusion in the eschatological events.[29]

28. Ibid., 297. Though the immediate context of this sentence is a discussion of the implications of Plato's "theophanic" experiences, it applies equally to the Pauline perspective.
29. Ibid., 315–16.

Whereas the Hindu differentiation left a static gap between ultimate reality and the "infinity of a cosmic process," one of the radical characteristics of the Judeo-Christian differentiation of transcendent reality is that it removes the last traces of creative self-perpetuation from the spatiotemporal universe: the world had a Beginning in divine creation, and will be brought by divine movement to its meaningful End. Worldly existence is not simply a process. It is History.

Thus, there is a historical bent to the Western involvement with the problems of transcendence—problems that include, not incidentally, the promise of immortality suggested by the revelation of human participation in a divine mystery beyond space and time. Of course, all religions centrally informed by the explicit discovery of transcendence grapple with the promise or lure of immortality. On an elementary level Taoists, Buddhists, and Hindus agree with Muslims and Christians that human beings are invited to engage in what Voegelin calls an "immortalizing [movement] toward the Beyond."[30] In the West, though, the "immortalizing movements" of human-divine participation have been linked not only with notions of a "liberation" from the cosmic process and a release from its sufferings through unification with its transcendent ground (as in Hinduism and Buddhism), but also with *the transfiguration of the world itself* and with personal contributions to the eschatological arrival. In Western cultures the promise of "eternal life" through responsive participation in divine transcendence has been intimately associated not only with the elimination of the uncertainties and sufferings of personal existence in time, as in Hindu and Buddhist teachings, but also with the end of the entire temporal struggle itself and the transfiguration of the world or universe into a divine, imperishable glory. The radical differentiation of time and eternity in Western thought, then, having revealed human existence to be an "in-between" where transcendence and immanence, God and individual, meet in the provocation of divine movement and the searching of human response, has allowed the line of meaning that "runs from time into eternity" to be conceived not merely in terms of each person's or community's relation to a transcendent ground of being, but also in terms of *a historical advance* toward a worldly consummation with eternal meaning.

In *The Ecumenic Age*, Voegelin takes pains to insist on the experiential authenticity and profundity of the insights underlying the Judeo-Christian and

30. Ibid., 62.

Greek differentiations of transcendence. Nonetheless, he also insists on the special dangers of misinterpretation and misapplication that they have generated. The radical completeness of these differentiations has given rise, he asserts, to equally radical possibilities of "deformation" in our understanding of the relationship of historical existence to eternal meaning. In particular, the discovery of the transfigurative process within reality has repeatedly led to the indulgence of letting *an image of a completed transfiguration* obscure the actual "in-between" condition of historical existence, where one suffers the unresolved tension of a reality "neither transfigured nor untransfigured but . . . engaged in a transfiguring movement."[31] Voegelin's analysis of "deformed" interpretations of human existence in the In-Between of immanence and transcendence is a prominent feature of *The Ecumenic Age,* and it sheds an exceptionally helpful light on Western obsessions—both secular and religious—with "ending" history. The next chapter, therefore, will offer a brief examination of three such deformations, each a significant contributor to what Voegelin calls the "stop-history movements" that have thrived in Western culture.

31. Voegelin, "Wisdom and the Magic of the Extreme: A Meditation," in *Published Essays, 1966–1985,* 336; see also *The Ecumenic Age,* 291–92.

4

DEFORMATIONS OF HISTORY

> If we think we have seized upon the total historic process as an object of knowledge, if we think that thus we have visualized wherein and whereby we exist, we have lost the sense of the encompassing source from which we live. . . . Whenever an observer thinks he knows what man is, what history is, what the self is as a whole, he loses his touch with the encompassing and thus is cut off from his origin and his essence.
>
> —KARL JASPERS, *NIETZSCHE AND CHRISTIANITY*

> [T]here is always a well-known solution to every human problem—neat, plausible, and wrong.
>
> —H. L. MENCKEN, "THE DIVINE AFFLATUS"

THE FOLLOWING look at the problem of deformed conceptions of history, conceptions arising in response to the discovery of transcendence, can do no more than hint at the scope and detail of Eric Voegelin's exposition of the problem. Still, its nature, and Voegelin's view of its centrality to a sufficiently critical philosophy of history, may be conveyed by looking briefly at three types of deformation with closely intertwined careers in Western intellectual and cultural history: apocalyptic consciousness, gnosticism, and postcosmological varieties of what Voegelin calls "historiogenetic speculation."

Apocalypse

A first type of deformation concerns the familiar Western notion of apocalypse. The radical completeness of the Judeo-Christian differentiation of transcendence gave occasion for the emergence of apocalyptic consciousness. Once divine reality had been experienced as the absolutely transcendent and loving Creator of the world, it became possible to imagine midhistorical divine interventions in which social disorder is adjusted and corrected by its perfect Creator. As this same Creator is the God of history, the "eschatological direction in the experience" could eventually express itself by imagining an ultimate divine intervention that will end history altogether and establish a perfect world of everlasting beatitude. The embrace of this image of the end of history and enthusiastic anticipation of the eschatological event are the essence of apocalyptic consciousness, the roots of which Voegelin traces in Hebrew prophetism.[1]

Voegelin explains how a prophetic faith that worldly order might be translated immediately into spiritual fulfillment had by the eighth century B.C.E. already found expression in the prophet Isaiah's demand that the king of Judah cease to rely on his armies in warfare, in order that the direct intervention of God might confirm the king's faith, and how by the second century B.C.E., in the Book of Daniel, prophetic faith of this sort had expanded to the proportions of apocalypse, that is, of a divine intervention to end history and set up an everlasting kingdom of God.[2] Thereafter, of course, apocalyptic consciousness received new impetus from responses to the epiphany of Christ, including Saint Paul's belief in the imminence of the Second Coming; since then, Christian apocalyptic expectations and attitudes derived from them have ceaselessly exerted an influence within Western culture.

The origin of apocalyptic consciousness, Voegelin explains, lies in an acute awareness of the ontological divide between worldly order and divine perfection that becomes exacerbated by "the conviction that history is a field of disorder beyond repair by human action."[3] Anxiety combines with eschatological yearning to produce an imagined completion to the transfiguring process of history, a divine intervention in the not-too-distant future that will resolve the human tension between worldly existence and divine lasting out-of-time by introducing a perfected order of existence that will endure forever.

1. Voegelin, *The Ecumenic Age,* 73. For a discussion of the background, origins, and development of apocalyptic consciousness up through the first century C.E., including an argument for the importance of Zoroastrian influences on Jewish and early Christian communities, see Norman Cohn, *Cosmos, Chaos, and the World to Come: The Ancient Roots of Apocalyptic Faith.*

2. On Isaiah, see 72–74 and Voegelin, *Israel and Revelation,* 501–8. On the Book of Daniel, see *The Ecumenic Age,* 72–73, 121, 373.

3. Voegelin, *The Ecumenic Age,* 373.

Why is apocalyptic consciousness a "deformed" response to the discovery of transcendence? Voegelin underscores two elementary errors upon which it is premised, the first involving an existential refusal of the limitations of human knowledge, the second reflecting a conceptual fallacy.

First, when apocalyptic consciousness assumes knowledge about the end of history—that it will occur, when it will occur, and what form it will take—it assuages historical anxiety only by "tampering with the mystery of meaning."[4] The mystery of history involves both the unknown facts of the historical future and our inescapable human uncertainty about the overall meaning and goal of the transfigurative historical process itself. Apocalyptic confidence prematurely and illegitimately settles these issues by announcing the solution to the mystery of historical existence.

Second, while apocalyptic consciousness is not mistaken in its apprehension of a transfigurative process of history oriented toward a transcendent ground, it improperly conceives of divine transcendence in terms of a transformed place and future time. Transcendent reality is distinct from worldly existence precisely in being neither spatial nor temporal. We always need to remember that transcendence and immanence—God and world—are experienced in their distinctness only *in consciousness*, only as differentiated *dimensions of meaning* within the one reality of experience, not as different places or things. Apocalyptic consciousness hypostatically dissociates the one reality of experience, with its tension between imperfection and perfection, into two separate thing-realities: (1) a disordered reality of historical existence to be followed by (2) a perfect order established through divine intervention. Under the pressure of eschatological imagination, the experienced "tension between order and disorder in the one reality dissociates in the phantasy of two realities following each other in time."[5] Such a response to the burdens of differentiated consciousness is psychologically understandable, but the promise rests on a confused projection of transcendent perfection onto the field of future historical existence. One might say that apocalyptic consciousness fails to adequately distinguish the line of meaning running from time into eternity from the line pertaining to historical advance. An uncritical desire for resolution to the mystery of history produces the apocalyptic

4. Ibid., 303.
5. Ibid., 373.

finale by imaginatively bringing the line that runs from time into eternity to a historical, sequential standstill.

Gnosticism

A second deformation, that of the ancient Gnostics, is also motivated by the desire to escape both the mystery and the disorders of human existence, but its solution to the problems of worldly distress and uncertain meaning is quite different, reflecting its different assumptions about what the ontological gap between finite world and divine transcendence signifies.

The ancient Gnostics responded to experiences of divine transcendence by concluding that the world itself is an alien and wicked place, the creation not of the true god of the Beyond but of an evil divinity, or of divine "lowly powers." Into this world each human spirit (pneuma) has strayed from its true source, but escape from alienation in the prison of the world and return to the true god of the Beyond is possible. At the individual level the imprisoning element is not just the body but also the soul, because for the Gnostics, Hans Jonas explains, not only the body but also the soul "is a product of the cosmic powers," so that through both "his body and his soul man is a part of the world and subjected to [worldly fate]." However, enclosed in the soul "is the spirit, or 'pneuma' (called also the 'spark'), a portion of the divine substance from beyond which has fallen into the world."[6] Salvation of one's spirit—one's spark of true divinity—may be attained by gaining correct knowledge (gnosis): knowledge about the pneuma imprisoned in each human being, knowledge about the true god of the Beyond and of the nature and origins of our worldly prison, and knowledge of the methods or techniques that, when practiced, will ensure deliverance.

6. Jonas, *The Gnostic Religion: The Message of the Alien God and the Beginnings of Christianity*, 42, 44. Jonas's is the standard text on the Gnostic sects of antiquity. Of these he notes: "Actually there were only a few groups whose members expressly called themselves Gnostics, 'the Knowing ones'; but already Irenaeus [ca. 125–200 C.E.] . . . used the name 'gnosis' . . . to cover all those sects that shared with them that emphasis and certain other characteristics. In this sense we can speak of gnostic schools, sects, and cults, of gnostic writings and teachings, of gnostic myths and speculations, even of gnostic religion in general. . . . [Nevertheless,] we can speak of *the* gnostic doctrine only as an abstraction [because the] leading Gnostics displayed pronounced intellectual individualism, and the mythological imagination of the whole movement was incessantly fertile" (32, 41–42).

In these teachings, experiences of divine transcendence have led to a radical conceptual split between two realities: that of cosmos-fate-matter-darkness and that of transcendence-gnosis-spirit-light. This "dualistic-anticosmic spirit" is a defining characteristic, Jonas explains, of all the ancient Gnostic movements:

> The cardinal feature of gnostic thought is the radical dualism that governs the relation of [true] God and world, and correspondingly that of man and world. The deity is absolutely transmundane, *its nature alien to that of the universe,* which it neither created nor governs and to which it is the complete antithesis: to the divine realm of light, self-contained and remote, the cosmos is opposed as the realm of darkness. The world is the work of lowly powers which though they may mediately be descended from Him do not know the true God and obstruct the knowledge of Him in the cosmos over which they rule.[7]

In *The Ecumenic Age,* Voegelin discusses the experiential origins of ancient Gnostic speculation. As a speculative form it certainly arose from an acute awareness of divine transcendence discovered through the search for a convincingly nonthingly (or "nonexistent") ground of consciousness. Just as certainly it reflects "eschatological consciousness" in its yearning for union with the divine Beyond. However, Voegelin cautions, it should not in itself be identified as a "differentiation of consciousness," like the Greek (noetic) and Judeo-Christian (pneumatic) differentiations. Why not? The answer becomes clear through remembering that in the breakthrough from cosmological into differentiated consciousness, a compact *wholeness* of reality in which divine being is still imagined as more or less commensurate with worldly things *differentiates* into (1) a divine transcendent ground and (2) a worldly order that, while no longer considered commensurate with the ultimate ground, is still transparent for its origin in divine transcendent being. In the Gnostic speculations, however, we do not find the one cosmos diffracted into complementary dimensions of divine transcendence and divinely ordered world. Rather, the created world, *along with its divine creator or creators,* is rejected as alien and evil, as a darkness in which personal sparks of pneumatic divinity originating in a "superbeyond" have become imprisoned. This is not a matter of distinct dimensions of the one cosmos, transcendence and immanence,

7. Ibid., 42 (emphasis added).

being grasped in their distinctness; it is a conceptual sundering of the oneness of reality by way of a demonization of the world and the divinity or divinities responsible for creating it. Therefore, Voegelin describes the Gnostic outlook not as a "differentiation," but as a "contraction of divine order to personal existence," where an extreme reduction of true divinity to a "superbeyond" discovered in consciousness—identified as the true God beyond the divine forces who created this world—entails a rejection of all worldly reality.[8]

Voegelin stresses that the motivations of ancient Gnostic speculations are highly complex. They are undoubtedly related to the misery and alienation resulting from the political catastrophes and civilizational destruction caused by imperial expansion in the Western ecumene during the centuries preceding and including the early Christian era. It is not difficult to recognize the appeal of the Gnostic message under conditions of unrelenting political disorder and cultural chaos, of warfare and breakdown of local institutions and beliefs in the wake of imperial conquest. The Gnostic "deformation of eschatological consciousness," Voegelin states, must be understood as a revolt against an existence experienced as so chaotic and miserable as to have lost any intrinsic meaning, a revolt against a world of apparently intractable darkness and evil.[9] As E. R. Dodds explains:

> To the majority of Gnostics it was unthinkable that such a world should have been created by the Supreme God: it must be the handiwork of some inferior demiurge—either, as Valentinus [ca. 100–165 C.E.] thought, an ignorant daemon unaware of any better possibility; or, as Marcion [ca. 85–165 C.E.] thought, the harsh and unintelligent God of the Old Testament; or again, as in other systems, some angel or angels in revolt against God.[10]

Voegelin's appreciation of the psychology of the Gnostic phenomena adds weight to his explanation of its shortcomings as an account of reality, which proceeds as follows. In the Gnostic deformation, the key misstep is the failure to acknowledge that existence in the cosmos is itself *the condition for* the

8. Voegelin, *The Ecumenic Age,* 67.

9. Ibid., 66; see also 66–73. The present discussion can only mention, not explore, Voegelin's rich treatment of the "pragmatic" history of the ecumenic age, the events of imperial conquest, exploration, cultural upheaval, and destruction that must be recognized as concrete conditions for the emergence of both eschatological consciousness and its deformations.

10. Dodds, *Pagan and Christian in an Age of Anxiety: Some Aspects of Religious Experience from Marcus Aurelius to Constantine,* 16.

search that discovers the truth of transcendence—that our longing for goodness and order and our search for the ground arise only through our participation in the one reality of our experience. To spell this out: our *questioning* about the where-from, the why, and the where-to of existence belongs to the capacities of the human intellective psyche, the operations of which depend successively on biological, chemical, and physical foundations. Only through our participation in each of these levels in the hierarchy of being do we participate as conscious questioners in the cosmic process. Consequently, any *answer* we discover about the ultimate ground or meaning of existence cannot logically be considered to pertain to a reality radically alien to the very conditions of our questioning, that is, our conscious participation in the cosmic process. As Voegelin states this point, in typically concentrated manner, toward the end of *The Ecumenic Age:* "The discovery of the [transcendent] ground does not condemn the field of existent things to irrelevance but, on the contrary, establishes it as the reality that derives the meaning of its existence from the ground; and inversely the [questioning search for ultimacy], as it ascends over the hierarchy of being, leads toward the ground because the ground is the origin of the hierarchy." The gnostic discovery of a "true God" in relation to which the given world and its divine creator or creators are condemned as evil and alien is an intellectual error, in which the search for transcendent goodness and perfection is irrationally "torn out of the context of reality in which it arises and made the autonomous basis for human action that will abolish the mystery" of cosmic participation with its suffering and iniquity. Blind to this error, the Gnostic teachings offer a psychologically disturbed "imagery of nonparticipation" that diminishes divine goodness to a "true God" so pure that it lies beyond this world's creator(s), and that contracts the goodness of the person to the supposedly nonparticipatory pneuma or imprisoned "spark" that is his or her point of contact with this true God.[11]

The Gnostic constructs—which in the ancient writings are mythically elaborated in vividly complex theologies and cosmologies—have their obvious psychological appeal. The essence of their appeal is that they sidestep the mystery of existence, offering definitive answers to human questions about how we have come to exist in a world full of suffering and evil, along with assurances that the world is not our responsibility and that our true destiny is to escape from it. These answers and assurances address and calm our

11. Voegelin, *The Ecumenic Age,* 64–65, 299, 397.

anxiety about the mysteries of human origin and destiny, of suffering and iniquity—but at the cost, Voegelin stresses, of an irrational and immoral refusal to acknowledge certain basic facts of existence, including both our duty to the world and the limitations of human knowing. Let us examine for a moment the contrast between false Gnostic certainty and existentially honest uncertainty.

It is our desire to have final answers—answers that explain our sense of alienation from the world, that relieve the pressure deriving from our ignorance about the ultimate purposes of existence, and that deliver us from historical responsibility—that override the objections of reason and produce the Gnostic posture of conviction. Without such answers, after all, we must endure being seekers without fully knowing the end of our search, creatures without a secure foothold in creation, lovers of goodness with nevertheless a duty to face up to what Hegel calls "the slaughter-house of history." That prospect—the prospect of acknowledging human existence for what it is—fills us with anxiety. However, anxiety is, we find, an elementary feature of human existence. It arises naturally in consciousness as an unease accompanying the awareness of our situation, which first of all is that we have emerged in reality without knowing why, and with no way to permanently secure our place in it. "Anxiety," Voegelin states, "is the response to the mystery of existence." Our efforts to make sense of our situation in the world are related to this fundamental anxiety: "The search of order is the response to anxiety."[12] Moreover, it is this very anxiety that leads the seeker to the Gnostic solution, to the insistence that the search for order is at an end and that the mystery of existence has been solved.

Anxiety over the mystery of existence, then, must be regarded as a central motive in the construction of the Gnostic systems. Indeed, they are among the most brilliant and elaborate of attempts to assuage this anxiety, through explaining away the mystery of existence and providing an escape route from world and history. "The construction [of a Gnostic system]," Voegelin asserts, "is meant to assuage the anxiety of a man who cannot face the Mystery of Reality."[13] Although the Gnostic choice is irresponsible, it remains that the anxiety and alienation that prompt it—whether under extremely miserable or only the typical dissatisfactory human conditions—are phenomena that

12. Voegelin, "Anxiety and Reason," in *What Is History?* 71.
13. Voegelin, *The Ecumenic Age,* 403.

must, after all, be existentially addressed. Dissatisfaction with the world and the yearning to overcome alienation will in general be guided in one of two directions. They can move toward escape from the given world, as with the Gnostics, or move toward trying to resolve the alienation through accepting responsibility for bringing oneself and the world—intractable as the materials are and accepting their imperfections—as fully as possible into harmony with a good acknowledged to have as its ultimate basis a dimension of transcendent meaning. With respect to anxiety, as Søren Kierkegaard has pointed out, one's choice is again one of two basic alternatives. One may attempt to flee from it, trying either to assuage it with illusory answers or to suppress it with drugs and diversions, or one may attempt to learn from it, allowing anxiety to become what Kierkegaard calls "a serving spirit" whose function is to constantly remind one of the uncertainties and challenges of existence.[14] However, such openness to the guidance of anxiety is insupportable without a strong trust in the value of striving to discover truth and realize goodness in the world; that trust in turn relies on trust in the value of the cosmic process itself, and this on trust in the divine ground of this process. Kierkegaard and Voegelin both call this trust "faith."

Faith is not gnosis. They are, in a sense, existential opposites. Faith is explicitly a posture of loving openness toward an ultimacy of meaning—understood to transcend human comprehension—regarding the cosmic process in which humans participate. It is the orientation proper to the human seeker, because no amount of human insight into the structure of reality can eliminate the basic mysteries, and because refusing the Gnostic rejection of the cosmos requires the fortitude of trust to sustain both the effort to understand the world and the commitment to work for its good. The Gnostic posture, by contrast, founded on alluring but false claims to definitive knowledge about the meaning of existence, is one of closure toward the world and our participation in it, prompted largely by anxiety, and oriented toward escape. Though it is tempting to believe that an escape is both possible and good, the temptation must be dismissed.

The ancient Gnostic speculations famously contributed to the development—and, Voegelin would say, to the deformation—of genuinely *differentiated* consciousness when they mingled with the Judeo-Christian tradition.

14. Kierkegaard, *The Concept of Anxiety,* 159. We shall return in Chapter 8 to Kierkegaard's analysis of anxiety and its function in the human relationship to transcendence.

The Gnostic writings—which employ symbols drawn from Persian, Babylonian, Egyptian, Greek, and Israelite sources, among others, and the precise origins of which are not well understood—had a considerable impact on Christian thinkers.[15] What attracted the two traditions to each other was in part, obviously, their mutually radical accent on transcendence. The Judeo-Christian God of origins so transcends the world that he is in fact its Creator; the Gnostic true God transcends not only this world but even the divine creator (or creators) of this world! Both traditions also emphasize the role of the divine messenger who promises reunion between the personal spirit and its divine source. Then there is the tendency in Christian teaching to devalue the things of the world—for example, its admonition to live as if one were "not of the cosmos," in imitation of the Christ who proclaimed himself both "not of the cosmos" (John 17:14) and "victorious over the cosmos" (16:33)—a tendency that has readily lent itself to Gnostic-style interpretation. Though the Gnostic vision of the world as an evil prison flatly contradicts the Christian doctrines of Creation and Incarnation, and so indicates the irresolvable divide between the two outlooks, Gnostic influences absorbed into the Christian tradition have nevertheless retained their potential to deform the Christian differentiation, obscuring the Christian view of history as a redemptive process of transfiguring incarnation by encouraging hatred of the world and a life-despising desire for a "redemptive exodus from the cosmos."[16]

15. "Modern scholars have advanced in turn Hellenic, Babylonian, Egyptian, and Iranian origins and every possible combination of these with one another and with Jewish and Christian elements. Since in the material of its representation Gnosticism actually is a product of syncretism, each of these theories can be supported from the sources and none of them is satisfactory alone; but neither is the combination of all of them, which would make Gnosticism out to be a mere mosaic of these elements and so miss its autonomous essence" (Jonas, *Gnostic Religion*, 33).

16. Voegelin, *The Ecumenic Age*, 73. The Johannine passages quoted above are discussed on 62–64. In the first centuries of the Christian era there were a large number of Christian Gnostic sects—including those grouped around the well-known Gnostics Valentinus (ca. 100–165), Marcion (ca. 85–165), and Basilides (second century)—though in the cases of some of them, as Jonas points out, "the Christian veneer is rather thin." Consequently, the struggle against Christian Gnostic heresy had a high priority in the writings of some of the early church fathers, and early patristic literature gives us a good deal of our information about Gnostic teachings, including the bulk of existing direct quotations from original Greek sources (*Gnostic Religion*, 37–38, 292). Gilles Quispel argues that the attempt to blend Gnostic convictions with Christian theology was bound to fail due to the biblical, and especially Johannine, attitude toward God and world. "Christian Gnosis," Quispel concludes, "was a premature attempt to Christianize a pre-Christian mysticism and did not succeed in adopting the characteristic trait of the Christian

Historiogenesis

A third type of deformation linked to the discovery of transcendence pertains to the phenomenon Voegelin calls "historiogenesis," described in the previous chapter. In order to discuss historiogenetic thinking informed by the explicit differentiation of transcendence, we need to first rehearse the manner of its emergence in predifferentiated, cosmological societies.

As we have seen, Voegelin explains that in some cosmological societies a distinctive type of mytho-speculation arises whose function is to relate how the speculator's existing social order came into being by extrapolating its development back to a point of cosmic-divine origin. As with other types of mytho-speculation—such as theogony and anthropogony—that show the impact of rational-critical analysis on mythic materials, historiogenesis is a late form of cosmological symbolization. Indeed, Voegelin notes, where it does appear it developed later than other mytho-speculative forms. As it is manifestly concerned with historical meaning in the sense of a linear sequence of unrepeatable events, its presence in cosmological societies should give pause, as we have noted, to scholars holding to the convention that the cosmological conception of time was only "cyclical" and that "linear" time was the discovery of the Hebrews. Still, Voegelin warns, historiogenesis in these societies should not be taken as evidence of *historical consciousness in the profounder sense*, where the discovery of transcendence has conceptually removed divine timelessness from the flow of temporal existence. The function of early historiogenetic speculation is still the cosmological one of linking the social order of the present with cosmic-divine origins and thereby with "the timeless serenity of the cosmic order itself."[17] Nevertheless, in its particular blend of myth, rational speculation, and historiography, cosmological examples of historiogenesis do reflect a *growing* emphasis both on rational-critical analysis and on historical contingency.

Wherever historiogenetic speculation arose in cosmological cultures—Voegelin cites its emergence in China and India as well as in Egypt, Mesopotamia, and elsewhere—it performed the same function: to respond to the experience of temporal unrepeatability by accounting for an existing social

tradition," namely, that God—and all that comes from God—is love ("Gnostic Man: The Doctrine of Basilides," 246).

17. Voegelin, *The Ecumenic Age*, 115.

order in terms of a direct line from divine origins, so that with regard to the flow of events "the present can be understood as the terminal situation into which the meaning flowing from the origin has issued."[18] Any such construction requires, of course, a good deal of pruning and straightening out of data, because the histories of other known societies must be ignored, or at best granted no more than a supporting role in the drama of truly significant events that have issued into the society in question. Also, the construction requires that myths of cosmic-divine origins and legends of gods and ancient heroes be arranged on a conceptual continuum with recent pragmatic events, a process that subverts the mythic function of the former by literalizing them into spurious "facts of history." Only through such fanciful manipulations can a society establish an unwavering line of meaning between itself and the original emergence of order in the cosmos. If the symbolism appeared frequently in the ancient world, the reason is readily understood. Historiogenesis answered a given society's need to affirm its significance in the face of an increasing awareness of historical contingency and vulnerability. An *intensifying* experience of unrepeatable time and existential contingency was the catalytic factor. The precariousness of a society's existence was, through historiogenesis, transformed into something seemingly solid and inevitable. The speculative lineage sought to confer on the existing social order the sanction of divine meaning, binding it as firmly as possible to the cosmic-divine ground.

This basic motive of historiogenetic speculation—the anxious concern to guarantee the meaning of one's existence by tying one's present social order to an eternal ground of meaning—certainly does not fade when the transcendence of the divine ground is discovered. Indeed, this anxious concern intensifies as the divine ground recedes into the mystery beyond space and time and the accent falls more heavily on the contingency of worldly existence. Therefore, it is not surprising that the phenomenon of historiogenesis does not disappear when the differentiating insights transform the cosmological perspective. The principles of historiogenetic construction in the new context remain the same, but the speculation, now establishing a direct line of meaning from a *transcendent* divine origin, makes the chosen social order (at least in Western contexts) the privileged carrier of *incarnation,* a society through whose achievements *history* is moving toward its goal of transfiguration.

18. Ibid., 134.

In this new, differentiated context, historiogenesis reveals its potential as a unique source of deformative influence on the understanding of the relationship of history to transcendent meaning. The potential is exercised when a linear sequence of societies in the past and one particular social order in the present are granted the status of unique and unequivocal carriers of eschatological significance. This "attribution of eschatological ultimacy" to specific events and societies in a unilinear succession, explains Voegelin, is an illegitimate attempt to solve the mystery of incarnational process by forcing the story of meaningful human response to the transcendent divine appeal onto a straight line and letting it end in the society of the speculator's present. An example of historiogenetic deformation from the early Christian tradition, he notes, can be found in the writings of Saint Augustine. Even as rigorous a thinker as Augustine succumbed to the temptation to ward off historical anxiety and "solve the mystery of meaning" by positing "an historiogenetic pattern whose unilinear history came to its meaningful end in the dual ecumenism of Church and Roman empire," leaving history with "no meaning but the waiting for the eschatological events" of the Second Coming.[19] The open, transfigurative process of history, as revealed through the differentiating insights, is restricted to a single and linear course of events that has come to its meaningful end in Augustine's own time.

Modern Versions of the Deformations

We have been discussing deformed interpretations of what it means to live in the historical "in-between" of immanence and transcendence, and the three types of deformation discussed—apocalyptic consciousness, gnosticism, and postcosmological historiogenetic speculation—have in common one most significant feature. Each constitutes an attempt to *escape* the tension of living in the historical "in-between," in the shadow of historical uncertainty thrown upon the world by the discovery of transcendence. Apocalyptic consciousness tries to resolve the tension by announcing the end of history. Gnosticism seeks to escape the tension by developing methods to liberate the personal pneuma from the world's intrinsic evil and ignorance. Postcosmological historiogenetic speculation, finally, by ignoring the plurality of lines

19. Ibid., 230.

of meaning in history and the open-endedness of history, attempts to replace the tension with a more manageable "specific faith in a concrete social order as ultimate."[20] Each attitude in its own way seeks to avoid the full implications of the discovery of transcendence by bringing eternal transcendent meaning somehow into human possession.

Because it was the discovery of transcendence that provided the occasion for these deformative responses to it, it might seem that with the modern waning of confidence in transcendence, or in the context of a modern secular perspective where transcendent reality is simply dismissed as an illusion, these deformative responses would have lost their point and their appeal. This has hardly been the case, though. Voegelin's account of how these deformations have influenced modern Western thought, not only through religious but also through secular imagination, is a prominent theme in *The Ecumenic Age* and other works. All three types of resistance to the "in-between" of existence have mutated and continued to thrive in Western cultures, while confidence in transcendence has dwindled, the reason being that the eclipse of transcendence does nothing to solve the problems of ultimate meaning and the mystery of history. Radical secularization does not undo the *impact* of the discovery of transcendence—it does not reawaken cosmological experiences of eternal divine ultimacy somehow interfused with the universe of things. Rather, it presents the challenge of finding in a *purely* temporal and finite world a *ground of meaning* that can convincingly substitute for the lost ground of divine transcendence. Likewise, radical secularization does not dissolve "epochal consciousness," the concern with historical transformation that arose from the differentiating experiences. Rather, when a firmly established historical outlook can no longer take its bearings from the vision of a transcendent context and goal for the transfigurative process, the purpose of history must be found in a purely worldly process of transformation with a purely worldly goal.

In other words, though transcendence may become eclipsed, historical existence is still experienced as an "in-between" of tension between imperfection and perfection, temporal and timeless meaning; the human search for the ground of history, and for attunement with that ground, does not abate. The suspicion of transcendence and of a transcendent mystery of eschatological fulfillment, therefore, leads only to efforts to find ultimate meaning in

20. Ibid., 402.

the temporal process itself, and, most notably, in efforts to endow existence in time with eschatological significance. So we can understand and notice why, in somewhat altered guise, apocalyptic, gnostic, and historiogenetic resolutions to the burden of historical existence have continued to flourish even in the most secular streams of modern thought.

Apocalyptic sentiment, for example, may be found in a thinker like Karl Marx, who holds to the core apocalyptic conviction that the presently disordered field of history will before long give way to a transfigured and perfected existence marking the end of history (the end of "prehistory," in his parlance). In Marx's view, of course, the end of disordered history and the introduction of the perfected realm will come to pass not through divine initiative, but instead through necessary laws of historical development—an immanent cause of the immanent realization of the ultimate meaning of historical existence. Here the apocalyptic procedure of imagining a definitive sequel to the history we actually experience remains unchanged; as Voegelin remarks, "[t]he phantasy of two realities has remained constant in Western history from antiquity to the present."[21]

Gnostic sentiments as well, Voegelin contends, not only may be found in Marx's thought, but in fact pervade much of modern political theory and cultural life. This claim might at first sound odd, because ancient Gnosticism, with its belief in an ultratranscendent divine Pneuma and its desire to abandon the world, would seem to offer little to a culture lacking interest in transcendence and dominated by a belief in worldly progress. However, Voegelin specifies as the core of the "gnostic attitude" the following convictions: that the world as it exists is a realm of alienation, that salvation from this world is possible, and that salvation is to be effected through human action based on knowledge. This core attitude is quite adaptable to a modern and secular perspective through conceiving of salvation from alienated existence not in terms of an escape from the world but in terms of a transformation of the world itself. Salvation out of the world becomes a salvation within it, with the saving knowledge that guarantees the transformation coming not from a god but from human deliverers. Defined thus, the "gnostic attitude" may be found, asserts Voegelin, in any number of modern and secular streams of thought. In his essay of 1960, "Ersatz Religion," he identifies gnostic elements in "progressivism, positivism, Marxism, psychoanalysis, communism,

21. Ibid., 374.

fascism, and national socialism," some of these showing also apocalyptic inclinations in their portrayal of a temporal solution to historical disorder. In the convictions and pronouncements of each of these movements Voegelin detects an anxious desire to end history in order to escape the *metaxy,* the "in-between" of unresolved historical existence. Promising a saving knowledge and a perfectable world, "the modern apocalyptic-Gnostic movements attempt to abolish the Metaxy by transforming the Beyond into this world."[22]

Merging in a dramatic way with these sentiments so pervasive in Western modernity, finally, is a historiogenetic element that gives ample testimony to the "human weakness of elevating one's own present into the purpose of history." Modern Western thinkers have been no less prone than their ancient forebears to speculatively secure the meaning of their own place and time by elevating it to a position of supreme importance in the historical process. However, their methods have had to become more complex. A vast increase in knowledge of world cultures, and especially of civilizational developments running parallel in time, has made it far more difficult to present historical materials convincingly as a single line of advance leading to one society in the present. Therefore, explains Voegelin, modern thinkers have had to resort to ever more "ingenious devices for straightening out obstreperous facts on a fictitious line" so that they will "unequivocally lead into the speculator's present." In *The Ecumenic Age* his principal example of such ingenuity is Hegel, who manages to portray the meaning of history as a chronological

22. Voegelin, *Science, Politics, and Gnosticism,* in *Modernity without Restraint,* 295; *The Ecumenic Age,* 302. Voegelin's characterization of many influential modern philosophies and political theories as "gnostic" in orientation is one of the most well-known features of his work. This is a central theme in *The New Science of Politics,* the work for which he first received broad attention as a political philosopher, as it is in the essays in *Science, Politics, and Gnosticism* (1960), both in *Modernity without Restraint.* His position in these works was amply criticized, both by specialists in ancient Gnosticism and by political theorists, in part for using the category of "gnosticism" too freely, and also for oversimplifying modern intellectual and political movements. Voegelin came to agree that in these midcareer writings, his use of the "gnostic" label involved oversimplification. Nonetheless, he maintained that its application to modern social and political phenomena was justified, if properly contextualized by recognizing also the impact of other esoteric traditions on modern streams of thought, traditions such as apocalypticism, Neoplatonism, Hermeticism, and alchemical thinking, all of them in their modern variations sharing the trait of desiring, or offering methods for, the transformation of an evil world into a perfected one. By the time of the writing of *The Ecumenic Age* (1974), Geoffrey L. Price points out, Voegelin was well prepared "to account for the otherwise confusing issue of the phenotypical differences between ancient and modern manifestations of gnosticism" ("Recovery from Metastatic Consciousness: Voegelin and Jeremiah," 187–88).

"westward march of empire toward ever-increasing freedom" by means of a sophisticated manipulation of civilizational data, carefully arranging "the errant materials on the straight line that leads to the imperial present of mankind and to himself as its philosopher." Hegel's historiogenetic speculation, however, is only the most brilliant and grandiose of a modern variation that proliferates in eighteenth- and nineteenth-century thought. Condorcet, Comte, Proudhon, Marx: each presents a "philosophy of history" that describes a single line of civilizational advance bringing history to a culmination *in the foreseeable future of his own society,* promoting it thereby "to the rank of a goal toward which all mankind had been moving from the beginning." The device of historiogenetic speculation, as always, wards off troubling questions about the mystery of history by narrowing it to a unilinear sequence that reaches a specific worldly conclusion.[23]

Of course, the "history" in these modern philosophies of history—the progress of civilization toward a perfection of knowledge and social organization—cannot, Voegelin points out, be "history" as understood by the philosophers and prophets in whom the consciousness of epoch came to sharp attention through the Greek and Judeo-Christian differentiations of transcendence. The history of divine appeal and human response—history as a story of human participation in the divine mystery with its movement of transfigurative incarnation—must be replaced by a history of purely human accomplishment if it is to lead to the modern and secular present. "[T]he reality of theophanic history," Voegelin states, "must be eclipsed by an imaginary egophanic history," a quite different story, which concerns the career of world-immanent entities called humans within a wholly immanent process of reality, a history much more conducive to human control and satisfactory outcomes than the mysterious process revealed in the differentiating insights.[24]

Significantly, though, upon inspection, one finds that the modern secular solutions to the problem of historical meaning have essentially the same structure as the Christian solution, a parallelism that is inevitable given that historical consciousness—the legacy of especially the Judeo-Christian differentiation—is eschatologically oriented, that is, involves some guiding vision of historical outcome. If the transfigurative movement constituting history

23. Voegelin, *The Ecumenic Age,* 47–48, 116, 287, 405.

24. Ibid., 327.

does not have its ultimate goal or telos in transcendent mystery, its goal must be a transfigured world order; if there is no process of "immortalizing" through conscious participation in a mystery of divine transcendence, there must be the attainment of everlasting truth through absolute knowledge and a perfected society; and finally, if there is no divine presence in consciousness to which appropriate response might save historical existence from meaninglessness, then there must be human saviors—intellectual and political leaders—to point the way out of the historical wilderness to the earthly promised land. Voegelin returns repeatedly in *The Ecumenic Age* and elsewhere to the theme of how modern philosophies of history mimic, in immanentized form, the classic and especially the Christian understanding of history as a process of transfiguration. "[T]he modern revolt," he says, "is so intimately a development of the 'Christianity' against which it is in revolt that it would be unintelligible if it could not be understood as the deformation of the theophanic events in which the dynamics of transfiguration was revealed to Jesus and the Apostles."[25] However, in contrast to the undeformed traditional view that the end of history remains an undisclosed mystery of eschatological fulfillment, the modern immanentist philosophers of history deformatively close the book on the story of transfiguration.

The immanentist histories are both harmful and dangerous, Voegelin explains, because they are a betrayal of the truth that human existence is lived in the *metaxy*, the divine-human "in-between" of transcendence and immanence. They are an existentially disorienting influence, flooding the culture with images that eclipse some of the most basic facts of existence: that every consciousness is given to itself from a ground that transcends full human comprehension; that human beings, while capable of vast understanding and mastery of the world, are still participants in a drama of reality whose ultimate meaning remains mysterious; and that history is open-ended both toward the future and toward its transcendent ground. Regarding the structure of history, they impose unilinear, constricted, and foreshortened models that force history to a false eschatological climax, stifle consideration of the parallel lines of meaning in history, and obscure the anxiety-inducing line that runs at every historical moment from time into eternity. In essence they are, Voegelin concludes, attempts to "stop history." Exposing the degraded nature of such models of history and granting full recognition to the lines of meaning

25. Ibid., 336.

they obliterate are among Voegelin's foremost aims, seen as crucial steps in developing a philosophy of history that is sufficiently critical of contemporary assumptions and properly responsible to the data at our disposal.

The "Stop History" Movements and the Need for Appropriate Historical Symbols

One of the most important lessons of Voegelin's *Ecumenic Age* is that a successful critique of the unilinear, immanentist, gnostic, apocalyptic, and nihilistic images of history that crowd the contemporary landscape must be based on a sufficiently solid understanding of the occasions and impact of the discoveries of transcendence during the "ecumenic age." Without an understanding of the experiences that "differentiated" the one reality of the cosmos into the two conceptual realms of immanence and transcendence, it is impossible to understand the very emergence of profoundly historical consciousness out of cosmological consciousness, that is, the emergence of a sense of human history as involving a "transfigurative movement" unfolding in constant relation to a transcendent ground of meaning. Once these experiences of differentiation and their symbolic legacy are adequately understood, it is possible to make sense of, and recognize the illegitimacy of, the deformed responses to them that we have been discussing. Finally, it is only when these deformations have been critically appreciated for what they are that both the background and the motivations of contemporary "stop history" movements, secular or religious, can be grasped, together with the futility of reactions to these movements by the philosophers of groundlessness, who seek to end the tyranny of dogmatic solutions to the mystery of history by ignoring transcendence altogether and reducing human experience to pure immanence and pure contingency. *The Ecumenic Age,* like much of Voegelin's late work, is a therapeutic effort to orient the reader in *true* historical reality through illumination of the historical "in-between."

The truth may set one free, but it is not always comforting. During the ecumenic age, human existence was discovered to have historical meaning, to be participation in a transfigurative movement whose ultimate meaning and outcome are uncertain. Nothing has changed. "Our present, like any present, is a phase in the flux of divine presence in which we, as all men before and after us, participate."[26] To attempt to bring the flux of presence to a standstill by

26. Ibid., 405.

assuming knowledge of its ultimate meaning, or by predicting its fulfillment in time, is an act of existential closure both against history in all its worrisome open-endedness and against the fact of transcendent meaning.

This act of existential closure against the fact of transcendence also constitutes a theoretical closure—in consequence if not in intention—against the idea of the solidarity of humanity. This is because the universality of humanity—that which makes all humans actors in a single unifying story—is precisely the transcendence of the one divine presence constitutive of human consciousness at all times and places. Humankind constitutes the subject of a single story only if all humans participate in a reality that transcends biological, psychological, and cultural differences. As Voegelin states: "A scattering of societies, belonging to the same biological type . . . is discovered to be one mankind with one history, by virtue of participation in the same flux of divine presence." The discovery of transcendence that makes explicit the line of meaning in history that runs from time into eternity, then, which contributes to making the order of history so much more complex than a single line of development, and which provokes so much anxious invention when it erupts into consciousness, must not be overlooked or oversimplified by the philosopher of history. Only careful appreciation of this line of meaning ensures that the idea of history is kept maximally open, embracing *all* human participants in "the Mystery that has no end in time."[27]

Finally, for this maximally open idea of history to become critically or socially effective, there must be available the appropriate images and concepts to represent it. For example, images of history that suggest its actual complex of diachronic, synchronic, and transcendent lines of meaning—like Voegelin's awkward but useful description of history as "a web of meaning with a plurality of nodal points"—must be available to replace the unilinear images of history that nations and cultures tend to foster. Above all, images that successfully evoke our lives in the personal and historical *metaxy,* in the In-Between of transcendence and immanence, must replace immanentist images of existence and history. This last development, Voegelin states, is crucial. Without the reemergence of a convincing sense of the universal presence of transcendent meaning, and a sense of human existence as a "tension" between time and timelessness, a realistic apprehension of the true structure of history is impossible. At present, he declares, the "great obstacle" to experiencing history in its genuine depth and meaning is the "massive block of accumulated

27. Ibid., 377, 407.

symbols" of existence and history that "eclipses the reality of man's existence in the Metaxy."[28]

Images and concepts that do manage to overcome this obstacle, that successfully illuminate the *metaxy* in which we live, not only reveal what is false in unilinear, immanentist, apocalyptic, and other deformed images of history, but also have the therapeutic effect of promoting what Voegelin calls "balanced consciousness." The balance at issue here is the existential equilibrium maintained in duly affirming and respecting both finite world and transcendent ground—for one may easily lose one's "balance" in the direction of either (1) denying the fact or implications of transcendence (the general problem of modernity) or (2) degrading immanence in favor of transcendence (more a classical and medieval tendency in the West, though fundamentalist religious attitudes keep the problem current).[29] We require, in other words, historical symbols and ideas that affirm the full value and complexity of the worldly enterprise—practical, technological, economic, political, cultural, moral—while keeping vividly apparent the mystery of transcendence.

Of course, one of the reasons for Voegelin's adoption of the Platonic term *metaxy* during the years he was working on *The Ecumenic Age* and for his reliance on it in all of his subsequent writings is that it helps to answer this need. Still, as a term that refers first of all to the ontological status of human consciousness as a reality "in-between" immanence and transcendence, *metaxy* is a symbol of extreme concision and abstractness, an abstractness that is not lessened when it is expanded into the notion of "the historical *metaxy*."[30] For an example of a more richly evocative symbol of our historical situation "in-between" time and timelessness, a symbol rich in connotations of cultural and moral aspiration, we may turn to an intriguing section of Bernard Lonergan's work *Insight*, in which he attempts to rehabilitate and press into contemporary service the classic philosophical idea of cosmopolis, the "universal city."

28. Ibid., 107.

29. Ibid., chap. 4, § 3, "The Balance of Consciousness" (291–302). For a summary account of this concept of Voegelin, and an exploration of its use in diagnosing misinterpretations of the fundamental structure of reality, see Glenn Hughes, "Balanced and Imbalanced Consciousness." On the same topic, see also Michael Franz, *Eric Voegelin and the Politics of Spiritual Revolt: The Roots of Modern Ideology*, 3–20. We will return to this concept in Chapter 6.

30. Voegelin, *The Ecumenic Age*, 230–31. On the *metaxy* as the structure of human history, see esp. 229–58.

Since its first use (according to tradition) by Stoic philosophers in the early centuries of the ecumenic age, the idea of cosmopolis has functioned to promote awareness of a transnational and transhistorical—and thus transcendence-grounded—element in human identity. At the same time it has served as a reminder that it is precisely as citizens *of the world* that we fulfill our distinctively human responsibilities. Lonergan's treatment of the notion of cosmopolis is in harmony with Voegelin's understanding of the transcendent ground of history and of the contemporary need for effective symbols of the historical *metaxy.* Let us turn, then, to Lonergan's account of cosmopolis, to consider how a symbol might function to impart and to protect a maximally open idea of human history. Because it will be helpful, once the idea of cosmopolis has been clarified, to explore how a sense of participation in the "universal city" might be culturally nourished, in the second part of the following chapter we will also examine how this purpose is served in a uniquely powerful fashion by artists and works of art.

5

COSMOPOLIS, CULTURE, AND ART

> I believe [that hope] is awakened, revived, nourished by millions of solitary individuals whose deeds and works every day negate frontiers and the crudest implications of history.
>
> —Albert Camus, "Create Dangerously"

> We flinch from the immediate pressures of mystery in poetic, in aesthetic acts of creation as we do from the realization of our diminished humanity, of all that is literally bestial in the murderousness and gadgetry of this age. . . . [W]e shall not come home to the facts of our unhousedness, or our eviction from a central humanity in the face of the tidal provocations of political barbarism and technocratic servitude, if we do not re-experience the life of meaning in the text, in music, in art. We must come to recognize . . . a meaningfulness which is that of a freedom of giving and of reception beyond the constraints of immanence.
>
> —George Steiner, *Real Presences*

Cosmopolis

BERNARD LONERGAN's provocative use of the notion of cosmopolis in his magnum opus *Insight* builds on a tradition reaching back to the Hellenic miracle. Diogenes Laertius's *Lives of Eminent Philosophers,* composed in the third century C.E., allows us to trace the idea of cosmopolis back to the eccentric philosopher known as Diogenes the Cynic (413–327 B.C.E.), a younger contemporary of Plato. This Diogenes, we read in the *Lives*, was a native of Sinope in Asia Minor, whence he had come in exile to Athens; however, "asked where he came from, he said, 'I am a citizen of the world' *(kosmopolites)*." Tradition has it that thereafter the concept of the *kosmopolites* was taken up and developed by the Stoic philosophers, as part of their argument that beyond all local laws there are universal standards of justice and reason to which each human being owes principal allegiance. Tradition, of course, is not always trustworthy. We cannot be certain that Diogenes actually called himself a *kosmopolites*, and it is not beyond question that the Stoics used the term. In the extant literature, its first appearance is in the *De Opificio Mundi* of Philo, a contemporary of Christ.[1]

Nonetheless, let us assume that Diogenes the Cynic did refer to himself as a citizen of the world. The sentiment expressed would have been primarily antinationalist; that is, in contrast to the typical Greek man of his time, Diogenes would have been pointedly refusing to identify himself in terms of allegiance to his place of birth or to political or group affiliations.[2] This implies, though, that his first loyalty is to something else. What is this something else? The *kosmopolites* is a citizen of the world *(kosmos)* community *(polis)*: of cosmopolis.

What *is* cosmopolis, though? What is "world community"? How is it constituted? When we imagine Diogenes saying, "I am a citizen of the world," we do not at once dismiss the notion by reasoning that until the world has been organized into a single overarching political institution, no one can be a "citizen of the world." We understand that a person can be a *kosmopolites* because of the nature of his or her allegiance and orientation to fellow humans. If a cosmopolitan can exist without all humanity being gathered under one political structure, then cosmopolis must be something other than a political structure.

1. Diogenes Laertius, *Lives of Eminent Philosophers*, 65. Cf. Voegelin, *The Ecumenic Age*, 77. In *De Opificio Mundi* ("On the Account of the World's Creation Given by Moses") Philo says: "[Moses gives] an account of the creation of the world, implying that the world is in harmony with the Law, and the Law with the world, and that the man who observes the law is constituted thereby a loyal citizen of the world *(kosmopolitou)*, regulating his doings by the purpose and will of Nature, in accordance with which the entire world itself is also administered" (*Works*, 7).

2. Martha C. Nussbaum, *Cultivating Humanity: A Classical Defense of Reform in Liberal Education*, 52–53; for a brief description of the idea of world citizenship in ancient Greek and Roman thought, see 53–67.

We can begin, then, to answer the question, What is cosmopolis? in the same manner that Lonergan does, by stating what it is not: it is not a political institution, or any army or police force that enforces or imposes adherence to the laws of any political institution.[3] Extending this observation, we can see that world community is also not just a matter of economic powers and relations. However tightly knit together at a global level of interdependence, the production, supply, and distribution of goods and services for producers and consumers are not what create cosmopolis. Finally, it is not a reality at the level of technology. People may be linked together through use of the same technologies, through increased speed of transportation and communication, through sharing a global information network, or through the electronic proximity of virtual reality, but none of this necessarily establishes a "world community." A community is not created simply by persons being in proximity, geographically or electronically, nor again simply through everyone being exposed to the same data.

As Lonergan explains, community is realized only through "an achievement of common meaning": not just experience of common data, but the common understanding of that data, common judgment about the truth and reality of what is understood, and—especially—subsequent common commitment to worthwhile action arising from common judgments of value. Any authentic community, then, local or national, involves more than shared institutions and communication links; rather, these are mere structural elements that serve in the constitution of community when they are genuinely integrated through shared apprehensions of significant truths and shared orientations toward significant values.[4] Furthermore, the notion of *world community*—cosmopolis—introduces still another criterion, in that it requires, beyond a commitment to any concrete community, dedication to an order of truth and value that transcends all local and national concerns and, indeed, all practical concerns.

3. For Lonergan's discussion of cosmopolis, see *Insight*, 263–67.

4. Lonergan, *Method in Theology*, 79. Albert Borgmann argues that vastly extended communication links may actually inhibit the achievement of community. For Borgmann, community arises in part from experience of the "commanding presence" of others. However, communication links diminish the presence of others to images we can call up or make vanish at will. So while the idea of advanced communications systems suggests that by "having our hyperintelligent eyes and ears everywhere, we can attain world citizenship of unequaled scope and subtlety," actually the possibility of community is undermined precisely through the world's losing "its force and resistance" (*Crossing the Postmodern Divide*, 105–6).

The aim of practical intelligence is the securing of instrumental ends: technology, economy, and polity are the tools and the organized cooperation of individuals in institutions that together serve practical needs and desires. Their complexity and their influence are an extraordinary testimony to the scope and ingenuity of human reason, and their presence is central to the realization of the human good, but they are nevertheless not the ultimate focus of human concern.[5] When Diogenes declared, "I am a citizen of the world," he was expressing his recognition of and allegiance to something higher than politics, and therefore to something higher in the scale of human values than the practical organization of society. What is higher than practicality?

However beneficial the fruits of practical intelligence, the deepest desires of a human being are not to live with absolute efficiency, and with every practical problem solved. Rather, those deepest desires focus on living a life that is meaningful and dignified. People do not live merely in order to develop technologies, economies, and polities; rather, they work hard at developing and improving these in order that their lives may be more rich, more full, more complete. As I have already described in the Introduction and as Lonergan emphasizes, the overriding concern of people is, in the end, with the dramatic meaning of their lives, with the "[d]elight and suffering, laughter and tears, joy and sorrow, aspiration and frustration, achievement and failure, wit and humor [that] stand, not within practicality but above it." Above practicality, then, there is the comprehensive artistry of one's performance in the drama of living, where the goal is not just to satisfy needs and desires, but to do so admirably, appealingly, beautifully, and with a sense of dramatic accomplishment. "Man is an artist. His practicality is part of his dramatic pursuit of dignified living."[6]

Culture

The same point may be made by saying that we feel our lives to be successful when our practical aims and accomplishments contribute to the realization of certain meanings and values. These meanings and values, which give us

5. On practical intelligence, see Lonergan, *Insight,* 232–39, 250–67; on social institutions as elements of the human good, see *Method in Theology,* 47–50.

6. Lonergan, *Insight,* 237, 261.

our sense of direction in life, are summed up in the word *culture*. Lonergan's definition of culture is precisely this: "the set of meanings and values that informs a way of life."[7] Culture makes sense of life. It reveals what our physical survival and our interactions with others and our practical devices are *for;* it answers our questions about what to live for, and how. It enlightens us as to what a good performance in the drama of living entails.

For a sample of everyday culture in the contemporary United States, one can turn to television, because its programs and especially its advertisements reflect so glaringly and so relentlessly the cultural habits and norms of our society. The advertisers in particular need to have a fine sensitivity for everyday culture if they are to successfully tap our quest for dignity by appealing to our desire to buy commodities that we deem will make our lives worthwhile, beautiful, and complete. For example, there is a television commercial from the 1990s that shows a daughter visiting home from college who finds herself sharing an early morning cup of coffee with her mother, and we witness their touching rediscovery of the goodness of life, of family, of love, and of the coffee that symbolizes all this: Folger's coffee. They lean together in the kitchen in the early morning light in their bathrobes, and what is it that gives their lives richness? Is it the technology of the coffeepot? Is it the economic system that brought these particular goods to the kitchen? Is it the political laws that keep rat feces out of the coffee and require warning stickers on the coffeepot about its proper use? No. All of these serve a higher end, which is living a life of emotional richness and dramatic completeness, and in our everyday culture, the ritual of drinking coffee together is widely considered part of a life well lived, in this case mediating the love between mother and daughter. The manufacturers of Folger's coffee and their advertisement company understood this well, which is why they constructed their commercial as a tiny heartwarming story. Their product will sell better if we associate Folger's coffee with deeply meaningful existence.

Beyond everyday culture there is a second, reflexive level of culture, a "cultural superstructure" (as Lonergan calls it). This consists of those elements of culture that reflect upon, explain, and evaluate human spontaneity and everyday culture, in addition to political and economic institutions, technological developments, and the conditions under which all these arise. The natural and human sciences, philosophy, theology, history, literary criticism, and art

7. Lonergan, *Method in Theology,* xi.

criticism are all parts of this cultural superstructure, and they in turn have an impact on human living, expressing and shaping hopes and convictions about what constitutes the right way to live—an impact that, we would do well to remember, is not always beneficial.[8]

Comprehensively, then, culture embraces and guides practicality, as it explains our world to us and expresses what is significant, appropriate, and valuable in our living.[9] Moreover, it is *only at the cultural level* that the phenomenon of world community, of cosmopolis, can begin to be realized. World community comes about when human beings recognize and dedicate themselves to meanings and values that pertain to the fulfillment of human beings as such—human beings universally. To rise above personal, family, group, class, and national interests and give one's first allegiance to that which dignifies every person, to those discoveries, reasoned arguments, ideas, and aspirations that would enrich everyone's lives, is to create cosmopolis. Cosmopolis, therefore, is not a material thing or an aggregate of things. It is not any kind of political setup. It is, as Lonergan states, a "long-standing, nonpolitical, *cultural* fact" that "transcends the frontiers of states and the epochs of history." It is founded upon a specific quality of orientation and allegiance to fellow human beings, one that has risen above immediate historical conditions and local cultural views to a disinterested concern with human fulfillment. Thus, Lonergan describes it as "a dimension of consciousness, a heightened grasp of historical origins, a discovery of historical responsibilities."[10]

When Lonergan states that cosmopolis "transcends the frontiers of state and the epochs of history," he is not being rhetorical. He means that world community is a function of human participation in the dimension of meaning that transcends space and time. One cannot concern oneself with human

8. On the two levels of culture, see Lonergan, "The Absence of God in Modern Culture," in *A Second Collection,* 101–3; and Robert M. Doran, "Cosmopolis and the Dialectic of Community," chap. 11 in *Theology and the Dialectics of History.* With regard to dangers arising from the influence of reflexive culture, Lonergan warns of "the disastrous possibility of a conflict between human living as it can be lived and human living as a cultural superstructure dictates it should be lived" (103).

9. "Over and above mere living and operating, men have to find a meaning and value in their living and operating. It is the function of culture to discover, express, validate, criticize, correct, develop, improve such meaning and value" (Lonergan, *Method in Theology,* 32).

10. Lonergan, "The Role of a Catholic University in the Modern World," in *Collection,* 109 (emphasis added); *Insight,* 266.

fulfillment as such unless one conceives of all human beings as united in a single story, where each life takes its meaning in part from its involvement with all of humankind. However, the notion of universal humankind makes sense only if environmental, biological, psychological, and social circumstances—that is, the conditions of human existence that are intrinsically conditioned by space and time—are not completely determinative for human identity. There is universal humankind only if we are all united in a mystery of transcendent being beyond space and time. As we have already noted, Eric Voegelin explains in *The Ecumenic Age* that the very notion of "universal humanity" can have originated only in experiences of participation in transcendent reality.[11]

As indicated in previous chapters, the most common error in interpreting symbols pertaining to transcendence is to take them as referring to some type of entity or place with imaginable contours or characteristics. This certainly holds true for the symbol of world community. It is all too easy to forget the dimension of transcendence in conjuring an image of cosmopolis, and to imagine universal brotherhood and sisterhood in exclusively social, political, economic, and technological terms. And when this happens, the ultimate human good envisioned by culture—as in much of influential modern thought, where transcendent reality is proclaimed to be an illusion, and the human drama portrayed as a strictly immanent course of events—is identified solely with physical and social conditions, themselves seen as increasingly subject to human control. Thus the mistaken view can take root that the realization of world community is a function not at all of participation in transcendence, but only and completely of humanly created institutions. So we arrive at modern visions of political utopia, as well as theories that justify the absolute authority of the State.

Images of political utopia are tremendously appealing to many people, and it is not difficult to understand why. They are symbols of the fulfillment of a united humanity, of an ultimate and redeeming oneness with others, and as such they respond to one of our most profound emotional needs: to orient ourselves in the search for proper direction in life through glimpsing a meaningful outcome to the human story. It remains, though, that all such utopian symbolism distorts the truth of universal humanity when it reduces it to purely immanent proportions; moreover, this distortion is genuinely dangerous, because the energy inspired by the half-hidden truth can become transformed into a political absolutism readily harnessed by leaders long on

11. See Voegelin, "Universal Humanity," chap. 7 in *The Ecumenic Age*, esp. 375–77.

self-confidence and grandiose plans for humanity but short on wisdom and scruples. The twentieth century has shown us the consequences of government based on the passionate conviction that world community, spearheaded by national community, can be created and sustained through political, economic, and technological means: in the name of liberation, a massive curtailing of liberty; an imposing of conformity through tactics of intimidation that extend to mass murder; and a thoroughgoing degradation of culture.

Culture is inevitably degraded in states run by governments working to build secular utopias, because in them all articulation of meanings and values that pertains to or derives from the recognition of transcendent reality must be suppressed, as that recognition gives the lie to the attempt to reduce the meaning of living to a series of practical problems and their definitive solutions. The critical function of culture—its responsibility to evaluate, to approve and disapprove, acclaim and denounce, the fashionable outlooks and ideas, and the prevalent institutions in a society—must be straitjacketed into loyalty to specific political goals. The famous attempt by the Soviet Union to restrict art to the style known as socialist realism exemplifies such a constraint of culture, under the assumption that full dramatic artistry in human living is identical with the establishment and enforcement of a specific economic and political situation.

These facts help to explain why Lonergan's discussion of cosmopolis dwells on its being something other than a political institution or achievement. Cosmopolis is "not a superstate," "not an organization," "not a police force," not "a court that administers a legal code," not "an unrealized political ideal." The genuine cosmopolis is a cultural community, a community "above all politics," that indeed has as one of its primary responsibilities the effective criticism of attempts to exalt the political and the practical to a position of supreme importance in human affairs.[12] Without such critique, in the form of science, philosophy, theology, literature and art, journalism, history, and the other forms of cultural analysis and communication, the reach of political power, influenced invariably by group interests as well as by a general bias against complexity, long-term solutions, and questions of ultimate meaning, can too easily grow too great.[13] What is necessary to prevent this, according to Lonergan, "is a cosmopolis that is neither class nor state, that stands above

12. Lonergan, "Role of a Catholic University," in *Collection*, 109; *Insight*, 263–64, 266.

13. On Lonergan's notion of "general bias," and its correction as a function of cosmopolis, see *Insight*, 250–67.

all their claims, that cuts them down to size, that is founded on the native detachment and disinterestedness of every intelligence, that commands man's first allegiance, that implements itself primarily through that allegiance, that is too universal to be bribed, too impalpable to be forced, too effective to be ignored."[14]

Now if cosmopolis is to command our first allegiance, there must be available in the culture images conducive both to our discovery of universal humanity as grounded in transcendence and to our commitment to a universal human fulfillment rooted in transcendent mystery, images as compelling as those of political utopias but without their immanentist distortion. Without such images, we would be incapable of sustained commitment to actions that disinterestedly promote universal human dignity. This is because (1) personal commitment depends upon regular apprehensions of specific values; (2) apprehensions of values are initiated and sustained by feelings; and (3) feelings are prompted by images. We are moved, impressed, delighted, awed, and inspired by images of universal dignity, truth and justice, self-sacrificing charity, and so on. Without such images there are not the responsive feelings that illuminate these values; without that revelation of values, there cannot be the shared judgments of value that actually create the community of shared commitments that is the basis of cosmopolis.[15]

Art

Where do the images that truly promote cosmopolis come from? From many sources, but here the role of the artist merits particular attention. Poets, novelists, painters, sculptors, composers and songwriters, filmmakers, photographers, and other artists have a peculiar responsibility to culture, in that artistic images have a unique power to inspire and persuade, a power

14. Ibid., 263.

15. Lonergan, *Method in Theology*, 37–38, 64–67. Lonergan is emphatic about the role that images play in the realization of values. The psyche has a constant need for what he calls "dynamic images" to call forth the feelings that are the "mass and momentum and power" of daily living, and that enable insights and judgments and decisions to "flow spontaneously into deeds no less than words" (*Insight*, 547–48; *Method in Theology*, 65). The poet and literary critic Robert Hass makes the same point when he states that "we all live our lives in the light of primary acts of imagination, images or sets of images that get us up and move us about our days" (*Twentieth Century Pleasures: Prose on Poetry*, 303).

Lonergan often acknowledged, as in his 1959 Cincinnati lectures on philosophy of education when he reminded his audience of the wisdom in the saying, "Let me write a nation's songs, and I care not who writes her laws." Let us focus momentarily on the question of what it is that gives art its power, disregarding here the distinction between "popular" or "low" art and "fine" or "high" art, but still distinguishing "art" in general from the manipulation of images for solely utilitarian or commercial ends and recognizing that there is a murky area where popular art shades off into what is mere advertising, mere entertainment, mere propaganda.[16]

First, art derives its power from the fact that its language is made up of symbols, of images rich in multiple meanings and the power to call up feelings. The symbols of art are suggestive, not final; they are allusively concrete, not dry and precise through abstraction; they are emotionally charged and not intellectually detached. In other words, art speaks the language of the normal dramatic artistry of everyday living, where we feel and think and decide and act in the mode of what Lonergan calls "symbolic consciousness." Symbolic consciousness is consciousness that allows words and other signs their spontaneous complement of image associations and feeling associations, and that is tolerant of multiplicity of meaning. Such is the consciousness of our everyday lives, full of feeling and apprehension, rich with the sense of free possibilities that belong to us as "actors in the primordial drama that the theatre only imitates."[17] By contrast, scientific or critically reflective consciousness seeks a language whose terms approach an ideally univocal, or at least carefully restricted, meaning, in the service of a dispassionate account of things. Everyday consciousness, however, uncritically employs a language full of emotion-laden images in the service of *dramatic* meaningfulness, a language meant to be evocative and at times ambiguous, an essentially symbolic language. Of course, the symbolic language of everyday living is not identical to the symbolic language of art. The latter is set apart by, first, its exploitation of the suggestive and communicative power of both nonverbal and verbal media through the formal refinement of their languages; second, the creation within

16. Lonergan, *Topics in Education,* 221. Greil Marcus highlights the bond between "popular" art and commercial interests by describing the former as "art made within a tradition the operating premise of which is to replicate a work and sell as many copies as possible as fast as possible" (*The Dustbin of History,* 142).

17. Lonergan, *Topics in Education,* 220–21; *Insight,* 211.

those media of internal patterns and overall compositions whose unities reflect unities within human living; and third, its extraordinary heightening or condensation of meaning by means of those patterns and compositions. Nevertheless, its symbolic language links art directly to the orientation and concerns of everyday living.

Next, and equally important, art is an exploration of the possible uses of human freedom, and as such it speaks directly to our concern with the quality of our performances in the drama of living. Art explores what Lonergan calls "potentialities for human living" through its presentations of images carefully selected and crafted to awaken wonder and emotion and to shake us out of both instrumental concerns and routine habits of perception. Its intended effect is to transport us beyond the "ready-made world" of practicality and domesticated culture in order to renew our sense of life's possibilities, to show us new ways to imagine and interpret ourselves, to quicken and explore our deepest longings and apprehensions, and, in doing all these, to reveal the mystery present at the heart of all things.[18] Thus, art brings us face-to-face with our open-endedness, our status as creatures engaged in self-making. We feel through art the strange majesty of freedom, and rediscover the beauty of the world, but only through simultaneously rediscovering that we can squander our capacity to be responsive to it, indeed *have* squandered it, and must try to amend our dullness and live more beautiful and dignified lives.

These purposes set art in natural tension with the prevailing social structure, in that it is precisely that structure with its established practical and cultural institutions, its entrenched attitudes and unquestioned assumptions, that art invites us to consider afresh from the perspective of a free exploration of human possibilities and values. Art exerts what Denis Donoghue calls "interrogative pressure" on the status quo: implicitly, and sometimes explicitly, it questions the way things are and the way things are done.[19]

This explains why art is feared. Artists are the natural enemies of those who wish above all to preserve the status quo, or who do not want a political regime, an economic system, or a moral or religious doctrine to be

18. Lonergan, *Topics in Education,* 222. On the revelatory function of art, Lonergan explains that it is serving its highest function when it "draws attention to the fact that the splendor of the world is a cipher, a revelation, an unveiling, the presence of one who is not seen, touched, grasped, put in a genus, distinguished by a difference, yet is *present*. . . . [J]ust as the pure desire to know heads on to the beatific vision, so too the break from the ready-made world heads on to God" (222, 224–25).

19. Donoghue, *The Arts without Mystery,* 27–28.

questioned. The freedom of art is above all such loyalties, and in fact to serve its true function must call those loyalties into question. It is intrinsically antagonistic, as Donoghue states, "not to reality but to any and every official knowledge of it," an antagonism that is appropriate "whether the official determination of society is bourgeois liberal, Marxist, aristocratic or Fascist." An understandable fear of art leads time and again, of course, to political efforts to suppress, dictate, or co-opt the work of artists, that is, to redirect the loyalty of the artist away from the free exploration of human possibility and into the service of the regime. "It is not surprising," notes Albert Camus, "that artists and intellectuals should have been the first victims of modern tyrannies, whether of the Right or of the Left. Tyrants know there is in the work of art an emancipatory force." When the Bolsheviks finally cracked down on the extraordinary flourishing of Soviet experimental art in the early postrevolution years, when in China Mao Tse-tung's regime of the mid-1950s performed its sudden and brutal about-face after briefly "letting a hundred flowers bloom" in artistic and intellectual life, they knew what they were doing. They knew that art not subject to political control was dangerous to them, because beauty, as Camus states, "cannot serve any party," but always sanctions the quest for greater liberty and dignity and condemns the effort to squeeze human meaning into practical programs and plans.[20]

Simply in performing its elementary function, then, art makes vividly and immediately clear that the aims of polity, economy, and technology do not exhaust the meaning of human living. Implicitly, every true work of art is a critique of practicalism. It reminds us, not dispassionately and discursively but with the emotional power and prediscursive immediacy of symbols, that the human drama is not reducible to practical ends. Given this fact, it is not surprising that artists have at times chosen as the explicit subject matter of their work the limitations of practical goals and practical achievements in

20. Ibid., 59; Camus, "Create Dangerously," 267, 269. David Walsh eloquently makes this same point in a chapter devoted to the crucial role that art and artists have performed in "publicly evoking the mystery of transcendent Being" during recent centuries: "No great art can be in the service of ideology. . . . The one-dimensional stridency of ideology, vainly masquerading as the fullness of reality, cannot withstand the probing of artistic openness. As soon as an artist puts himself at the service of a closed political system he has sold his soul. Almost by definition, the vocation of the artist calls him to resist all closure of the openness to the horizon of mystery" (*Guarded by Mystery: Meaning in a Postmodern Age,* 149, 151; see chap. 7, "Cultural Transparence," 147–73).

answering the deepest human needs. In contemporary art we see explicit critiques of this kind across the spectrum of media, reflecting different degrees of concern: from Charlie Chaplin's *Modern Times*, with its gentle ridicule of the tyrannies of modern technology and market demands for ever increasing productivity; to George Orwell's *1984*, with its warning vision of a humanity enslaved to absolute political predictability; to (in some interpretations) Dmitry Shostakovich's appalling evocation of the rise of Soviet totalitarianism in his *Seventh Symphony*. These are works of art that not only themselves liberate us from the world of utilitarian concerns, but also take for subject matter the need for that liberation and, more particularly, the degradation involved in consciousness being trapped, by accident or design, in a world bounded by practical or political goals.

Another, brief and accessible, example of such artistic critique is a poem written toward the end of his life by W. B. Yeats. The poem is a short lyric written in the ominous year of 1938, one that at first glance seems little more than a casual jibe but whose title and epigraph reveal it to have deeper importance to the poet. The title is "Politics," and the epigraph is a statement made by Thomas Mann as he witnessed Hitler and Europe heading for war: "*In our time the destiny of man presents its meaning in political terms.*" Yeats's reply is this:

> How can I, that girl standing there,
> My attention fix
> On Roman or on Russian
> Or on Spanish politics?
> Yet here's a travelled man that knows
> What he talks about,
> And there's a politician
> That has read and thought,
> And maybe what they say is true
> Of war and war's alarms,
> But O that I were young again
> And held her in my arms![21]

On a basic level the poem reads as a lyric confession of momentary feeling, in which the poet admits that, just now, the allure of physical beauty and

21. Yeats, *The Collected Poems of W. B. Yeats*, 348.

romantic love means more to him than all the political good in the world. The poem reminds us of similar moments in our own experience, and through its unembarrassed directness, the poet indirectly absolves us of any self-aimed charges of "inhumanity" over such momentary feelings.

There is more going on, though. Yeats's inclusion of the epigraph alerts us to the fact that, to Mann's general statement about human destiny, his poem is a counterstatement. The poem denies that at any time, "the destiny of man presents its meaning" only "in political terms," and the denial or counterstatement takes the form of a symbol: a concrete occurrence of the poet being unable to focus on politics because of his spontaneous attraction to a beautiful girl. To admonish the poet for selfishness, romantic self-indulgence, moral immaturity, or—given the reference in the poem to advanced years—an undignified lapse into nostalgia for the passionate transports of adolescence would be to mistake his symbol for mere factual report, or, even worse, for a moral declaration. (The ideologue or the philistine reads the poem and exclaims, "How dare the poet assert that a fleeting romantic passion is more important than political justice!") The poet's being distracted by beauty symbolizes all human longing for a life made brilliant and immortal through love, a life fulfilled through the realization of that happiness of which eros is the universal promise. The momentary distraction of the poet symbolizes the impossibility of political concerns ever finally holding the attention of our most searching desires, and thus the impossibility of their constituting the meaning of "the destiny of man."

Any art contributes toward the realization of cosmopolis when it promotes reflection on the shortsightedness of merely practical, merely group, or merely national interests. It does so as well when it encourages our identification with others in the human drama not because they are our kin or belong to any specific nation, class, or race, but just because they are human. Then, too, there are works of art that give us images that specifically focus attention on our common humanity and pointedly awaken the feelings that would sustain giving cosmopolis our first allegiance. One thinks of the Great Depression photographs of Walker Evans, of Ingmar Bergman's *Seventh Seal,* of Arthur Miller's *All My Sons,* of Beethoven's *Ninth Symphony.*

For an early example of such art, we might return to the Greek world of Diogenes, specifically to the Athens of an earlier generation, that of Aeschylus. Soon after the Persian Wars from which the Greeks miraculously emerged victorious, with his native city still in ruins from the conflict, Aeschylus in his drama *The Persians* presented the defeat of the enemy in terms of a tragic fall from their own greatness, brought on by the pride of the Persian rulers. This willingness to explore and sympathize with the humanity of the enemy is an example, as Voegelin says, of "[t]he sense for the dramatic unity of mankind." It is a somewhat early example of that sense, though, and not a pure and unqualified articulation of it, reflecting the fact that—Diogenes and Plato and the Stoic philosophers notwithstanding—insight into the essential unity and spiritual equality of all human beings never reached complete and radical differentiation in classical Greek culture.[22] In the Western world, it was the Judeo-Christian experiences that brought this insight to full clarity, and so quite naturally we find some of the most profound and effective Western art that inspires an allegiance to universal humanity to be that devoted to the symbolic communication of basic elements of the Christian story.

It is not surprising, of course, that religious insights into universal personal dignity and the common divine ground of our joy and suffering should be the source for artistic images that invite the realization of cosmopolis. We must nonetheless remember that the images of art are concrete, local, and specific, and that the universalist meanings are contained in them. It is, for example, the artistic representation of this man, Jesus, healing the sick or suffering on the cross, that invites us to recognize our common humanity in and through him. Likewise, the local and concrete in many other contexts provide the symbolic material for cosmopolitan enlightenment. Images derived from experiences of personal happiness or misfortune, from family life, or loyalty to one's group or nation can do so, providing they are crafted to evoke awareness of and responsibility to human fulfillment as such. This is an important point: devotion to the local is not intrinsically antagonistic to loyalty to the world community. On the contrary, only *through* commitment to the concrete and the local can one participate in cosmopolis. To take an example from popular art, when Woody Guthrie wrote the song "This Land

22. Voegelin, *World of the Polis,* 406–7. The incompleteness of the differentiation is reflected in a passage in bk. 5 of Plato's *Republic* (466e–471c) in which Socrates is urging Glaucon and his fellow discussants to agree that a well-ruled polis at war with another Greek city should not treat it in the same way as it properly treats a barbarian enemy—that is, it should not strip the corpses of defeated warriors, ravage the lands, raze the houses, and enslave the civilian population. In Plato's time, Voegelin notes, "[t]he idea of personal membership in a community of the spirit . . . was still in its infancy; it had just begun to express itself, in the fourth century, in the form of philosophical schools" (*Plato and Aristotle,* 172).

Is Your Land," he was, of course, writing about the vastness and beauty of the United States and every citizen's right to enjoy its gifts, but not merely that. The song is about human rights and human dignity as well as being about the United States. The chorus's last line, "This land was made for you and me," does not mean "and it was not made for the Canadians and Mexicans." It means, most important, that everyone's homeland belongs as much to him or her as to every other inhabitant, because all human beings—each of whom lives concretely in some nation—are ultimately brothers and sisters. Art that promotes cosmopolis affirms the value of the specific and the local while revealing through that affirmation our involvement in and our proper allegiance to world community.

The availability and efficacy of such art vary from culture to culture, of course. For different reasons and in different ways, the potentially most liberating art can become a diminished and marginal power. The best art can be politically repressed and much of the rest forced into ideological molds, producing a state-controlled art of homogenized propaganda. Or, the concerns and modes of expression of the strongest artists can get out of touch with popular culture and comprehension, so that their work speaks only to other artists in a self-conscious contempt of the broader community, while in response, popular resentment grows against a high art that flaunts its alienation and inaccessibility. Or, the power of the finest art can be poisoned through its control by and marriage to commercial interests—at present, we might consider the absurdly inflated prices of the international art market, not to mention such inanities as Van Gogh neckties and Verdi soundtracks to car advertisements.[23] Or, a massive technology-driven entertainment industry can channel taste toward the immediately exciting and superficial, producing a popular culture of sensational, sense-drenching images that leaves no room for, and undermines the willingness to engage in the self-discipline required for, refinement of aesthetic response. In all of these cases, cosmopolis itself

23. Robert Hughes has described how the huge prices that art can now command have infected our relationship to works of art: "The art-market boom has been an unmitigated disaster for the public life of art. It has distorted the ground of people's reaction to painting and sculpture. Thirty or even twenty years ago anyone, amateur or expert, could spend an hour or two in a museum without wondering what this Tiepolo, this Rembrandt, this de Kooning might cost at auction. Thanks to the unrelenting propaganda of the art market this is no longer quite the case, and the imagery of money has been so crudely riveted onto the face of museum-quality art by events outside the museum that its unhappy confusion between price and value may never be resolved" (*Nothing If Not Critical: Selected Essays on Art and Artists,* 20–21).

suffers from the loss of invigorating artistic visions that would help guide a culture toward a proper sense of its historical place and responsibility. Which brings us to the question, where does contemporary Western culture, led by American culture, stand with respect to the availability and efficacy of artistic images conducive to the building of cosmopolis?

One of the most artistically ambitious filmmakers of recent decades, Werner Herzog, has expressed his view of the matter with typical intensity: "The simple truth is that there aren't many images around now. . . . You practically have to start digging for them like an archaeologist to try to find something in this damaged landscape." Herzog is aghast at what he calls the "lack of decent images" in the culture, warning that "[w]e urgently need images to accord with the state of our civilization, and with our own innermost souls."[24] These remarks point, I think, to a genuine problem: the artistic images that would serve cosmopolis, inviting us to realize our common ground in transcendence and our higher historical responsibility, are not easily found or felt in our culture, are not efficacious in many lives. Let me suggest briefly two reasons for this.

First, our daily lives are ever more inundated by the exciting images produced by technological gadgetry meant to entertain and, of course, to encourage the purchase of every kind of commodity. We are bombarded by images pouring from televisions at home, in restaurants, bars, laundromats, and airports; from radios and CD players at home and in our cars; from home entertainment centers stocked with videos and DVDs; from personal computer screens with their increasingly rapid, exotic, and exhilarating games and tools and inducements to electronic interaction; from sound systems in malls, restaurants, lobbies, waiting rooms, and elevators; from advertisements on billboards and walls and buses that promote the blockbuster movies that everyone is talking about; and from the flashing, screeching, pounding computer games ever more prevalent in commercial establishments and public waiting areas. The list could go on. And the principal defining characteristics of all these images is their triviality and dispensability: few of them mean anything beyond the stimulation of a few moments. They constitute, as the filmmaker Wim Wenders has said, "an invasion of and inflation of meaningless images" that numb the capacity for reflection on artistic images of any

24. Quoted in Wim Wenders, *The Logic of Images: Essays and Conversations*, 64.

high order, artistic images that in their stilled concentration of references and purposes require us to slow down and focus and reflect, images that demand and reward sustained attention and contemplation.[25]

Though it is nothing new to say so, the most destructive element in this onslaught has been television, about which the art critic Robert Hughes has remarked:

> In 1989 the average American spent nearly half of his or her conscious life watching television. Two generations of Americans . . . have now grown up in front of the TV set, their consciousness permeated by its shuttle of bright images, their attention span shrunken by its manipulative speed. . . . The power of television goes beyond anything the fine arts have ever wanted or achieved. Nothing like this Niagara of visual gabble had even been imagined a hundred years ago. American network television drains the world of meaning; it makes reality seem dull, slow and avoidable. . . . It tends to abort the imagination by leaving kids nothing *to* imagine: every hero and demon is there, raucously explicit, precut—a world of stereotypes, too authoritative for imagination to develop or change. . . . It is stupidly compelling, in a way that painting and sculpture, even in their worst moments of propaganda or sentimentality, are not.[26]

In other words, the drama of living is to a large extent taking its cues about its own meaning from the content of television and the act of watching television, contributing to what Wenders describes as "the rule of empty images over the country called 'America.' "[27] The artistic images that might evoke transcendence and sustain a commitment to universal fulfillment tend to get uprooted and swept along in the flood of dazzling distractions.

A second obstacle to the efficacy of such art has to do not with the technologization and commodification of the search for meaning, but with the impact of some of the currently influential ideas about community, dignity, and power. The rejection of transcendent meaning by the philosophers of groundlessness and others among the intelligentsia has made widely popular the notion—although it has been around since the time of Socrates—that human community is ultimately no more than a power-sharing arrangement

25. Ibid., 22.

26. R. Hughes, *Nothing If Not Critical,* 14.

27. Wenders, *Emotion Pictures: Reflections on the Cinema,* 143.

among individuals or factions. In other words, if there is no transcendent ground uniting human beings, then world community is finally no more than a mutual accommodation among participants in their respective struggles for dignified living. This outlook on world community has been supplemented by a correlative, and more genuinely modern, notion that all products of intellectual and cultural achievement, including works of art, are to be considered primarily as creations that serve the interests of personal or group power. While there are obviously valuable insights to which these notions point—insights that, extracted from their embeddedness in the dogmas of immanentization, can serve as important tools of cultural critique—as blanket notions they are reductive and oppressive, distorting the spiritual aims of the drama of living. To the extent that in an unqualified form these notions shape one's response to works of art, the efficacy of symbols of transcendence and universal humanity is subverted by a supercilious reduction of their meaning to expressions of will to power. If we must remain suspiciously on guard against Picasso's *Guernica*, against Mozart's *Requiem*, against *Hamlet* and *King Lear*, lest by forgetting the self-serving interests and limitations of their authors and societies we fall into ideological traps, then such works will not illuminate our hearts and lives or help to reconcile us to the transcendent mystery that is the only possible ground of human unity and of any unguarded and unqualified commitment to universal fulfillment.

The fact is that world community or cosmopolis is a cultural fact founded on transcendence, and art is one of its sustaining elements. Artistic images that serve cosmopolis and historical responsibility can still inspire and convert us, even amid the racket of modern life, and in spite of our era's reductionist and immanentist political and philosophical doctrines that, as Lonergan says, "have done not a little to make human life unlivable." Many important artists of the past century have recognized this, and have worked with a powerful sense of responsibility to create art that opens clearings where the transcendence that grounds universal humanity may be felt or glimpsed. In the visual arts, Kandinsky, Mondrian, Klee, Malevich, Brancusi, Noguchi, Rothko, Newman, Reinhardt—all, in writings and conversations, made clear that a central concern in their work was to express spiritual truths and to evoke what are traditionally called "religious experiences." Strange as it sounds, witness to transcendence has been one of the major motives in the history of modern pictorial and sculptural art, a fact that has been so overlooked in standard accounts that it constitutes, in Roger Lipsey's words, a "hidden side of modern artists."[28] Likewise, novelists such as Mann (especially in his great tetralogy *Joseph and His Brothers*) and Joyce (in his concern with mythical time) have concerned themselves with the problem of modern access to the reality of "timelessness." Composers from Mahler to Arvo Pärt; poets such as Eliot, Auden, Rilke, and Machado; and filmmakers on the order of Bergman, Herzog, and Tarkovsky have placed the fact of transcendence at the hearts of their works. All of these artists have endeavored, in one fashion or another, to find and examine a "balance of consciousness" between world and transcendence as a genuine possibility in contemporary life.

Such artists have produced, as I suggested at the start of this book, what one might call private mythologies, artistic visions of and elaborations on the human relation to transcendence that, while recognized and loved by the few or the many, have made little impact on the predominantly immanentist mood of the epoch. For all of them it can be said, as Lipsey says of the painters and sculptors mentioned above, that "the culture at large has been amazingly unreceptive to the spiritual aspect of [their] thought and work."[29] Their work and its greatness stand in a distinctly uneasy tension both with the standard view of modernity as the age of science and secularism and with the denunciations of transcendence and deflating ironies of so-called postmodernism. Because they are artists, because they embody in their work their culture's sensibilities, conflicts, and confusions—because they are, in Ezra Pound's words, the "antennae of the race"—the difficulties and at times agony of their search to honor and explore the fact of transcendent reality are reflected in their creations. One of the reasons a close study of these artists is so rewarding is that the complexities and insufficiencies of their works reveal how forceful the illusions of immanentism and reductionism are, how atrophied or bankrupt many traditional symbols pertaining to transcendence have become, and what efforts of attention and cultural education are required to

28. Lonergan, *Topics in Education,* 232; Lipsey, *An Art of Our Own: The Spiritual in Twentieth-Century Art,* 2. Lipsey's book examines at length a number of major twentieth-century artists who sought to create an art that would be both profoundly contemporary and profoundly spiritual, an art of new spiritual vision that would keep a sense of transcendence alive in the modern age. This aim of much important modernist art has been widely ignored or denied, and Lipsey offers a deeply researched and convincing argument that "[m]any of the universally respected artists whose works are altogether familiar and whom we feel we understand have in fact escaped understanding because we haven't yet penetrated the spiritual history of modern art" (2). On the evocation of transcendence and the divine in modern art, see also Robert Rosenblum, *Modern Painting and the Northern Romantic Tradition: Friedrich to Rothko.*

29. Lipsey, *An Art of Our Own,* 3.

break through the obstacles of dogmatic closure and dead symbols to the recovery of a sense of the *metaxy,* of human existence as life "in-between" finite world and transcendent mystery.

Ezra Pound is a particularly forceful example of an artist whose work evidences this struggle. In Pound a fascination with the structure and meaning of world history, and an unusually powerful vision of world cultures as grounded in the one flux of divine presence, is compromised by various strains of modern bias, most notably the attraction to immanentist solutions to the problems of civilization (exhibited most famously in his active support of fascism in wartime Italy and in his anti-Semitism). Again, in Pound an extraordinary sensitivity to the historical and spiritual dimensions of language—his ear for the live and dead word or text, his attunement to the importance of consciousness-forming symbols and myths—is linked to a typically modern resistance to the mystery of history, in the form of his conviction that civilizational progress can be guaranteed through a precise control of language together with fundamental changes in economic and political policy. His work and life epitomize an artist's heightened awareness of the need for balance between commitment to the worldly enterprise and responsive openness to transcendence, but they also, with frightening vividness, epitomize the disorientation, and collapse into fury and despair, that characterizes Western failure in the twentieth century to maintain that balance. The next chapter will be devoted to examining this peculiarly representative mixture of insight and oversight, success and failure, in Pound's struggle to give artistic expression to truths of history and transcendence.

6

EZRA POUND AND THE BALANCE OF CONSCIOUSNESS

M'amour, m'amour
what do I love and
where are you?
That I lost my center
fighting the world.
The dreams clash
and are shattered—
and that I tried to make a paradiso
terrestre.

—Ezra Pound, *The Cantos*

The human mind is so constructed that moral issues, if we are honest with ourselves, cannot be resolved. The conflicts between ideality and practice, between love and justice, are everlasting, at least in finite intelligence.

—Hayden Carruth, "The Time of Falling Apart"

THE MOST EFFICIENT way to approach Ezra Pound's artistic struggle with the problem of transcendence will be to use Eric Voegelin's philosophy of human existence and history to analyze some of Pound's guiding ideas about divine reality, history, language, and political order, especially as they shape and inform his epic poem *The Cantos*. To a reader familiar with both Pound and Voegelin, this might seem an odd pairing, not least because

Voegelin's philosophical achievement and outlook contrast so glaringly with the trajectory and incoherences in Pound's poetic vision and personal life. In fact, though, some of Voegelin's basic theoretical principles regarding divinity, consciousness, and history have their reflections in Pound's deepest convictions. If it is true that Voegelin's exploration of these principles and their implications leads to a coherent philosophy and a sound political realism (with a complete rejection of totalitarian aims and principles), whereas Pound's thought and work deriving from them wind up an inconsistent mixture of compelling vision and appalling oversight (symptomized by his support of Mussolini's Fascist government), still the range of their agreement on fundamental insights testifies to a certain shared brilliance. Furthermore, it makes Voegelin's philosophy an exceptionally useful instrument for explaining why Pound's is a mangled greatness.[1]

The aspect of Voegelin's thought most helpful for a critical appreciation of Pound pertains to Voegelin's portrayal of human existence as conscious participation in the *metaxy*, the In-Between of reality. We have been emphasizing the basic, ontological sense of *metaxy* as existence in-between immanent world and transcendent mystery, time and timelessness, finite and nonfinite reality. However, the *metaxy* of human existence is also, we remember, a cognitional in-between, as all of our understanding and deciding occur in-between complete ignorance and complete knowledge; an affective in-between, living continually as we do in the tension between longing and satisfaction, hope and fulfillment; and a moral in-between, in that we struggle between imperfection and perfection. All of these pairs of "poles" in-between which existence unfolds are implied in the statement that the *metaxy* is the place of human-divine encounter. To be human is to be aware of, and to be drawn in tension toward, that divine transcendence (nonfinite and timeless, perfect in goodness, knowledge, and love) in which we understand ourselves to participate. The in-between or *metaxy* of human existence, then, is summarily the in-between of human-divine encounter, where a person's search

1. We will not address here the vexed topics of Pound's trial for treasonous broadcasts during the Second World War; his notorious, at times rabid, anti-Semitism; or his mental instability and incarceration at St. Elizabeth's Hospital. For a plausible psychological sketch exploring how Pound's famous generosity, his aesthetic principles, his economic views, his anti-Semitism, and his political stance during the war may have been linked in his imagination, see Lewis Hyde, "Ezra Pound and the Fate of Vegetable Money," chap. 10 in *The Gift: Imagination and the Erotic Life of Property*, 216–72.

for the ground of meaning meets the transcendent origin that moves the person to search for it, in a constant revelation of both their identity and their differences. "The In-Between," as Voegelin puts it, is " . . . the meeting ground of the human and the divine in a consciousness of their distinction and interpenetration."[2]

In cosmological consciousness, we recall, divine reality is conceived in ways that do not with full critical clarity penetrate beyond the horizon of spatiotemporal imagination. When in various cultures the insights and symbols are introduced that conceptually separate reality into divine transcendence and worldly immanence, they bring with them, as we have seen, enormous problems both for speculative thought and for the informing of cultural and political institutions whose role is to promote the human good in light of a full awareness of human purpose and destiny. Especially—it cannot be emphasized enough—transcendence is misconceived as a faraway place or superpowerful entity. This in turn provokes the countermisconception that because there is indeed no such faraway place or superpowerful entity, the symbol *transcendence* must refer not to fact but to nonsense, to nothing at all. To counter such misconceptions, Voegelin devotes many pages to the experiential origins of insights into transcendence, returning time and again to

2. Voegelin, "On Hegel: A Study in Sorcery," in *Published Essays, 1966–1985,* 233. On the human-divine *metaxy* as situated between various sets of "poles," and on Voegelin's warning that these "poles" in-between which consciousness moves must not be misconceived as objects independent of the tension within which they are experienced, see esp. Voegelin, "Equivalences of Experience," 119–23, and "Reason: The Classic Experience," 279–82, both in *Published Essays, 1966–1985;* and "Eternal Being in Time," 320–33, and "What Is Political Reality?" 373–81, both in *Anamnesis.* Voegelin is aware that this analysis results in the term *human* becoming fundamentally ambiguous, insofar as it must refer both to the finite creature who apprehends himself or herself as distinct from the ground of being *and* to the "in-between" where immanence and transcendence, "world" and "divine," interpenetrate. This ambiguity of the term *human* is inevitable, deriving as it does from the paradox of consciousness as *participation* in the divine ground, as the experienced simultaneity of human nonidentity *and* identity with the ground of being. Voegelin suggests that we may keep the two meanings of the term *human* clear by distinguishing between human consciousness as (1) the time-bound, finite "sensorium" of experience and (2) the "site" of the experienced interpenetration of immanence and transcendence: "[W]hen man discovers his existence in tension, he becomes conscious of his consciousness as both the site and the sensorium of participation in the divine ground. As far as consciousness is the site of participation, its reality partakes of both the divine and the human without being wholly the one or the other; as far as it is the sensorium of participation, it is definitely man's own, located in his body in spatiotemporal existence. Consciousness, thus, is both the time pole of the tension (sensorium) and the whole tension including its pole of the timeless (site)" ("Immortality: Experience and Symbol," in *Published Essays, 1966–1985,* 90).

the crucial point that the terms *transcendence* and *immanence* do not refer to places or worlds or entities but are rather explanatory notations or "linguistic indices" that denote the structural elements of the in-between of consciousness. The elements and the relationship indicated by the terms are *essentially abstract,* deriving from consciousness discovering the ontological conditions of its own questioning and intending. Such symbols are misunderstood when taken descriptively as referring to imaginable objects or places; as Voegelin emphasizes, they "are exegetic, not descriptive."[3]

However misunderstood, and however popular the misunderstandings, the differentiation between immanent world and transcendent ground is well established in cultural and linguistic horizons both East and West. And everywhere it poses the same challenge to people who must make sense of their existences in light of this differentiation: the challenge of not letting the discovery of transcendence cause one to lose one's balance in relation to the immanent and transcendent "poles" of reality. I have already, toward the end of the fourth chapter, mentioned Voegelin's diagnostic notion of "balanced consciousness." The "balance of consciousness" consists in not letting the discovery of transcendent meaning draw one into either (1) degrading immanent reality in light of the more perfect being of transcendence or (2) denying the fact or the implications of transcendence. This balance of consciousness is not easy to maintain, as it requires admitting the permanent imperfection of finite existence—including all of our efforts to realize justice, order, and beauty in our lives—in relation to a perfection or fulfillment that is "beyond" all that we can know or imagine; at the same time it requires that we not despair of the meaningfulness of our efforts, as we seek to attune imperfect reality as best we can—through rational discernment, careful judgment, attentiveness to conscience, love, meditation, prayer—to permanently transcendent standards. One grows weary of this existential tension. Thus one is led to despise or ignore the world in favor of a perfection imagined to be elsewhere or later, or one impatiently seeks the realization of perfection in the here and now. In either case, the balance of consciousness is lost, and the vision of human existence as a movement in the In-Between of imperfection and perfection, of time and timelessness, of human and divine, is eclipsed and replaced by an image less troubling and mysterious.

3. Voegelin, "Beginning and Beyond," in *What Is History?* 185.

Before turning to Pound's work, let us clarify and expand upon the relevant elements in Voegelin's analysis, bringing together a number of points made in previous chapters. First of all, the timeless ground is real. The structure of reality includes the transcendent ground of meaning, which we experience through participation. It is a "flow of presence" in all human consciousness, whether we attend to it or not, affirm it or not, and however sophisticated or unsophisticated our imaginative or conceptual portrayals of it. Ancient peoples experienced this presence as "the gods," manifest entities encountered in the forces and regularities of the natural universe; increasing clarity about the transcendence of divine presence gradually "dedivinized" nature, and forced the resymbolization of the divine as a presence simultaneously more recondite (in not being perceivable by the physical senses) and more universal (in being everywhere and, of course, nowhere). It should be stressed that this dedivinization of nature that accompanied waning belief in the cosmological gods involved an emotional or experiential, but not a philosophical, removal of divine *presence* from finite reality. Indeed, the logic of the discovery of transcendence even more thoroughly irradiates both consciousness and nature with divine presence, because that presence is understood precisely as the nonfinite condition for the existence and good of every finite thing. Every place becomes the place of the intersection of the timeless with time. And human being is where that intersection comes to self-recognition and self-realization, where the flow of eternal divine presence orients temporal existence, through human consciousness, toward timeless meaning and truth. Human beings, then, always "remain in the 'in between,' in a temporal flow of experience in which eternity is nevertheless present. This flow [of divine presence] cannot be dissected into a past, a present, and a future of world-time, for at every point of the flow there persists the tension toward eternal being transcending time."[4]

Second, we recall the consequence of this for a proper understanding of history. History as it is generally conceived, as a linear course of events unfolding through time, is a jejune simplification that ignores the fact of timeless presence. The essential data of history, the significant events and patterns of events worth remembering, include, above all, human struggles to attune social and personal life to timeless divine truth; of particular significance are

4. Voegelin, "Eternal Being in Time," in *Anamnesis,* 329.

the breakthroughs in that struggle on occasions of the discovery of transcendence. History, then, takes its meaning first of all from the epochal events of divine-human encounter—one might list the names of Lao-tzu, Buddha, Moses, Jesus, Socrates, Plato, and Mohammed—that have ramified over centuries and millennia into personal lives and into the fields of social and political institutions and relations. Also, the fact of timeless presence means that history is not something that is merely "past." History is a "web of meaning" in which all humanity is implicated through the common flow of divine presence, and in which humans at all times and places are linked in a contemporaneity through participation in and orientation toward timeless meaning.[5] History is not simply the unfolding of time; it is the intersection of the timeless with time. Historical progress, consequently, is not simply movement forward on a time line. It is, most essentially, success in attuning social and personal life to the truths of timeless meaning, a success that waxes and wanes in human communities, progress oscillating with decline in a historical process whose ultimate meaning and outcome remain a mystery.

This understanding of history in turn implies that a respect for tradition and earlier wisdom, a willingness to explore and preserve the insights and achievements of our predecessors, is a central civilizing impulse, insofar as we must use it to take our bearings in relation both to our position in history and to our situation in the In-Between of existence. Of course, the intellectual, artistic, political, and spiritual achievements of earlier persons and cultures found expression in symbolic forms peculiar to their times and places. However, the ultimate human contemporaneity in the struggle for attunement, grounded in our common participation in timeless meaning, assures us that the recovery of the meanings of those symbolic expressions of various types of truth is possible and worthwhile—and even necessary, if we are to respond with utmost effectiveness to the civilizational challenges of our own place and time, because the best of our cultural inheritance articulates the high points of insight into the human struggle for meaningful existence in the In-Between.

A final implication of Voegelin's analysis concerns the origins of true order in political and social life. Society becomes well ordered, that analysis reveals, only through the insights, decisions, and influence of individuals who have attained a clear understanding of what is possible and worthwhile in human affairs. Such individuals find their evaluative standards in the transcendent

5. Voegelin, *The Ecumenic Age*, 106.

perfection that they accept as the measure of their own actions and goals. Thus, true order may be said to flow into society through the wisdom of individuals attuned to transcendent truths. This, of course, is the principle reflected in Plato's account of the philosopher-king in the *Republic*, which, Voegelin reminds us, is not so much an argument for or against specific types of government as it is an exposition of the insight that order or disorder in society reflects the order or disorder in the souls of its leaders, and of the fact that the wise are few and the foolish many.

Pound on Divine Reality and Historical Truth

Turning now to Ezra Pound, we find that his work reveals a remarkable range of agreement with Eric Voegelin's philosophical account of existence in the In-Between. To begin with, for Pound the gods are real, and so for him as for Voegelin experiences of human-divine encounter are a fact of existence. As Voegelin is a mystic philosopher in an age profoundly suspicious of mystery, so Pound is a genuinely religious poet in a generally irreligious age. As George Kearns points out at the start of his excellent guide to Pound's *Selected Cantos*, divine reality is constantly affirmed in his epic poem, through repeated descriptions and evocations of " 'magic moments,' visions of the light, divine energies, paradisal states of mind," an affirmation that must not be misinterpreted as a mere "literary conceit."[6] Divine energy is the font of reality, the source of all things, the force that draws into patterns of beauty and order both the works of nature and those of human invention. This is true now, as it has always and everywhere been true. Because it is true now, Pound's task as an artist in a secular age includes the special responsibility of *remembrance* of this fact, poetic witness to the fact of divine mysteries. Because it has always and everywhere been true, the hierophanies of all cultures and religions should be respected, Pound holds, and one of his poetic aims is to show that sacred stories and images from different traditions will, when juxtaposed, reveal archetypal equivalence through their common root in the constants of human-divine encounter. For Pound it is through the visions of hierophanic experience that we ascend to the realm of the timeless, the transhistorical dimension of divine presence, the metaphysical realities that do not change,

6. Kearns, *Guide to Ezra Pound's "Selected Cantos,"* 9.

although their appearances to us do, bound as our perceiving is to the finite and imaginable. In sum, Pound confirms the human dwelling place to be the In-Between of time and timelessness, of immanence and transcendence.

For Pound the poet, such remembrance is a matter of visions preserved and revisited, and visions consist of images. "[T]he images of the gods," he asserts, ". . . move the soul to contemplation and preserve the tradition of the undivided light."[7] Images of divine presence erupt in lyric passages throughout *The Cantos,* images drawn from a variety of cultures but principally those of Greek, Roman, and Chinese mythology, and from the Neoplatonic tradition including its Christian strands. Even detractors of Pound's general poetic achievement have tended to admit the power of these passages, which reveal not only his openness to the sacred but his powers of artistry as well:

> Gods float in the azure air,
> Bright gods and Tuscan, back before dew was shed.
> Light: and the first light, before ever dew was fallen.
> Panisks, and from the oak, dryas,
> And from the apple, mælid,
> Through all the wood, and the leaves are full of voices,
> A-whisper, and the clouds bowe over the lake,
> And there are gods upon them,
>
> (3/11)[8]

> And in thy mind beauty, O Artemis,
> as of mountain lakes in the dawn,
> Foam and silk are thy fingers,
> Kuanon,
> and the long suavity of her moving,
>
> (110/778)

> there came new subtlety of eyes into my tent,
> whether of spirit or hypostasis,
> but what the blindfold hides
> or at carneval
> nor any pair showed anger
> Saw but the eyes and stance between the eyes,
> colour, diastasis,

7. Pound, "A Visiting Card" (1942), 307.

8. References to *The Cantos* will be given in the form (3/11), which means Canto 3, p. 11, in *The Cantos of Ezra Pound.* All further quotations from the poem will be from this edition.

careless or unaware it had not the
whole tent's room
nor was place for the full Ειδὼς
interpass, penetrate
casting but shade beyond the other lights
sky's clear
night's sea
green of the mountain pool
shone from the unmasked eyes in half-mask's space.
(81/520)[9]

They also reveal a polytheistic enthusiasm that rushes to embrace every kind of hierophany, every species of "magical moment," as long as it speaks to Pound of genuine encounter. As Guy Davenport explains, the poet "was in love with so many religions that we have to accept him as a pagan who couldn't have too many gods on his hearth."[10]

For Pound, without imaginative vision there is no ascent to the timeless; our feeling and apprehension of divine reality are impossible without the mediation of images. This outlook explains his antipathy to both Hebraic and Protestant iconoclasm, as well as to theological doctrine and speculation in the form of philosophical abstractions. We ascend to the divine through image and contemplation; both the suppression of images and abstruse theological argumentation destroy religion. "Tradition *inheres* . . . in the images of the gods, and gets lost in dogmatic definitions."[11]

Pound's attraction to experiences and symbols from the world of cosmological myth, as well as his aversion to much of the Christian tradition, is explainable to some degree by that world's openness to nature as a medium of revelation and its pluralistic tolerance for differing symbolic expressions of equivalent experiences of the divine.[12] Pound approves of all images and

9. Ειδὼς means "form."

10. Davenport, "Ezra Pound, 1885–1972," in 173.

11. Pound, "A Visiting Card," 322.

12. The pluralism inherent to the cosmological perspective is discussed by Voegelin in the introduction to *Israel and Revelation.* There he explains: "If anything is characteristic of the early history of symbolization, it is the pluralism in expressing truth, the generous recognition and tolerance extended to rival symbolizations of the same truth. . . . The early tolerance reflects the awareness that the order of being can be represented analogically in more than one way. Every concrete symbol is true insofar as it envisages the truth, but none is completely true insofar as the truth about being is essentially beyond human reach" (45–46).

myths that help us to discover and contemplate the divine reality and the truths of human-divine encounter. His attitude recalls the words of the pagan philosopher Maximus of Tyre (second century C.E.): "If Greeks are stirred to the remembrance of God by the art of Phidias, or the Egyptians by paying worship to animals, or others by a river, or others by fire, I will not quarrel with their differences. Only let them know, let them love, let them remember." Along with suppression of images and theological abstractions, then, Pound resists any kind of exclusivism that tries to secure a monopoly of religious truth for one tradition, to bring the timeless mystery under dogmatic control, or to restrict our experiential access to it. He is convinced that if we cannot apprehend, in some way or another, the divine as the formative and transformative ground of the natural world we ourselves experience, then we are not apprehending nature as it really is at all. The lyric passages in *The Cantos* describing or invoking divine appearances in nature, so odd to modern sensibility yet so poetically convincing, aim to remind us of our existence in the In-Between, to release our sense of the natural world from the fiction of pure immanence and reveal it as it truly is: saturated with the mystery of the divine and with potency for revelation. Thus, for Pound, Hugh Kenner declares, "[t]o see gods was a way to see nature, not to use an antique way of talking." When people lose their capacity for visions of the divine and the sense of the timeless fades, then according to Pound the invigorating heart of culture withers. "Without gods, no culture. Without gods, something is lacking," he states tersely.[13]

Pound's recognition of the crux of human existence as the encounter with timeless reality leads him to a sense and view of history that is similar to Voegelin's in many respects. They both reject the popular notion of history as a steady march of civilizational progress, not simply on empirical grounds, but because if the divine is real, then meaning in history lies essentially in the attunement of any and all persons, and any and all social orders, with the divine ground of truth, goodness and beauty. Such attunement is gained and lost over time, both by individuals and by societies, and so history is an oscillation of progress and decline, or rather an unfolding over time of multitudes of oscillations among many persons and societies. Pound does not

13. Maximus of Tyre translation by Frederick C. Grant, in his *Hellenistic Religions,* quoted in Mircea Eliade, ed., *From Primitives to Zen: A Thematic Sourcebook of the History of Religions,* 541; Kenner, *The Pound Era,* 30; Pound, *Guide to Kulchur,* 126.

imagine, therefore, anymore than Voegelin does, that history is headed inexorably toward some enlightened or perfected social order that marks the end of history. There have been, Pound believes, places and periods of civilization where exceptional good order, exceptional success in realizing the good and the beautiful in civic life, has been achieved. They have faded or disappeared, though, and were bound to do so, for the "conspiracy of intelligence" cannot ever be broadly effective for long against the forces of disorder—at the forefront of which Pound usually places "stupidity"—though it may live on underground. So although Pound works hard at his self-appointed task of helping a new civilization "*as good* as the best that has been" to rise out of what he sees as a chaotic and decadent Western culture, he does not labor under the illusion that any civilizational gain achieved will be permanent. "Earthly paradises for Pound are various and have come and gone, for they are effective spiritual or social contexts gained at points of time"; and as time passes, the achievement invariably erodes, the orienting vision loses efficacy, the ordering energy is dispersed.[14]

However, past achievements vivid in the remembering mind are in a real sense not past at all, for Pound. His understanding of divine presence in history enables him to recognize that the popular conception of the historical past as having receded irretrievably into a distance of time is a misconception based on a failure to appreciate human participation in timeless realities, and to appreciate that all who grasp and enact those realities are brought together in immediate and true contemporaneity. Kenner notes that Pound's early thought and poetry reflect a Romantic fascination with "the magic of time" and the "romance of temporal distance," but that this fascination soon evaporates. All of his mature and influential work reflects an anti-archaizing assumption that there are crucial human experiences and insights that, though conceived or written about or realized in different forms by different people in different cultures, are genuinely common and enduring because rooted in the timeless, and that, when we intelligently engage such experiences and insights in whatever image-form they are manifest, the "past" is in a sense obliterated; to put it somewhat more accurately, the "historical" comes into being in its simultaneous temporality and timelessness. It is precisely this understanding of history and culture that guides *The Cantos,* both in the method

14. Pound, *Guide to Kulchur,* 263; Pound quoted in Kearns, *Guide,* 23; Eugene Paul Nassar, *The Cantos of Ezra Pound: The Lyric Mode,* 30.

of the poem's construction and in Pound's aim for it to be a "tale of the tribe" that helps us find meaning in history.[15] The most striking, and initially disorienting, structural feature of the poem is its often sudden juxtapositions of events, persons, phrases, or images drawn from throughout history that Pound considers to be "subject-rhymes" revealing a common insight or element in reality. These are juxtaposed to create ever augmenting leitmotifs of complex images that are intended to reveal significant, repeated, underlying patterns of energy, constructive and destructive, in human affairs. These images Pound famously compares to ideograms built up from multiple units of meaning, organized to express the richest concentrations of meaning that the poet can achieve. For example, in Canto 74, Greek wisdom concerning the importance of an exact and authentic use of language is juxtaposed with Chinese wisdom on the same topic:

> . . . because as says Aristotle
> philosophy is not for young men
> their *Katholou* can not be sufficiently derived from
> their *hekasta*
> their generalities cannot be born from a sufficient phalanx
> of particulars
> lord of his work and master of utterance
> who turneth his word in its season and shapes it
> Yaou chose Shun to longevity
> who seized the extremities and the opposites
> holding true course between them
>
> (74/441–42)[16]

With this method Pound celebrates the distinct wisdoms of diverse cultures and great individuals and simultaneously annihilates the time and distance that separate them, turning history from a linear course of events into, in Voegelin's phrase, a "web of meaning with a plurality of nodal points" whose ultimate reference is a transcendence known in the flow of timeless presence and its ordering influence. By forging in this way what Kenner calls "an ecumenical reality where all times [can] meet without the romance of time," Pound hopes to help us find our bearings in our own historical situation,

15. Kenner, *The Pound Era,* 30, 141; Pound, *Guide to Kulchur,* 194.

16. *Katholou* means "universal"; *hekasta* means "singulars (individual experiences)."

through understanding our relation to other civilizations as well as to their common ground.[17]

It follows that one of Pound's deepest convictions is that anything excellent in present achievement must be founded on diligent retrieval of the best of the past. The poet whose language and style more than that of any other writer stand for the invention of a revolutionary modernism invariably in his work expresses contempt for the idea of novelty for its own sake. The motto he adopts from a Chinese emperor, "Make It New"—

> Tching prayed on the mountain and
> wrote MAKE IT NEW
> on his bath tub
> Day by day make it new
> (53/264–65)

—signifies not the artist's duty to reject tradition, but rather the obligation to reclaim, revivify, and apply energetically to the present the best of tradition. The slogan, as Donald Davie observes, "is a recipe for conservation, for protecting past monuments in all their potency."[18]

We can do this only if we respect and meditate carefully on the language, the symbols, in which any such wisdom has come down to us. A respect for careful interpretation and use of terms, insistence on the need to attend to the experiential perceptions and insights that words and other symbols convey, again unites Pound and Voegelin. Language can become bankrupt through laziness or corruption of mind, can degenerate into cliché (disastrous to poetry), can even be used "to conceal thought and to withhold all vital and direct answers." When this happens, when "the application of word to thing goes rotten, i.e. becomes slushy and inexact," Pound asserts, " . . . the whole machinery of social and individual thought and order goes to pot." A precise use of language is the only means by which we can maintain and use our understanding of the important truths carried down to us by tradition and pass them on to those who come after us. This is a view of language that presumes, of course, that there is a metaphysical stability behind language (the presumption that is the bane of the philosophers of groundlessness),

17. Voegelin, *The Ecumenic Age,* 106; Kenner, *The Pound Era,* 552.
18. Davie, *Ezra Pound,* 100.

that there are enduring truths of natural process that include "enduring constants in human composition." Pound is never reticent about expressing his confidence that such constants exist, as here in "Patria Mia": "One wants to find out what sort of things endure, and what sort of things are transient; what sort of things recur . . . to learn upon what the forces, constructive and dispersive, of social order, move; to learn what rules and axioms hold firm, and what sort fade, and what sort are durable but permutable, what sort hold in letter, and what sort by analogy only, what sort by close analogy, and what sort by rough parallel alone." This reads like a gloss on Voegelin's description of his own work as involving a "search for the constants of human order in society and history."[19] This search is their common concern because, for both men, exact knowledge about such constants, gained through penetrating to the original perceptions underlying the symbolic formulations in which the greatest of our predecessors have expressed themselves, is the key to sustaining individual and social order.

The agreement extends further, because both men also give the same response to the question as to how that knowledge becomes socially or politically effective: it does so through the guidance and influence of leaders—political and cultural—whose enlightened minds and sensibilities, moral virtue, and steadiness of will constitute an achieved order of the personal soul attuned to unchanging truths. Order flows into society through the medium of great individuals, who as rulers can move the people toward a civic order in harmony with the divine and with natural human ends. However, if Voegelin turns to Plato and Aristotle for the foundational articulation of this truth, for Pound it is provided in the teachings of Confucius (K'ung-Fu-tzu), whose formulation of the core principle Pound briefly paraphrases in the beautiful Canto 13:

> And Kung said, and wrote on the bo leaves:
> If a man have not order within him
> He can not spread order about him;
> And if a man have not order within him

19. Pound, "Interview: Ezra Pound," 328; *Polite Essays,* quoted in Hugh Kenner, *The Poetry of Ezra Pound,* 42; *Guide to Kulchur,* 47; "Patria Mia" (1913), 125; Voegelin, "Equivalences of Experience," in *Published Essays, 1966–1985,* 115.

His family will not act with due order;
        And if the prince have not order within him
He can not put order in his dominions.
(13/59)

This theme runs right through *The Cantos,* and both there and in the rest of Pound's writings Confucius remains its central image, the paradigm of political authority and enlightened source of civic order. Pound's fascination with Confucius may seem curious to a Westerner, but nevertheless explainable. More troubling for Pound's reader is his choice of certain other "great individuals" whom he holds up for admiration and emulation, most notably Mussolini. In fact, if we compile a brief list of Pound's heroes—Confucius, Sigismondo Malatesta, Voltaire, Jefferson, John Adams, Mussolini—and note that such figures as Plato, Jesus, Buddha, Augustine, and Aquinas are absent, we find a significant clue to the parting of the ways between Pound and Voegelin. The list indicates a decided bent on Pound's part toward confidence in what can be achieved through direct political action. It suggests a feature of Pound's character and thought that is finally decisive, from the point of view provided by Voegelin's analysis, in distorting his vision of human existence in the In-Between: his distrust of transcendence in its full radicality, and, in his representation of the human situation, his habitual collapsing of transcendence into the quasi immanence of that which can appear to human intellect and imagination and can appear in and through human action. For all his insight into timeless reality, Pound slips away from "the balance of consciousness" in the direction of an immanentist construction of reality and human purpose.

Pound's Resistance to Radical Transcendence

Pound's brand of immanentism, of course, is quite different from those of philosophical materialists or secular progressivists: it has ample room for the divine and its mystery, but still at a certain limit Pound balks at the full implications of transcendence. The closest he gets to an embrace of radical transcendence is his approving use of the light symbolism he finds in the Neoplatonic mystical tradition, the notion of the "undivided light" of which all visible things are but manifestations.

Shines
in the mind of heaven God
who made it
more than the sun
in our eye.

(51/250)

Light tensile immaculata
the sun's cord unspotted
"sunt lumina" said the Oirishman to King Carolus,
"OMNIA,
all things that are are lights"

(74/429)[20]

Pound is comfortable with the notion of the divine mind, the Platonic Nous, as an original "light" that both constitutes reality and is refracted in the "light" of human understanding, and he gives credit to Plato for establishing the symbolic tradition: "What we can assert is that Plato periodically caused enthusiasm among his disciples. And the Platonists after him have caused man after man to be suddenly conscious of the reality of the *nous*, of mind, apart from any man's individual mind, of the sea crystalline and enduring, of the bright as it were molten glass that envelops us, full of light." Yet in Platonic and other mystical traditions there is a further level of affirmation where Pound will not follow, in which the acknowledged participation of the human mind in the divine light greets a border of unyielding darkness, a "beyond" that is only darkness to our understanding: Plato's "being beyond being," the mystery of the mystery.[21] Voegelin refers to this reality in *Anamnesis* as "the ineffable," of which we can know only that it lies beyond what we can know. As he says, "[I]n the tension toward the [divine] ground we have experience of a reality that incomprehensibly lies beyond all that we experience of it in participation," and we "can speak of the incomprehensible only by characterizing it as reaching beyond the symbolic language of participation." It seems that when Pound is faced with this "tension between symbol and ineffability," his agreement turns to suspicion. Kenner addresses this when he states that

20. The "Oirishman" is Scotus Erigena (810–877), whom Pound is quoting: "Omnia quae sunt, lumina sunt" (all things that are, are lights).

21. Pound, *Guide to Kulchur,* 44; *The Republic of Plato* 509b. For Voegelin's analysis of this and other Platonic symbols of transcendence, see, for example, *The Ecumenic Age,* 292–300; and "Beginning and Beyond," in *What Is History?* 212–22.

Pound's openness to mythic symbolization ends when the symbols begin to differentiate a dimension of reality that cannot be addressed in terms of appearance, that Pound was "never willing to concede a shift of dimension between crystalline myth and the polymorphous immediate." So the radically transcendent God of Hebrew and Christian faith is notably absent from *The Cantos;* the "divine beyond" of Moses and Jesus that has been understood as condemning other gods and other revelations to falsehood or irrelevance is unacceptable to Pound, who sees its worship as having undermined our abilities to perceive the divine in nature and to seek out and trust in our own ecstatic experiences. Therefore, as a guide to the divine he will "substitute for the Moses of the Old Testament the Ovid of the *Metamorphoses,* with [the latter's] recognition of the vivifying personal immediacy of supernatural forces and the constant penetration of the supernatural into the natural."[22] Buddhism and Taoism likewise for Pound place too much stress on an otherworldly transcendence, so that in his view their teachings easily degenerate into the promotion of superstitions, such as the belief that magic rituals can guarantee personal immortality. In *The Cantos* we find the rigorous, realistic Confucianists contrasted with the passive Buddhists and degenerate Taoists (whom Pound derisively calls "taozers"):

> And there came a taozer babbling of the elixir
> that wd/ make men live without end
> and the taozer died very soon after that.
> (54/288)

> And of Taosers, Chu says:
> concerned neither with heaven, earth
> or with anything on the square
> but wholly subjective, for the Dragon moaning,
> the screaming tiger, mercury, pills, pharmacopia,
>
> And the Bhud rot: that floaters eat
> without maintaining their homesteads
> (99/696–97)[23]

22. Voegelin, "What Is Political Reality?" in *Anamnesis,* 395–97; Kenner, *The Pound Era,* 15; Clark Emory, *Ideas into Action: A Study of Pound's Cantos,* quoted in Donald Davie, *Ezra Pound: Poet as Sculptor,* 216.

23. Pound firmly chooses one side in the age-old conflict in Chinese culture between the "realistic" Confucian concern with human affairs and social ideals, with its confidence in the

Pound's frustration with feverish otherworldliness is understandable: he realizes it to be a self-comforting or self-aggrandizing fiction in which the experienced unity of the In-Between of human existence is imaginatively split into distinct entities; he abhors the superstitious mind that seeks magical powers over nature or avenues to personal immortality, ignoring the sufficient beauty and mystery of natural processes—

> Hast'ou seen the rose in the steel dust
> (or swansdown ever?)
> (74/449)

—and abandoning the concrete conditions of existence, with their real challenges and opportunities for personal and social improvement. This last point should be underscored. At the core of Pound's refusal to affirm a radical transcendence is his conviction, buoyed by the popularity of images of other worlds and immortal delights, that such affirmation vitiates our interest in and energy for purposeful action in the world. "The concentration or emphasis on eternity is not social," he grumbles, and what is needed is "a sense of social responsibility."[24] It is an understandable irritation: he is fighting against the loss of the balance of consciousness in the direction of ignoring or degrading immanent reality in light of the perfection of transcendence. However, it pushes Pound into an opposite imbalance, in which recognition of the ultimate transcendence of timeless standards of truth, beauty, and goodness is replaced by an impatient desire and effort to realize those standards in the In-Between. This denial and impatience manifest themselves in a number of related aspects of his thought and work, yielding a specifically Poundian idiosyncratic mixture of insights into the human-divine truth of the In-Between and oversights about the full implications of transcendence.

Returning to the question of history, while Pound is no naive progressivist and understands that civilizational progress alternates with decline, in the

potentials of human intelligence and virtue, on the one hand, and the "transcendentalism" of Taoism and Chinese Buddhism, on the other. On the introduction and impact of Buddhist thought in China, and its relation to Confucian teachings and principles up through the great Neo-Confucian synthesis of the twelfth century, see Wm. Theodore de Bary, *East Asian Civilizations: A Dialogue in Five Stages*, 21–61. For a brief description of Confucian humanism versus Taoist and Buddhist transcendentalism in relation to Chinese poetry, see Burton Watson, *Chinese Lyricism: Shih Poetry from the Second to the Twelfth Century*, 73–74, 124–26, 169–72, 203–6.

24. Pound, *Guide to Kulchur*, 38–39.

bulk of his work he still portrays the ultimate telos of human community in terms of a civic order to be built by leaders with sufficient wisdom and strength of will. He is not inclined to accept Saint Augustine's distinction between the city of God and the earthly city, nor the Platonic insight that the perfectly just city exists only as "a pattern . . . laid up for the man who wants to see and found a city within himself on the basis of what he sees," and that it "doesn't make any difference whether it is or will be somewhere."[25] Whether it exists "somewhere" on earth does make a difference to Pound. And out of that stance comes his support of Mussolini and Italian Fascism. Pound's writings present Mussolini as a leader who understands what the people truly need, and who is willing to take action unhampered by degenerate "democratic" scruples deriving from ignorant fear and resentment of exceptional talent—*"Democracies electing their sewage / till there is no clear thought about holiness"* (91/613–14)—a ruler who respects the role of higher culture in establishing civic order, who can shape society along the lines of Confucian principles. For Pound, such a leader is justified in imposing his vision on society, as he is a lover of order, not of power, and he asserts his belief

> that the Duce will stand not with despots and the lovers of power but with the lovers of
>
> ORDER
>
> τὸ καλὸν.[26]

However, the faith in Mussolini must be seen as part of a larger pattern of judgment reflecting Pound's long-held conviction that social injustice, war, indeed all human evils following on the misuse of will, can be alleviated or eliminated through proper government—at least for a time—if only the ruler's vision is clear enough and the will is strong enough. As Guy Davenport states, "Pound has always gone on the principle that if a thing can be thought it can, by golly, be done. One can animate the dead past and make it live again in a poem *(The Cantos),* one can find out the causes of wars, one can educate the people and make them noble."[27] The key word in this description of Pound's energetic optimism is *educate.* Like Socrates, Pound is

25. *The Republic of Plato* 275 (592b).
26. Pound, *Jefferson and/or Mussolini,* quoted in John J. Espey, *Ezra Pound's "Mauberley": A Study in Composition,* 87. τὸ καλὸν means "beauty, moral virtue."
27. Davenport, "The Pound Vortex," 167.

convinced that evil arises from ignorance, not from perverted will; if governmental leaders are sufficiently educated, and implement policies—especially economic policies—that in turn guarantee adequate guidance and education of the populace, the causes of disorder in human society will surely diminish, and a just society, reflecting timeless principles of order and beauty, begin to flourish.

Marion Montgomery and others have pointed out that this political confidence of Pound, manifest in his idealization of Fascism and Mussolini, is based in part on his faith in language itself: a conviction that when language is exact, and communicates perfected knowledge, it has an essentially irresistible power to transform and guide the individual will. To Pound, says Montgomery, ideal language "is an infallible medium that transubstantiates external existence in such a way that the mind is powerless to disgorge it," the result being that by a kind of causal necessity, proper intention and action follow from "the right word spoken."[28]

Voegelin has no such confidence in the power of language. Pound's view of it would appear to him a dream of sorcery, reflecting the desire for a magically infallible means of transmuting disordered into ordered wills. Voegelin would reply that one must never forget not only the extent to which the efficacy of language depends on the recipient having had, or being able to have, the experiences and insights of which the language is the symbolic expression, but also that even understood language can be rejected by a perverse will, by a will committed to self-assertion, dominated by disordering desires, or overwhelmed by the anxieties of existence. To imagine that the will's imperfection is correctable by human language, however exact and authentic its use, is, for Voegelin, a symptom of the refusal to accept the human situation in the In-Between as a *tension toward* transcendent perfection.

Voegelin's analysis suggests that Pound's confusion about the perfectibility of the will is linked to his resistance to radical transcendence, because it is only within the logic of affirming that divine perfection is somehow "beyond being" that human moral imperfection, including deviance of the will, can be understood and accepted in the permanence of its tension toward what cannot be perfected within the known conditions of existence. The resistance of the will to its own good is a mystery, and this is at least one mystery that Pound seems unwilling to accept. In his assessment of the human condition

28. Montgomery, "Ezra Pound: The Quest for Paradise," 84.

there is no mystery of iniquity, no reflection of the Christian doctrine of the perversion of the will; "original sin," as George Kearns states, is not a term in Pound's vocabulary.[29] Consequently, Pound's view of evil, like his view of transcendence, is not radical enough: he does not acknowledge the fact of moral impotence, that the mind can know what is good yet still not act on that knowledge, or can act in violation of it. For Pound accurate knowledge of the good immediately results in—essentially *is*—moral goodness; it is a moral force (Pound's primary symbol for it is *virtú*) that is the source of right order in self and society, a force that operates with the inevitability of a law of physics. Proper knowledge of the nature of *virtú* is obscured, he believes, by the teachings of religions characterized by worship of a radically transcendent divinity, which substitute a "mystery" of evil for clear understanding that evil is no more than the selfish ignorance correctable by the ordering force of moral knowledge:

> The principle of good is enunciated by Confucius; it consists in establishing order within oneself. This order or harmony spreads by a sort of contagion without specific effort. The principle of evil consists in messing into other peoples' affairs. Against this principle of evil no adequate precaution is taken by Christianity, Moslemism, Judaism, nor, so far as I know, by *any* monotheistic religion. Many "mystics" do not even aim at the principle of good; they seek merely establishment of a parasitic relationship with the unknown.[30]

One consequence of this view of good and evil is that there is something distressingly abstract about Pound's diagnoses of problems in human affairs and his proposed solutions for them. His eager equation of moral knowledge with moral goodness and his denial of the perversity of the will lead him to undervalue the significance of the struggle for moral maturity at the personal level, to ignore the mess and mystery of the concrete individual existing in the concrete tension between ordering and disordering influences, who may or may not support the better angels of his nature. This abstracting from the concrete individual is what enables Pound to believe in systematic solutions—economic, political, cultural—to human problems, a belief in systems that Voegelin would argue is another signal that Pound has lost the balance of

29. Kearns, *Guide,* 64.
30. Pound, "Prolegomena" (1927).

consciousness in the manner of trying to draw transcendent perfection into the range of cognitive and practical control.[31] Such an effort always entails eclipsing the full mystery of the "beyond," and along with it the truth of personal order as a tension of existence in faith toward a transcendent ground.

If we consider now the various immanentizing components of Pound's thought, they help to explain a major feature, and failure, of *The Cantos.* The mythic vision they present is finally incoherent, not adequate either to Pound's insights into the In-Between of human-divine existence or to Pound's ambitions to tell the "tale of the tribe." As moving and convincing as the mythic elements in the poem are, they do not unite into a compelling vision of the meaning in human history in relation to the Whole: as Michael Bernstein asserts, Pound's "insights into magic moments . . . cannot . . . adequately engage historical reality on its own terms." Our analysis suggests that one of the reasons Pound ends up with only fragments of a mythos is that he fails to resolve the contradictions between his love of the divine and his resistance to the full depth of its mystery. He recognizes that existence unfolds in the intersection of temporal with timeless reality, but is not willing to affirm that timeless reality reveals itself in human consciousness only by revealing itself as reaching into the In-Between from an unknowability beyond human consciousness. To put it another way, he wants the gods that appear, but not the God who does not. With regard to history, Pound recognizes that its essence is the history of the waxing and waning struggle for attunement with divine truth, but continues for much of his life to envision the perfected community in terms of that which can be fashioned on earth. Even in his poet's devotion to language, a related contradiction lurks: along with Voegelin, he understands that important and needed language symbols can become detached from the underlying experiences and insights that they were intended to express, and that one must work to penetrate to an exact understanding of what Voegelin would call their "engendering experiences," but at the same time he ignores the very possibility of that gap between experience and symbolization when he assumes that right words will of their own accord produce right knowledge and right action. From the perspective of Voegelin's philosophy, a visionary, poetic mythos adequate to the structure of history in the In-Between would have to move us to a sense of ultimate

31. On the construction of "systems" as a symptom of revolt against the transcendence of the ground, see Voegelin, "Anxiety and Reason," in *What Is History?* 82–83.

community (of cosmopolis) that transcends adequate figuration in terms of an earthly city; to a sense of human-divine encounter that embraces not only ecstasies, but also the opening of the soul to radical transcendence, where faith embraces also the episodes of unmet longing and waiting, "the periods of aridity and dullness, guilt and despondency, contrition and repentance"; and finally, to a sense of the ineffable divine grace that is the alpha and omega of the transfigurative process of history.[32] In sum, such a mythos would be characterized by something in notably short supply in *The Cantos:* religious humility.

Coda

It is in short supply, but still it is not absent; it comes suddenly to the fore in the *Pisan Cantos* (Cantos 74 through 84), the part of the poem written by Pound after he had been arrested by Allied troops in Italy and held at the Detention Training Center near Pisa—first in an outdoor cage, until he had a breakdown, and afterward in a tent—while awaiting transport to a U.S. court to be tried on charges of treason. The *Pisan Cantos* show Pound reviewing the course of his life and his learning, reconsidering his convictions and commitments, sifting through his memory to try to find where he has been right and where he has gone wrong. They register an awareness of personal failure, of pride-induced blindness, and also a new degree of existential openness, a readiness to relax the will:

> Pull down thy vanity, it is not man
> Made courage, or made order, or made grace,
>   Pull down thy vanity, I say pull down.
> Learn of the green world what can be thy place
> In scaled invention or true artistry,
> Pull down thy vanity,
>
> (81/521)

This note of humility deepens in the final drafts and fragments Pound composed for the poem during his late years, as the writing increasingly reflects

32. Bernstein, *The Tale of the Tribe: Ezra Pound and the Modern Verse Epic,* quoted in Lillian Feder, "Pound and Ovid," 23; Voegelin, *The New Science of Politics,* in *Modernity without Restraint,* 187.

a recognition that his epic poem does not, in fact, add up to a convincing vision of human history and divine reality:

> But the beauty is not the madness
> Tho' my errors and wrecks lie about me.
> And I am not a demigod,
> I cannot make it cohere.
>
> (116/795–96)

> To confess wrong without losing rightness:
> Charity I have had sometimes,
> I cannot make it flow thru.
>
> (116/797)

And he pointedly confesses the misplacement of energy and love in his devotion to building the heavenly city on earth:

> M'amour, m'amour
> what do I love and
> where are you?
> That I lost my center
> fighting the world.
> The dreams clash
> and are shattered—
> and that I tried to make a paradiso
> terrestre.
>
> (117/802)

Paradiso there is indeed, but *terrestre* it is not. Pound's inability or unwillingness to embrace transcendent meaning in the fullness of its mystery, it would seem, is at the center of the intellectual and artistic misjudgments that he came to see as having seriously marred his life and work. The failure of *The Cantos* as a convincing vision of human history and divine reality haunted Pound's last decade, the years between 1961 and 1972 during which he rarely spoke, withdrawn into silence and self-doubt. During this time a reporter asked him, "Where are you living now?" Pound replied: "In hell."[33]

Pound's complex achievement in *The Cantos* displays, in its idiosyncratic way, the terrible difficulty facing twentieth-century artists or thinkers who

33. Hall, *Their Ancient Glittering Eyes*, 255.

want to remain true both to the justice, order, and beauty that exists, has existed, and may yet be achieved in world and history, and to the fact of a divine reality that has manifested itself in many different guises to peoples of all places and epochs. Pound's loss of the balance of consciousness occurs not because he attempts to *stop* history, as do the apocalyptists or modern gnostics or historiogenetic exclusivists who either claim special knowledge of divine being or try to absorb transcendent meaning fully into human insight, or because he closes himself off to transcendent meaning, as do the historical immanentists and the philosophers of groundlessness. Rather, because in Pound the dynamism of wonder and inquiry that draws him toward transcendence balks at the *ultimate* mystery, at the transcendence of transcendence, his vision of history and divine reality does not cohere but fragments into beautiful and curious splinters. His pluralistic embrace of religious epiphanies turns aside from the Buddhist, Upanishadic, and Taoist insights into radical transcendence, and he resists the radically transcendent God of Judaism, Christianity, and Islam. His understanding that history involves a waxing and waning of personal and social attunement to the divine ground hesitates at the recognition that divine reality lies ultimately *beyond* history. The erotic energy that informs his artistic evocations of divinity stops short of the revelation of the transcendent mystery as absolutely unrestricted love. Consequently, he remains "essentially a religious poet," as Lewis Hyde notes, whose "work displays a curious incongruity: it is framed by clear declarations of erotic and spiritual ends which it does not achieve."[34]

If this critique is accurate, then the achievement of truly balanced visions of history and divinity must rest on ideas and images that give (1) the finite world, (2) the radical transcendence of the ground, and (3) human existence as the site of their conscious interpenetration their full and proper due. In the next chapter, therefore, we will examine characteristics of such visions, addressing the problem of responding to divine presence in the finite or immanent world while still affirming the radical transcendence of the divine ground. Following it, a final chapter will concentrate on the contemporary challenge of acknowledging human consciousness as the site where finite being and divine transcendence interpenetrate.

34. Hyde, *The Gift*, 219, 223.

7

COSMOLOGY

The Problem of Divine Presence in the World

—And these Things,
which live by perishing, know you are praising them; transient,
they look to us for deliverance: us, the most transient of all.
They want us to change them, utterly, in our invisible heart,
within—oh endlessly—within us! Whoever we may be at last.

—RAINER MARIA RILKE, *DUINO ELEGIES*

THE ENDURING power of poetic evocations of nature-divinities and of the divine within nature, such as those of Pound—or of Rilke, Blake, Mary Oliver, Allen Ginsberg, James Wright, and many other poets—indicates that the gods of the cosmos, the gods experienced in transformative encounters with things and persons in the world, the gods of polytheistic myth, have not been simply obliterated by the discovery of the transcendence of the divine ground of reality. Despite the discovery of the Tao, Brahman, nirvana, and the God of the Beyond, the intracosmic gods are not completely dead—that is to say, despite the convincingness of experiences of divine transcendence, experiences of divine presence in the things of the world are still part of human life.

However, the fact of divine presence in finite reality after the differentiation of transcendence constitutes a problem—actually a tangle of problems, which merely to unravel to the point where they can be clearly articulated is a challenge for the most astute of thinkers, as Eric Voegelin's repeated grappling with the task in his late writings reveals. We may begin our own analysis by considering some of Voegelin's insights into the matter, starting with his firm assertion: "Even when the Beyond has revealed itself to the questing mind of man as the One that is truly divine, the cosmos remains full of gods," followed by the crucial question: "What is this surplus of divine reality represented by the intracosmic gods even when the divine Beyond has revealed itself?"[1]

The fundamental issue is this: the explicit recognition of divine transcendence does not, either by force of logic or on the basis of experience, simply dedivinize or desacralize the world of things. That the victory of transcendent symbolizations of divinity over cosmological symbolizations has led to a widespread interpretation and experience of the world as merely profane, as radically empty of divine presence, is certainly true. However, according to Voegelin, such interpretation and experience are a perversion. Explicit appreciation of transcendence dissolves belief in the traditional cosmological gods as adequate symbols of divine ultimacy, but it leaves intact the fundamental experience of *divine formative presence* in the things of the world, and it does not eliminate the human need to symbolize that presence through imaginative figuration.[2] The discovery of transcendence reveals no more than that the *ultimate* source of worldly divine presence is a Beyond of things—that, as Voegelin puts it in one context, the "divine reality that reveals its presence in the meditative act is both within Being as its creative core and outside of Being in some Beyond of it." So the postcosmological notion of a world emptied of divinity is an error—and a psychologically damaging error, because it has a direct impact on the management of existence. Voegelin abbreviates the issue as follows:

> Under the cosmological style of truth, man is still fully conscious of the gods being present in the cosmos. When, however, an experience of transcendence concentrates divinity in a Beyond of the world, this primary consciousness may suffer damage. By a non sequitur, immanence may become

1. Voegelin, "Beginning and Beyond," in *What Is History?* 223.

2. Once the *cosmos* has conceptually split into *worldly (secular)* reality and *transcendent* reality, both realms may still be—and to balanced consciousness still are—regarded as sacred. Eugene Webb clarifies the point: "The sacred is only in part an intellectual concept: it is also a mode of experience. And its opposite is not, properly speaking, the secular, but the profane. The secular, which is to say, the world of life in time, may be experienced as either sacred or profane" (*The Dark Dove: The Sacred and Secular in Modern Literature,* 4). The other-than-sacred is not to be equated with secular or worldly reality, but rather with whatever appears to be *profane* reality—that which lacks truly significant meaning, or that which is meaningless, or that which is evil.

> perverted from a world empty of the gods of polytheism to a world empty of divinity. If the intracosmic gods are an obstacle to understanding the transcendent God, their disappearance may become no less an obstacle to understanding divine presence in the world. The primary experience of the cosmos thus has hold of a truth that may become obscured or even obliterated under the impact of a spiritual outburst [focusing attention on divine transcendence].[3]

This obscuring of divine presence in the things of the world may be abetted by the vocabulary of *transcendence* and *immanence*, Voegelin admits, because in "conventional usage" these two terms are often understood as referring respectively to divine reality and to a dedivinized and profane world. The original creators of symbols of transcendence, he emphasizes, did not intend this kind of distinction. Plato, for example, used the term *Beyond* to symbolize "the goal of a meditative act that transcends the [still] divinely permeated reality of the 'cosmos' "; neither does the "Christian act of transcendence" dedivinize the world, Voegelin states, but leaves it, if not full of gods, still (in Gilson's phrase) "full of God."[4] The conventional misunderstanding of the language of transcendence and immanence, Voegelin would say, derives from a lack of familiarity with the experiential basis of that language. Behind the word-symbols lie the meditative and reflective acts that gave rise to them. Because it is only the exercise of similar meditative and reflective acts that can clarify the actual meaning of the distinction between transcendence and immanence, the following section traces the results of such a meditative reenactment. Necessarily, it begins with a remembrance of the historical starting point for all interpretations of reality: the constant that Voegelin calls "the primary experience of the cosmos." Already introduced and discussed in Chapters 2 and 3, we will now concentrate on this experience one final time, in somewhat more detail than before.

The Primary Experience of the Cosmos

To understand the primary experience of the cosmos—the first and fundamental human experience of reality, both in terms of history and in terms

3. Voegelin, "Beginning and Beyond," in *What Is History?* 221; "Anxiety and Reason," in *What Is History?* 78.

4. Voegelin, "Beginning and Beyond," in *What Is History?* 218.

of personal experience—we have to recall that human existence is always experienced as a "tension." We find ourselves aware of, and full of wonder and anxiety about, our situation within a reality that created us and that encompasses us. From the beginning human consciousness is "conscious of being constituted by the reality of which it is conscious," and we want to understand and make contact with the ultimate basis or ground of whatever it is that we are participants in. So we find our very selves to exist as a "tension" of inquiry and concern oriented toward the ground of meaning, toward ultimate reality, toward sacred power.[5]

Now, our first intimations of the superabundant meaning of the ground are not thoughts of something apart from nature, but rather are apprehensions of a mystery and sublimity *present in the world* that appears through our senses. The world we encounter as children—of vast earth and sky, endless varieties of plants and animals, night following day in the revolving seasons, families and societies with their activities and rituals—is, we find, a world of potential epiphanies: every item of it is part of a *completeness of meaning* that can serve as a reminder of the ultimate meaning of the whole. The glittering sky on a clear night, a glimpse of a mare nursing her foal, or the welcome home after a trip might be the cause of a sudden apprehension of the depth of significance, of the whole of meaning, that transcends and encompasses world and life. Both in human history and as individuals, we first experience reality as a *whole*, as a completeness we are immersed in, and of which every part is alive with the potential to bring us into contact with the absolute. It is the experience of living in a *cosmos:* an ordered totality of meaning. With regard to this experience the size of the physical universe and the length of time it has existed are irrelevant. It is an experience of reality as *narratively* complete.

The "primary experience of the cosmos," then, is an experience of all of reality as an interpenetrating oneness. And "cosmological" cultures—which include all early human cultures—are those in which the apprehension of the natural world is still *dominated* by a sense of its oneness with ultimate meaning. In these cultures, therefore, divine reality is symbolized, without any sense of impropriety, as a multiplicity of cosmic forces and things, including divine personages manifesting themselves as earth, sky, celestial objects, winds, waters, animals, plants, humans.

5. Voegelin, "Remembrance of Things Past," in *Published Essays, 1966–1985*, 312.

Jorge Luis Borges, in a lecture on poetry delivered at Harvard in 1967, offers an example of cosmological perception (though he does not call it this), in which a natural phenomenon and divine presence are as yet "compactly" blended together, not yet imaginatively or conceptually separated:

> Let us take the word "thunder" and look back at the god Thunor, the Saxon counterpart of the Norse Thor. The word *thunor* stood for thunder and for the god; but had we asked the men who came to England with Hengist [in the fifth century C.E.] whether the word stood for the rumbling in the sky or for the angry god, I do not think they would have been subtle enough to understand the difference. I suppose that the word carried both meanings without committing itself very closely to either one of them. I suppose that when they uttered or heard the word "thunder," they at the same time felt the low rumbling in the sky and saw the lightning and thought of the god. The [word was] packed with magic; [it] did not have a hard and fast meaning.[6]

In Borges's excellent example, linguistic meaning reflects the compact experience and understanding of reality. In cosmological perception, nondivine things and divinity still flow together. Thus, the symbolic vehicles through which all ancient societies make sense of existence and explore the question of the ground of reality are those cosmological myths that evoke the mutual involvement—the consubstantiality and, to some degree, interpenetrability—of sacred powers (gods), world, society, and individual.

As discussed in previous chapters, though, there came a time in the development of cultures, initially in a few societies, when cosmological myths came to be found wanting. The cause of this disquiet was a shift in the perception of the structure of reality based on a new understanding, which recognized that the superabundant meaning of the divine ground had to be something radically other than what could be represented in terms of cosmic things, and indeed radically other than what could be communicated in human language. This new insight into the radical transcendence of the divine ground eventually caused the cosmological myths to be abandoned as inappropriate vehicles for truly explaining the human situation in reality. The recognition of the ultimate ground as a Beyond of all finite reality—and so of its essential incomprehensibility to human understanding—required new forms of image,

6. Borges, *This Craft of Verse,* 80.

story, myth for telling truly the story of human existence. However—and this is now the crucial point—nothing in this discovery negated the human experience of *the oneness of reality.* Humans still found themselves participants in a comprehending whole that included the divine ground. So, in Chinese thought, the transcendent Tao and the world of "ten thousand things" still constitute one whole of reality. Or again, in Christian thought, God and creation still constitute one whole of reality. The oneness of reality is a given.

In Chapter 2 we discussed the human search for the ground of reality as the search for a necessary mode of being. In order to bring that analysis to bear on the present topic, and to supplement the descriptive language of cosmos, gods, world, and God with the explanatory, philosophical language of contingency and necessity, let us now recast our description of the basic "tension" of existence in terms of human consciousness being a "tension" of contingent existence aware of, and longing for, necessary being.

First, it would be a mistake to conceive of our contingent consciousness—with its wonder, anxiety, longing, and doubt—as *needing to seek out a relationship* to perfect and necessary being. On the contrary, such a relationship is present from the beginning. As Voegelin puts it, "[t]here is no doubting contingency without the tension toward the necessity which makes the doubt evident as such."[7] (Just as there is no existential longing for the Good without the actual tension toward perfect reality that makes the longing evident as such.) The tension between contingent and necessary being is a *given structure* of human consciousness.

Just how, though, is necessary being encountered? We are aware of the contingent status of our bodies, perceptions, and cognitive experiences; our individual particularity is contingent through and through. How, then, do we experience necessity? The answer lies in the fact that our individual particularity is not all that we are. Consciousness is indeed experienced as bodily located and distinct from the rest of reality (what Voegelin calls the "intentional" experience of consciousness), but it is simultaneously experienced as an emergence within, and as belonging to, the comprehending reality in which it participates (what Voegelin calls the "luminous" experience of consciousness).[8] We are our distinct selves, but we are also parts of the one

7. Voegelin, "Quod Deus Dicitur," in *Published Essays, 1966–1985,* 380.

8. On *intentionality* and *luminosity* as structural dimensions of human consciousness, see Voegelin, *In Search of Order,* 28–33; and G. Hughes, *Mystery and Myth,* 34–37.

reality from which everything comes and which embraces all things. And it is this latter aspect of our experience—our consciousness of oneness with the comprehending reality—that is the source of our *given* awareness of noncontingent, necessary being. As derivative and contingent beings who are conscious, we always, at least inchoately, apprehend the noncontingent being that grounds our contingent existences. So we strive to deepen our connection with that permanent being, that necessary actuality, that we encounter as the "ground" of the comprehending reality from which we have emerged. The human search for the divine is for that permanent ground of meaning with which we are always concerned due to our awareness—however vague, sophisticated, or repressed—of our *participation* in it.

The crucial point, then, is that the primary human experience of reality, whether explained in the descriptive language of cosmos and gods or in the philosophical terminology of contingency and necessity, is always of a *whole, a completeness.* While in cosmological cultures—and in the consciousness of every child—this whole is not yet differentiated into the realms of transcendence and immanence, it is an experience that such differentiation *does not eliminate, but rather relies upon,* as it diffracts the cosmos into its constitutive components of transcendence and immanence. Though we have come historically (and may come personally) to clearly distinguish contingent and necessary being as, respectively, the universe of things and a transcendent ground of being beyond all worldly things, this distinction *always presupposes the fact and the truth* of the prior apprehension of a comprehending whole within which these distinctions are made.

This means that the experience of the cosmos *as a cosmos,* a oneness, is a constant in human experience. So, while cosmological myths are discredited by later insights into the structure of reality—insights that sharply distinguish between contingent and necessary being—still the experience of the oneness of reality remains. "Compact *symbolisms,*" states Voegelin, " . . . may become obsolete in the light of new insights, but the *reality* they express does not cease to be real for that reason. . . . Even though we should have to reject all traditional symbolizations of cosmic reality as incompatible with our present mode of experience, we still are living in the reality of the cosmos."[9]

9. Voegelin, "Immortality: Experience and Symbol," in *Published Essays, 1966–1985,* 93 (emphasis added).

The constancy of the experience of the oneness of reality corresponds to the fact that although the divine ground transcends the world, divine presence is still the creative and formative essence of the world. It is, after all, the divine presence in the contingent things of the world, including in our own bodily and psychological existences, that provides the experiential condition of experiences of transcendence. Worldly things, then, are never really just things. If seen for what they are, they always retain what Voegelin calls a "divine aura," that is, they *participate* in transcendence, which is why, as John D. Caputo says, "[t]he simplest things can become occasions of transcendence and hence can become deep." To put it another way: things are not permanent, but the permanence of meaning that grounds them may be discovered in things. And this "more-than-themselves" dimension of the meaning of worldly things, this lastingness of their meaning through their participation in a meaning beyond worldly perishing, also needs to be evoked and remembered if worldly things are not to be cut off imaginatively from the divine ground and reduced to what Rilke in one of his letters calls "empty, indifferent things, pseudo-things, DUMMY-LIFE." Rilke goes on in the same letter to say that we have the responsibility of preserving things in their "human and laral worth," explaining that he uses the word *laral* "in the sense of household-gods."[10]

Which brings us back to the gods of polytheistic myth, the gods who have not been simply obliterated. The human need to symbolize the divine presence in finite reality is a permanent need. If it is not addressed, there is a crucial lacuna or disruption in the human experience of reality. "If we let any part of reality drop out of sight by refusing it public status in the world of symbols," says Voegelin, "it will lead a sort of underground life and make its reality felt in intense moods of alienation, or even in outright mental disturbances." Thus, some sort of mythic evocation of divine presence in the world will always be a part of healthy human living, because there are "fundamental experiences of reality that require for their expression the language of the gods even when, in the process of differentiation, the many gods are superseded by the One God."[11]

10. Voegelin, *In Search of Order,* 93; Caputo, "Being and Mystery," 110; letter to Witold von Hulewicz, November 13, 1925, quoted in Rilke, "Appendix 4: The Task of Transformation," in *Duino Elegies,* 129.

11. Voegelin, "Immortality: Experience and Symbol," in *Published Essays, 1966–1985,* 93; *In Search of Order,* 94.

Myth, Aberrant Myth, and Neopaganism

Before the spiritual outbursts that focused attention on the radical transcendence of the divine ground, cosmological myths successfully carried the burden of ultimate meaning. Once a rigorous notion of transcendence emerged, however, the cosmological myths—concerning, for example, the divine pantheons of Sumeria and Egypt, or the Olympian gods of ancient Greece—ceased to be convincing explanations of the structure of reality as a whole. The essence of divinity became a transcendent principle or God. This released the finite world from its close identification with divine essence or divine immediacy, and made possible its analysis as an autonomous field of intelligible objects and relations—it became "nature" or "the physical universe," eventually examined and explained by the various natural sciences. This *conceptual* autonomy of the physical universe, which to our outlooks is second nature, does not, however, reflect an *ontological* autonomy. The finite universe is not, through the discovery of divine transcendence, sundered from its divine ground. Rather, the finite universe has taken on the status and value of being the *manifest* aspect of the one cosmic reality—the showing-forth, in the dimensions of space and time, of a reality whose essence is divine transcendence. The entire finite universe has become, in the words of Eugene Webb, "a sacramental sign speaking analogically of the *infinite* Being that is its ground."[12]

Because the natural universe is rooted in a mystery of transcendence, and because it bespeaks the mystery of transcendence, the human need for myth does not simply vanish once the older cosmological myths have ceased to be convincing accounts of the whole of reality. Myth, as Voegelin points out, remains the "adequate and exact [symbolic] instrument of expression" for our understanding of the process of reality as a whole. Why is this so? First, it is because the suggestive ambiguity of mythic symbols conveys simultaneously our insights into transcendent meaning and our awareness of the incompleteness of human knowledge regarding its mystery. Second, it is because the yearning, love, and awe expressed in and evoked by the emotion-laden imagery of myth bring us psychologically closer to the divine mystery than can any conceptual knowing. And third, it is because in the form of cosmic, or encompassing, myth—as, for example, in Plato's great myths or in the *divina*

12. Webb, *Dark Dove*, 257 (emphasis added).

commedia of Christian faith—it tells an overarching story that makes sense of our deepest intimations and longings by affirming that all human lives are elements in one cosmic and divine drama.[13]

After the clarification of transcendence, of course, myth can no longer be embraced as the most direct expression of divine ultimacy. Abstract terms denoting the radical transcendence of the divine ground—such as the "being beyond being" of Plato's *Republic,* or the mystical notion of the *Urgrund,* or the Buddhist nirvana, or the Chinese Tao, or Voegelin's symbol of the "Beyond"—take its place. Nonetheless, myth remains the elementary and necessary language *for relating human and worldly meaning to divinely transcendent meaning.* Myths compatible with the truths of transcendence remain needed as "relay stations," as Voegelin puts it, "on the way to the . . . differentiated absolute ground."[14] As humans, as embodied creatures who are aware of participating in transcendent being, as seekers who live in the in-between of immanence and transcendence, we require the stories and symbols of myth to satisfy our basic need to have the divine meanings of things expressed in terms both imaginable and mysterious, in a manner that promotes what Voegelin calls balanced consciousness, wherein we honor and attend to the sacred character of the world while at the same time honoring divine transcendence.

Myths available to us that promote the balance of consciousness come in many forms. To begin with, there are the grand myths of the major religious and wisdom traditions, which focus on the divine Beyond and offer to orient us within the process of reality as a whole by giving imaginal and narrative form to the invisible mysteries of original creation, divine intent, and transcendent destiny.

In addition to these grand myths of the Beyond, however, we also require symbolic evocations of divine presence in the natural world, of *divine immanence.* Without these evocations, we run the risk of experiencing the world

13. Voegelin, *Revolution and the New Science,* 56. This is an oft-repeated theme of Voegelin: "The reality of things . . . cannot be fully understood in terms of the world and its time; for the things are circumfused by an ambience of mystery that can be understood only in terms of the Myth" ("Beginning and Beyond," in *What Is History?* 175).

14. Voegelin, "Anxiety and Reason," in *What Is History?* 79. The term *God* is itself, of course, a mythopoetic symbol, an analogical evocation, that in a single word enables "the mystery that lets all meaningfully structured stories within the process [of reality] be experienced as substories of the comprehending story" (Voegelin, *In Search of Order,* 98).

as drained of divine significance, as profane, as merely mechanical. This is why Voegelin makes the slightly startling assertion that even after the discovery of divine transcendence, the "intracosmic gods . . . are not expendable." In healthy living, he argues, experiences of sacred presence corresponding to ancient experiences of the intracosmic gods remain, in a wide variety of post-cosmological epiphany. Sometimes it is natural phenomena—animals, landscape, light, sea, and sky—that elicit experiences of sacred presence, as they resonate with and suggest a value and beauty more profound and enduring than the world. We associate certain writers and artists with such experiences; one thinks of Wordsworth, Blake, Turner, or Friedrich. Sometimes myths, tales, and images inherited from cosmological, or borrowed from tribal, cultures serve to evoke a sense of the sacred in nature and in everyday life. Artists attesting to such experiences would include Joyce, Pound, Picasso, and Brancusi. Sometimes works of art themselves perform this service—it being the principal purpose of the artist, as W. H. Auden has remarked with regard to poets, "to preserve and express by art what primitive peoples knew instinctively, namely, that, for [human beings], nature is a realm of sacramental analogies," so that through art divine presence in the world is mediated and thus recollected.[15] Then there are artifacts such as Buddhist stupas, venerated icons, and holy shrines. In all of these cases there is functioning an experience of "myth," however rudimentarily, that is, finite objects are expressing or communicating, in a satisfyingly concrete manner, experiences in which places and things, sights and sounds and actions, are transfigured with a sense of transcendent significance and radiate a sense of transcendent purpose.

The apprehension of divine presence in worldly things, the experience of some kind of mythic "play of divine presence, always presupposing, and leading toward, the divine ground ultimately intended," is not an expendable element in healthy human living, *because without it the sense of divine transcendence itself becomes lost.* Divine transcendent being is not of the world, but it is encountered only by human beings who long for and discover it as the fullness of meaning implied and signified by the things of the world. It is only in and through the things of the world that we approach the divine being that transcends the world. Experiences of the sacramental character of certain places, things, and persons are requisite, therefore, for keeping alive a conscious and balanced relationship to divine transcendence. Acknowledgment of this fact

15. Voegelin, "Anxiety and Reason," in *What Is History?* 78; Auden, *Secondary Worlds,* 131.

appears in what Voegelin calls the "psychological tact" shown by the Catholic Church in providing "Christian versions of holy places, miracle-working images, and rituals, and . . . a host of saints to substitute for the gods." Awareness of it also lies behind much of the energetic upsurge of literary and scholarly interest in myth throughout the nineteenth and twentieth centuries. The work of scholars such as Frazer and Eliade, the appreciation of myth by Jung and his followers, the literary creations of writers such as Joyce and Mann—all of these constitute a healthy recognition that a consciousness of transcendent divine mystery can be nurtured only through the mythic evocation of divine presence in the world.[16]

The figures just mentioned are generally understood to have been engaged in an action of recovery, of regaining lost truths about the human situation and the human psyche that had become obscured by the modern scientific and ideological flattening of the world into a merely profane "physical universe" and the corresponding reduction of human consciousness to just another "thing" among immanent things. What the success of the modern immanentist ideologies shows, among other things, is that if the divine presence in the things of the world becomes too obscured, a loss of convincing awareness of divine transcendence will follow. Eugene Webb has stated the point with precision: "One might say that it is the transcendent pole of the sacred that is the source or ground of its sacral quality and that the immanent is its vehicle, the means by which it becomes accessible to man. *If either were missing, the sacred would vanish from human experience.*"[17] The skepticism about and rejection of transcendence by immanentists and materialists corresponds to the disappearance of convincing experiences of sacramental places, things, actions, and persons that attune one to the mystery of transcendence through the efficacy of "myth."

Let us focus briefly on the cultural landscape of Western modernity, with its "heap of broken images," in order to consider some of the consequences of the inefficacy or absence of myths that effectively mediate divine transcendence.

16. Voegelin, "Anxiety and Reason," in *What Is History?* 79–80. In a late analysis of Plato's *Timaeus,* Voegelin points out how "Plato carefully stresses that 'the divine' cannot be discerned by itself alone; there is no participation in 'the divine' but through the exploration of the 'things' in which it is discerned as formatively present" (*In Search of Order,* 120). Voegelin, "Anxiety and Reason," in *What Is History?* 78, 84.

17. Webb, *Dark Dove,* 9–10 (emphasis added).

First, as discussed in our first two chapters, when a sense of the world as a "sacramental sign" pointing to transcendence is lost, the human search for an ultimate ground of meaning will not cease. Rather, it will find some feature of immanent reality—a material good, a power within nature, a future historical state, a political leader, a nation—and invest it with the value of the infinite. If the true divine is eclipsed or rejected, some parts of finite being will be inflated to the status of gods. Our given human awareness of the necessary and perfect ground of being will project these qualities of necessity and perfection onto something or someone contingent and imperfect—perhaps a Hitler or a Mao. If we lose sight of genuine sacred reality, the world of objects, human constructions, and human heroes will always draw toward itself the supercharge of infinite value that our longing for the true ground always provides. This is an inevitability explained eloquently by both Saint Augustine and Søren Kierkegaard, as more recently by Paul Tillich in his analysis of the dynamics of "ultimate concern." The outcome is that proper myths—which function as symbolic expressions guiding and orienting one in relation to the mysterious depths of transcendent meaning—are replaced by *disguised* myths, aberrant or degrading myths, stories about reality as a whole that contract our native fascination with mystery into service of some *worldly* apotheosis—of national triumph, for example, or civilizational progress, or scientific omnicompetence. Because guiding myths of some kind remain a permanent human need—because by nature we are related to, and long for, the *mysterium fascinans et tremendum* of transcendent meaning—the immanentist or materialist eclipse of divine mystery only ensures the cultural dominance of aberrant myths.[18]

18. See Tillich, *Dynamics of Faith*, 1–29. "So it is," Lonergan notes, "that the full range of interpretations [of ultimate meaning] includes not only the whole gamut of religions but also the opposite phenomenon of antireligious feeling and expression, not only antireligious views but also the intense humanistic idealism that characterized liberal display of detachment from all religious concern, not only elevated humanism but also the crudely naturalistic nationalism that exploded in Germany under the fascination exerted by a Hitler, not only such social aberrations but also the individual aberrations that led Jung to declare that very commonly psychoneural disorder is connected with problems of a basically 'religious' character. In brief, there is a dimension to human experience that takes man beyond the domesticated, familiar, common sphere" to the "known unknown" of "the undefined surplus of significance and momentousness" toward which we are always emotionally and cognitively oriented. "Man is by nature oriented into mystery, and *naturam expellas furca, tamen usque recurret* [expel nature with a pitchfork, nevertheless it always comes back]" (*Insight*, 556–57, 570).

A second consequence ensues from such dominance. When the stories and images belonging to the traditions of the world religions, and when nature and art, fail in their proper mythic function due to the eclipse of divine mystery, and when secular forms of aberrant myth gain sway over the cultural imagination, there follows a loss of critical control with regard to the meaning of experiences of sacred power and presence. The experiences themselves do not disappear; divine presence always exerts its influence. However, in a landscape where divine mystery has been occluded, where the relation of worldly things to their transcendent ground has been lost to critical awareness, there will inevitably be a failure of critical assessment in the interpretation of experiences of worldly enchantment, of fascination arising from the aura of absoluteness and necessity evoked by something (or someone) contingent. The interpretive tools fall into disuse that would distinguish the false from the true matter of inspiration, the genuinely and profoundly spiritual from the magically exotic or the charmingly occult or the demonically intoxicating. So—whether the phenomena under consideration are the cults of Lenin, Stalin, Hitler, and Mao, or more benign discharges such as an obsession with UFOs or the deification of movie or pop music stars—a naively immanentist or materialist landscape is invariably a field of spiritual disorientation and false adoration, where the human longing for the divine ground is misdirected and misapplied.

Finally, as recent years in particular have shown, a loss of critical perspective and control with regard to experiences of the divine, together with a nostalgic reverence for the palpable gods of time and space, can lead to a romantic attempt to revive a cosmological experience of nature as sacred. Lacking a clear grasp of the historical process of the differentiation of transcendence in cultures East and West, as well as of the philosophical distinctions and complexities involved in the recognition of transcendence as a realm of meaning always implicit in human experiences of ultimacy, there are some who blame the religions of transcendence (especially Christianity) and Western scientific thought, together, as responsible for the loss of a sense of sacred presence in the world. In their view, the Western religions of transcendence successfully imposed on their societies a notion of divine being that strictly separates it from the natural world, allowing "nature" to be seen as a realm empty of the divine and thus of value solely as a field for scientific knowledge and control. Thus (they argue) has been produced a soulless, materialist vision of the universe, under the influence of which our capacities for awed humility and wonder before the sacraments of nature have been perverted into the proud and destructive worship of science and technology. What is seen as needed is a renewed sense of sacred presence in the world through a revival of cosmological religion, or "neopaganism." The current popularity of this attitude in Western societies deserves additional comment.

There are at present many who grieve about our culture's loss of a sense of nature as sacred, and some who consequently have taken it upon themselves to take direct action in awakening attention to divine presence in earthly, natural things. Some are writing about rocks, rivers, and trees as conscious or sentient beings; some are enacting Druidic or other ancient rites; some are going to symposia on Gaia armed with data on the interdependence of organic and inorganic subsystems in a given bioregion. They all share an awareness that something has gone badly wrong when cultural traditions drain divine reality from the physical universe so effectively that no humble respect for nature and no experience of awe or mystery before it remain, and this shared awareness is educated by increasing knowledge about the nature-oriented religious experiences and mythical legacies of cosmological (including Native American) cultures. Looking for the roots of modern arrogant disdain for the natural world, some of them vilify Christianity and Western philosophy as principal culprits in the successful installation of a falsely degraded, or merely mechanized, view of nature. Thus, the foundations of specifically Western culture—the Jewish and Christian heritage and the Greek philosophical and scientific traditions—are perceived by them as poisonous, as hiding within their achievements the seeds of our present withered spirituality, our exploitation of the environment, and our contemptuous indifference to the divine powers that (they assert) nevertheless live in and around us. Sometimes the remedy proposed is the reinstallation of ancient gods and goddesses as objects of worship; sometimes it is the paying of religious homage—through old or new rituals—to the earth, heavenly bodies, sacred places, and natural beings; and sometimes it is the renewal of ancient practices, including traditions of magic, that presumably gave our ancestors spiritual stability and joy, grounding them in the cosmos and uniting them with divine wisdom and power.

One may deeply sympathize with such attitudes, grounded as they are in desolating experiences of a radically dedivinized world—a world where gods and goddesses, epiphanies and numinous encounters, all the mysteries of sacred enchantment, have been banished, and where the very idea of the divine has been restricted to "God," interpreted as a purely transcendent absence. If attending church or temple has become an empty routine for millions, in which symbols and rituals meant to mediate a living divine presence have ceased to be effective, then those among the millions who refuse to put up with spiritual death and go in search of a convincing experience of the sacred are to be admired, at least for their insistence that experiences of human-divine encounter lie at the heart of proper human living, and for the recognition that, in some way or other, an experience of sacred respect for the created natural world is central to proper spirituality.

On the other hand, one's sympathy may be tempered by the naïveté so frequently in evidence among those hoping to create a renewed nature-centered religiosity. Writing passionately of goddesses and angelic sprites in the world of nature or in our inner selves; praying to Gaia; donning masks and dancing in the forest in order to ask forgiveness of the sacred spirits for our rapacious exploitation of the land—for all the personal satisfaction such rituals and prayers may provide, they finally have a rather limited cultural potency. Why?

The religions and myths of ancient peoples express the primary experience of the cosmos before that experience was broken by the explicit discovery of the transcendent realm of meaning and the accompanying discovery of the scientific realm of meaning that explains the structures and laws of a conceptually autonomous natural universe. In cosmological cultures, sun and moon, earth and sea, winds, rivers, animals, plants, groves, springs—not to mention kings, pharaohs, and other persons—could all be experienced as divinities, and conversely the divinities could be satisfyingly understood as capable of assuming any number of natural forms. It was inevitable, though, that the religions and myths whose essential forms of divine symbolization and worship came from experiences of divinities-in-nature and divinities-as-nature would be left behind as inadequate, or as "superstitions," after the explicit differentiation of divine transcendence. The gods, goddesses, sea nymphs, wood spirits, and all the other divinities identified with the natural world might still be honored or appreciated as ways in which divine reality has in the process of history revealed itself to peoples, but they could never be perceived by inheritors of the differentiated religions and philosophies, including us, as they once were, as *adequate figurations of divine ultimacy.* They will have lost what Voegelin calls "the magic of their transparency for the unseen order" once the essential unknowability of divine transcendence has come into focus.[19] This was an outcome settled, it must be stressed, on the level of experience, not of theology or institutional dictate. As the discoveries of divine transcendence permeated their original cultures and spread to surrounding ones, the cosmological divinities simply lost their convincingness for more and more people.

This is not to deny the aggressive and irrational elements in the doctrinal battles fought by partisans of religions of transcendence against cosmological beliefs and rituals (in addition to those fought against each other)—of Jews against "idolators," of Christians against "pagans," of Muslims against "infidels." A refined appreciation of the historical and cultural pluralism of genuine experiences of the sacred, such as we have already heard expressed by Maximus of Tyre in the last chapter—"If Greeks are stirred to the remembrance of God by the art of Phidias, or the Egyptians by paying worship to animals, or others by a river, or others by fire, I will not quarrel with their differences. Only let them know, let them love, let them remember"—is an all too rare wisdom of tolerance. From the ecumenic age to the present day, it has been hard for people to accept what Voegelin once called the "last word" of Plato's wisdom: that every myth has its truth.[20] Still, the general success of the religions of transcendence was not the result of coercion. The victory of the new insights was a foregone result, secured by their experiential and rational convincingness—by the *repeated personal discovery,* by ever more people, that the human longing for divine presence legitimately leads to recognition of a radically nonfinite, nontemporal, nonspatial, nonfigurable reality of ultimate meaning.

Where does this leave the natural world? From Greek culture science arises as the investigation of a world no longer directly animated by sacred power and intention but rather a world formed, or in-formed, by divine Intelligence (Nous), with "nature" understood as a realm of intelligible structures governed by intelligible laws. In the Jewish and Christian traditions the world is the creation of the transcendent Creator, to be cherished as God's handiwork but not to be worshiped as divine in itself. In the Buddhist outlook finite reality is the realm of duality, impermanence, and cravings, from whose

19. Voegelin, *Israel and Revelation,* 48.

20. Maximus of Tyre quoted in Eliade, *From Primitives to Zen,* 541; Voegelin, *Israel and Revelation,* 50.

temptations and entanglements enlightenment will liberate us. But in each of these traditions nature remains the place of the *showing-forth* of the sacred. The discovery of divine transcendence does not of itself relegate the natural world to irrelevance or simply desacralize it. On the contrary, nature properly appreciated in light of the discovery is still sacred, though it has lost its status as being identical with, or commensurate with, the divine essence or ground. The natural world is in each of these traditions the location and occasion where transcendent divinity gives and reveals itself, where the sacred is offered to and participated in by creatures, including the human creatures who in the course of their development eventually discovered and specified the transcendent mystery at the core of all things.

These facts indicate why the principal aim of neopaganism—the attempt to reawaken a sense of the divine in nature in line with cosmological perception—is bound to be frustrated. Whether or not people acknowledge the fact, the discovery of transcendence is now thoroughly and irrevocably embedded in our perceptions and conceptual outlooks as a consequence of our cultural and linguistic heritage. It is a fait accompli, and for all the difficulties it has introduced into human living, it cannot be wished away. Nostalgia for an era when divine reality was indistinguishable from the natural world is understandable, and there are those who pursue neopaganism or "cosmological consciousness" with deep sincerity, but therein lies no solution to the spiritual ills of the age.[21]

If the discovery of divine transcendence has in fact led, in certain traditions, to both indifference toward and contempt for nature, the fault nevertheless does not lie in the logic of the discovery itself. Transcendence is not the problem, and willful insistence that divinity should be worshiped in an intracosmic fashion does not address the problem. The revivification of a sense of nature as sacred—of nature as a showing-forth of the divine that deserves our humble respect and careful stewardship—will have to take forms other than the revival of ancient religions, mythologies, and practices, or the ad hoc invention of rituals based on those models. Transcendent meaning cannot be squeezed back into nature.

21. "One [can]not go back of revelation and play existence in cosmic-divine order, after the world-transcendent God [has] revealed himself. One [can]not pretend to live in another order of being than the one illuminated by revelation [of transcendence]" (Voegelin, *Israel and Revelation,* 518).

Ambient Vision

The balance of consciousness is difficult to maintain. The acknowledgment of the divine Beyond always threatens to drain worldly reality of its divine aura, to eliminate from the experience of worldly things and history all sense of their participation in divine goodness and purpose. Correspondingly, the conceptual isolation of the immanent universe always carries the danger that the transcendent ground—ineffable, impalpable, nonimaginable—will be forgotten, ignored, or rejected. One or the other error, either the eclipse of divine worldly presence or the eclipse of transcendence, has characterized many of the attitudes, East and West, that have emerged in the wake of the discovery of transcendence.

The eclipse of divine presence and meaning in the world is noticeable in a variety of familiar attitudes. For instance, the world has frequently been regarded, especially by religious fundamentalists, as *irrelevant,* as unworthy of deep concern, as we are urged not to let worldly matters (such as poverty, injustice, or environmental concerns) distract us as we stay focused on our transcendent destiny. Again, worldly reality has been portrayed as an *illusion,* as in the Vedantic tradition of Hinduism that subsumes all finite reality under the heading of maya (cosmic illusion).[22] The world (or the material realm) has been rejected as *evil,* as in the ancient Gnostic and Manichaean teachings. Or finally, the universe has been described as nothing more than

22. In Hindu thought the term *maya* corresponds roughly to "the manifest world." Maya is, according to Heinrich Zimmer, "the measuring out, or creation, or display of forms; *māyā* is any illusion, trick, artifice, deceit, jugglery, sorcery, or work of witchcraft; an illusory image or apparition, phantasm, deception of the sight; *māyā* is also any diplomatic trick or political artifice designed to deceive. The *māyā* of the gods is their power to assume diverse shapes by displaying at will various aspects of their subtle essence. But the gods are themselves the productions of a greater *māyā:* the spontaneous self-transformation of an originally undifferentiated, all-generating divine Substance. And this greater *māyā* produces, not the gods alone, but the universe in which they operate. All . . . the planes of being and the creatures of those planes . . . are made manifest by a play of *māyā*" (*Myths and Symbols in Indian Art and Civilization,* 24–25). In the Vedantic tradition deriving from the philosopher and mystic Shankara (788–820), "the phenomenal world is a collective illusion shared by all souls which have not yet attained to liberation [from ignorance]; and this illusion is the product of *māyā* and of God who is the author of *māyā*" (Zaehner, *Hinduism,* 76). In this view the manifest world is "illusion pure and simple, with neither more nor less objective existence than has the stuff of dreams" (R. C. Zaehner, *Mysticism Sacred and Profane,* 143).

an intricate mechanism, created and abandoned by its divine inventor who remains apart from and uninvolved in its functioning; by the seventeenth and eighteenth centuries, such a view of world (immanence) and God (transcendence), which hypostatizes the world and its divine ground, not just conceptually distinguishing but also ontologically divorcing them from each other, had entered Western popular imagination.

Contrariwise, transcendence as well can be dismissed as irrelevant (by the agnostic, who thus unwittingly promotes the divinizing of finite goods); as illusory (as with Feuerbach, Marx, Nietzsche, Freud, and the postmodern philosophers of groundlessness); or as evil (in the "Promethean attitude" that recognizes divine power as real, but regards it as an encroachment on human freedom and dignity and so defiantly refuses to give it allegiance).[23] Or, transcendence can fall into eclipse through the insistence that it is not in any real or significant way distinct from the finite realm, as in the pantheistic identification of divinity or God with the totality of things, or in the neopagan attempt to reverse the historical displacement of the cosmological gods and goddesses by the world-transcendent God and to reevoke experiences of, and reestablish forms of worship relating to, intracosmic divinities.[24]

Each of these imbalanced outlooks slips away from the truth that the finite universe and the Beyond of the ground are, while meaningfully distinct, still *one reality,* and that full openness to the whole of reality must therefore remain faithful both (1) to divine formative presence in the worldly order and (2) to the divine transcendence disclosed to human consciousness. There is a need, then, for mythic images of the whole of reality, or what might be called "ambient visions," to help us stay balanced and oriented in the In-Between of immanence and transcendence and to counteract the images corresponding to the mistaken outlooks mentioned above.

23. In Greek tradition, Prometheus was a divinity who rebelled against the community of gods by stealing the divine fire and giving it to humans, a transgression for which Zeus, leader of the gods, imposed a terrifying punishment. Aeschylus, in *Prometheus Bound,* portrays a chained Prometheus staunch in his defiance: "In one word, I hate all the gods who received good from me and wrongfully returned evil" (ll. 975–76, quoted in Voegelin, *World of the Polis,* 334). The "Promethean attitude," then, is one that rejects divine authority for the sake of pure self-determination. Franz, in *Voegelin and the Politics of Spiritual Revolt,* identifies "Promethean revolt" as one of the basic forms of "closure against transcendent experience" (10).

24. The preceding two paragraphs summarize my lengthier analysis of eleven attitudes toward reality that reflect imbalanced consciousness, in "Balanced and Imbalanced Consciousness," 170–80.

The basic criteria for ambient visions of cosmic participation that reflect balanced consciousness are readily identified. First, such visions will affirm and elicit fidelity toward the divine mystery that surpasses human understanding and is the alpha and omega of reality. Second, they will indicate the value of the world as a sacramental analogy, as a bodying-forth of divine goodness and purpose, thus promoting love of the world while acknowledging it to be rooted in transcendent meaning. Third, they will evoke awareness of the drama of universal humanity, of the fact that the meanings of the lives of all peoples of all times and places are united in one supervening story by virtue of their participation in the one flux of divine presence, in the divine fulfillment of meaning that transcends the conditions of space and time. Finally, fourth, such visions at their most sophisticated will entail symbolic recognition that history is an open-ended process in which finite and perishable being *participates through human consciousness* in the imperishable being of the divine ground, a process in which the things of the finite world are constantly being translated, as it were, through human consciousness and its differentiations, into a more eminent mode of participation in the transcendent ground of meaning. Visions meeting all four of these criteria will not only foster a balanced awareness of immanent and transcendent being, but also encourage a properly universalistic and pluralistic conception of humanity and history. Thus, they will appropriately discredit unilinear and exclusivistic images of history, promote participation in cosmopolis, and even allow the eschatological intimations of Western differentiations their due without letting them imaginatively foreclose on the transcendent context and open-endedness of history.

Examples of ambient vision meeting some or all of these criteria can be found throughout the religious, philosophical, literary, and artistic heritages of postcosmological Eastern and Western cultures. For instance, in the *Isha* Upanishad of Hindu scripture (eighth through seventh centuries B.C.E.), we find the following verses:

> In dark night live those for whom the Lord
> Is transcendent only; in night darker still
> For whom he is immanent only.
> But those for whom he is transcendent
> And immanent cross the sea of death

With the immanent and enter into
Immortality with the transcendent.
So we have heard from the wise.

(12–14)[25]

The emphasis here is on the importance of recognizing both divine formative presence in the world and the ultimate transcendence of the Godhead, without letting either fact reduce the other to insignificance; and also on the importance of realizing that human attunement with eternal divine truth—Aristotle's process of "immortalizing as much as possible" (*Nicomachean Ethics* 1177b31–35)—can be achieved only through this dual recognition and dual fidelity. Like many passages in the Upanishads, the pedagogical aim is to orient us amid the conceptual and existential difficulties introduced by the sharp specification of divine transcendence, and especially to remind us that the world of manifest forms, including preeminently human consciousness, is in its deepest identity one essence with the divine ground.

A complementary vision, but one that emphasizes the moral dimension of our participation in transcendent being, is found in Plato's *Gorgias*, arising from the argument between Socrates and Callicles about whether it is preferable to commit or to suffer injustice. The argument raises a question unavoidable in any serious analysis of moral experience: does human consciousness truly participate in eternal being, and is there consequently, in some mystery beyond our knowing, a moral resolution to the human drama? Is it reasonable to believe that, in Martin Luther King Jr.'s words, "the arc of the moral universe is long, but it bends toward justice"? Plato addresses the question by concluding the *Gorgias* with Socrates telling a tale about judgment after

25. Easwaran, *The Upanishads*, 209. Easwaran's use of the language of "immanence" and "transcendence" appears to take some liberties of translation, but these do not seem unwarranted. Compare the more literal translation of Swami Nikhilananda: "Into a blind darkness they enter who worship only the unmanifested prakriti [reality-principle prior to the manifestation of names and forms]; but into a greater darkness they enter who worship the manifested Hiranyagarbha [one of the names of the creator-god, Brahma; literally, 'golden egg,' the first manifestation of the Absolute in the relative, manifold universe, and in potency all future forms and individual consciousnesses]. . . . He who knows that both the unmanifested prakriti and the manifested Hiranyagarbha should be worshipped together, overcomes death by the worship of Hiranyagarbha and obtains immortality through devotion to prakriti" (verses 12, 14) (*The Upanishads*, 91–92; see also 42–44, 47–48, 90 n. 15, 91 n. 23, 370.

death—"a very fine tale," Socrates states, which his listeners may consider "fiction," but which he intends to recount as if it were "actual truth" (523a).

After a person dies, the tale goes, the soul endures, and he or she must stand before divine judges (the "sons of Zeus") for moral examination and subsequent deliverance to deserved rewards or punishments. Sound judgments are possible because of the soul's "nakedness": once the soul has been stripped by death of its body and all physical possessions and adornments, there are no distractions to hinder the judges from making an accurate assessment of its true state of moral health or corruption. Everyone must stand before the judges, the judgments are fair, and no escape or deception is possible. The tale, with its vivid details, persuades us "that we should be more on our guard against doing than suffering wrong," and encourages us "to live and die in the pursuit of righteousness and all other virtues." Socrates concludes his account, and the dialogue, by urging his listeners to take the story to heart (523a–527e).[26] Plato clearly wishes us to do the same, not as a statement of known facts, but as a story that points toward an ultimate truth. As a fable that brings the question of justice to imaginative completion, the myth of judgment testifies to Plato's confidence that the known facts of human moral struggle in this world suggest a meaningful resolution, but testifies at the same time to his recognition that such a resolution is a mystery beyond worldly and historical experience.

Fifteen hundred years after Plato, in the teachings of the great Sufi mystic and poet Jalāl ad-Dīn ar-Rūmī (1207–1273), a vision of cosmic justice grounded in transcendence is articulated in terms of divine love, with the finite universe presented as a hierarchy of being that in its totality is an incarnation of God's love:

> It's waves of love that make the heavens turn
> Without that love the universe would freeze:
>   no mineral absorbed by vegetable
>   no growing thing consumed by animal
>   no sacrifice of anima for Him
>   Who inspired Mary with His pregnant breath
>   Like ice, all of them unmoved, frozen stiff
>   No vibrant molecules in swarms of motion
> Lovers of perfection, every atom

26. Translations are from *Gorgias*, 303–7.

turns sapling-like to face the sun and grow
Their haste to shed their fleshly form for soul
sings out an orison of praise to God
(*Masnavi* 5:3853–59)

Rūmī adds to his vision an explicit pluralism that sees human beings of all religions in all cultures as authentic partners in the unfolding drama of human-divine encounter. The search for the divine ground of existence is universal, deriving from God's universal love, which, as it expresses itself in the cultural particulars of language, creed, and ritual, unites those particulars as it transcends them. God urges us, in Rūmī's verses, to recognize that all worshipers respond to the same flux of divine presence:

I have given everyone a character
I have given each a terminology
(*Masnavi* 2:1754)

Hindus praise me in the terms of India
and the Sindis praise in terms from Sind
I am not made pure by their magnificats
It is they who become pure and precious
We do not look to language or to words
We look inside to find intent and rapture
(*Masnavi* 2:1757–59)

Every prophet, every saint has his path
but as they return to God, all are one
(*Masnavi* 1:3086)

Love's folk live beyond religious borders
The community and creed of lovers: God
(*Masnavi* 2:1770)[27]

27. Translations by Franklin D. Lewis in his *Rumi—Past and Present, East and West: The Life, Teachings, and Poetry of Jalâl al-Din Rumi,* 406, 417. The *Masnavi,* or *Mathnawi* ("Spiritual Couplets"), is Rūmī's magnum opus, a twenty-six thousand–line work of Persian poetry in six books, which combines theological explication, folk stories, lyric flights, wild humor, spiritual direction, and more. Besides the *Masnavi,* Rūmī left a large collection of shorter poems. One of the most loved and influential figures of the Muslim world, revered by many as a saint, Rūmī was trained as a preacher and jurist, and was the founder of the Sufi order called the Mevlevi, or Whirling Dervishes. His verse often expresses an ecstatic spirituality, deeply grounded in the religious traditions of Islam, Christianity, and Judaism. Recent decades have seen an explosion

Here we find a vision of the finite world, divine transcendence, and the drama of humanity that fulfills the first three of our criteria, while hinting that history is essentially a transfigurative process involving the transformation of finite being, through the medium of human knowing and loving, into conscious participation in transcendent being.

Such a vision of the transfigurative function of human consciousness is explicit in the poetry of Rainer Maria Rilke (1875–1926), in whose masterpiece, the *Duino Elegies* (1923), we find the following passage:

> . . . *truly* being here is so much; because everything here
> apparently needs us, this fleeting world, which in some
> strange way
> keeps calling to us. . . .
>
> . . . Perhaps we are *here* in order to say: house,
> bridge, fountain, gate, pitcher, fruit-tree, window—
> at most: column, tower. . . . But to *say* them, you must
> understand,
> oh to say them *more* intensely than the Things themselves
> ever dreamed of existing. . . .
>
> *Here* is the time for the *sayable, here* is its homeland.
> Speak and bear witness. . . .
>
> Earth, isn't this what you want: to arise within us,
> *invisible?* Isn't it your dream
> to be wholly invisible someday?—O Earth: invisible!
> What, if not transformation, is your urgent command?
> (*The Ninth Elegy,* 11–13, 32–36, 43–44, 68–71)[28]

Rilke's vision confirms that the life of balanced consciousness is that of mediating—of functioning as a loving intermediary between—the truths and values of the finite world and their transcendent source and fulfillment, and of

of English translations of his work, many by the American poet Coleman Barks. In 1997 the *Christian Science Monitor* reported that he had become the best-selling poet in the United States (Lewis, *Rumi,* 1). Lewis's book is the best scholarly overview on Rūmī available in English to date, situating his teachings, life, and poetry in its original context of Muslim tradition; explaining its impact on the Muslim world; and presenting a history of Rūmī scholarship that includes an account of his reception in the West and an assessment of English translations.

28. Rilke, *The Selected Poetry of Rainer Maria Rilke,* 199–203.

embracing one's part in the mystery of transformation that human knowing and loving entail.

Finally, we may consider the vision of T. S. Eliot's *Four Quartets* (1936–1942), a sequence of four poems constituting a Christian meditation on existence, time, death, and tradition. As with Rūmī, and true to Christian teaching, the ground of reality is affirmed to be transcendent divine love, itself beyond time and desiring, that nonetheless suffers manifestation as desire in the divinely caused movement of creaturely longing and love:

> Love is itself unmoving,
> Only the cause and end of movement,
> Timeless, and undesiring
> Except in the aspect of time
> Caught in the form of limitation
> Between un-being and being.
> ("Burnt Norton," 163–68)

Human consciousness, where finite reality participates knowingly in transcendent freedom and love, is the place where immanent being is directly permeable by divine action—where creatureliness can know and conform to divine presence in consciousness, as Jesus is understood to have actualized in fullness, although most of us barely comprehend his, or our, condition:

> The hint half guessed, the gift half understood, is
> Incarnation.
> Here the impossible union
> Of spheres of existence is actual,
> Here the past and future
> Are conquered, and reconciled . . .
> ("The Dry Salvages," 215–19)

Past and future are ultimately embraced and transcended through the participation of incarnate human consciousness in the timeless meaning of divine being. Recognizing this, we can come to see that history is more than a mere process of chronological development:

> It seems, as one becomes older,
> That the past has another pattern, and ceases to be a mere
> sequence—

> Or even development: the latter a partial fallacy,
> Encouraged by superficial notions of evolution,
> Which becomes, in the popular mind, a means of disowning the
> past.
> ("The Dry Salvages," 85–89)

History, rather, is the worldwide unfolding in time of the participation of existing, situated human beings in timeless meaning. It is "a pattern / Of timeless moments" ("Little Gidding," 234–35).

To be sure, to radically transform oneself in attunement with the hint and gift of Incarnation, to embody in one's life the vision of transcendence, belongs only to spiritual genius:

> Men's curiosity searches past and future
> And clings to that dimension. But to apprehend
> The point of intersection of the timeless
> With time, is an occupation for the saint . . .
> ("The Dry Salvages," 199–202)

And saints are rare. Still, though, every human consciousness has its moments of apprehension, its intimations of the depths, when the timeless perfection of meaning that grounds the universe is glimpsed—moments of personal vision that, if remembered, can inform and inspire our everyday lives:

> For most of us, there is only the unattended
> Moment, the moment in and out of time,
> The distraction fit, lost in a shaft of sunlight,
> The wild thyme unseen, or the winter lightning
> Or the waterfall, or music heard so deeply
> That it is not heard at all, but you are the music
> While the music lasts. These are only hints and guesses,
> Hints followed by guesses; and the rest
> Is prayer, observance, discipline, thought and action.
> ("The Dry Salvages," 206–14)[29]

As with the previous examples, the ambient vision of *Four Quartets* reminds us that, in Voegelin's words, "[t]he divine reality that reveals its presence in the meditative act is both within Being as its creative core and outside

29. Eliot, *Four Quartets,* 122, 132, 136, 144.

of Being in some Beyond of it," and it urges us to be faithful to our roles as loving mediators between world and divine ground.[30] In addition, through its meditation on historical meaning, it assists us in resisting the deformed notions of history—unilinear, immanentist, gnostic, apocalyptic, and nihilistic—that in their dominance of contemporary thought eclipse the truth of the human condition, blunting and misguiding our desires.

This sampling of visionary insights from four civilizational traditions indicates that we are hardly bereft of images, symbols, myths, art, literature, and philosophical and religious guidance to remind and inspire us with regard to our situation as participants in the In-Between of reality. On the contrary: as never before, the discoveries and teachings of the world's wisdom traditions are available in abundance, amid the general glut of information, in bookstores, libraries, and, with a few clicks, on our computer screens. And despite the contemporary absence of convincing public myths, despite the fragmentations of community, the confusions about the relation of scientific to religious truth, the suspicions about metanarratives—despite all these, the hunger for insights into experiences of transcendence pervades our culture. A widespread and energetic, if largely uncritical, search for spiritual bearings is a hallmark of the age. As David Walsh states, "Our cultural self-understanding may not have the same substantive grasp on the symbols of spiritual illumination [that prior cultures have enjoyed] . . . but this does not mean that it is tone-deaf to the call of transcendent truth."[31]

Of course, the call of transcendent truth will be able to shape balanced imaginations only if certain conditions are met. For those already inclined toward spiritual insights, the pitfalls of fundamentalism, "New Age" fantasies, neopaganism, occultism, and other misguided spiritual enthusiasms will be difficult to avoid unless the culture at large becomes more successful at providing individuals with the tools of critical discernment that make possible interpretations of experiences of transcendence that are both philosophically nuanced and historically responsible.

The more basic problem, though, is the skepticism about transcendence that lies at the heart of modernity. Due to the overwhelming success of modern images of world and self as parts of a self-contained immanentist universe, any "call of transcendent truth" tends to be treated categorically as a

30. Voegelin, "Beginning and Beyond," in *What Is History?* 221.
31. Walsh, *Guarded by Mystery,* 150.

matter of "blind faith," by which is meant a willed belief in what fully contradicts both reason and common sense. And so the idea of transcendence, whether given credence or not, is typically conceived as referring to some kind of superbeing beyond the universe, a "beyond" of which we could not possibly have any experience, but which our hopes and fears could lead us to have a blind, irrational "faith" in. A balanced response to the call of transcendent truth must involve some degree of recognition that transcendence is not an "out there," *but a realm of meaning in which we immediately participate*—a realm of meaning that, even as it points toward a divine ground beyond all participation, is immediately present, both as the formative divine presence in finite reality and as the flux of divine presence in human consciousness.

Above all, the immanentist model of human consciousness must be recognized for the deformation it is. Both the modern image of the self as a "thinking thing" *(res cogitans)* inside a body thing and the postmodern image of the person as a purely temporal and contingent project of narrative construction are fundamentally misleading, because they eclipse the fact that human consciousness is an incarnate Question whose deepest identity is participation in the Mystery of radical transcendence. Nevertheless, the modern and postmodern models of the person are not easily overcome, deeply rooted as they are in cherished sentiments of progress. Our next chapter, then, will consider some of the difficulties involved in revising the modern and postmodern anthropologies, so as to recover a balanced awareness of human consciousness as the In-Between of time and timelessness, of finite insight and transcendent presence.

8

ANTHROPOLOGY
The Problem of Divine Presence in Human Consciousness

> [I]t is peculiar to the nature of man that it unfolds its potentialities historically. Not that historically anything "new" comes up—human nature is always wholly present—but there are modes of clarity and degrees of comprehensiveness in man's understanding of himself and his position in the world.
>
> —Eric Voegelin, letter to Robert B. Heilman

A NUMBER of twentieth-century philosophers in addition to Voegelin have worked to establish a sophisticated philosophical anthropology, a philosophy of human nature, that reveals human consciousness as the In-Between of time and timelessness, of localized individual existence and transcendent divine presence. Prominent among them are the phenomenologist Max Scheler, the existentialists Karl Jaspers and Gabriel Marcel, and the Jewish philosopher and "trans-phenomenologist" Emmanuel Levinas.[1] Each of these anthropologies is indebted to that of Søren Kierkegaard (1813–1855), especially as presented in his "psychological expositions" *The Concept of Anxiety* (1844) and *The Sickness unto Death* (1849), intricate works that analyze the

1. For introductions to these philosophical anthropologies, see Scheler, *Man's Place in Nature;* Jaspers, *Philosophy;* Marcel, *The Mystery of Being;* and Levinas, *Ethics and Infinity: Conversations with Philippe Nemo* and *Basic Philosophical Writings.* The term *trans-phenomenologist* comes from Adriaan T. Peperzak's preface to the latter volume. For an astute analysis of the problems of twentieth-century philosophical anthropology with particular attention to Scheler and Voegelin, see David J. Levy, *Political Order: Philosophical Anthropology, Modernity, and the Challenge of Ideology.*

problematic of human existence as "a synthesis of the infinite and the finite, of the temporal and the eternal," and of human consciousness as the place "whereby time constantly intersects eternity and eternity constantly pervades time."[2] Among Kierkegaard's successors it is Voegelin, I would argue, who has gone furthest in following up and providing answers to the questions that such an anthropology raises regarding political philosophy, philosophy of history, and a truly global philosophy of religion—questions that must be addressed in order to speak to the increasingly historical-minded and global culture of our time.

Literary counterparts to these philosophical anthropologies can be found, as we have seen, in the writings of modern masters such as Yeats, Mann, Pound, Eliot, Rilke, and Auden. Still, one may say that, altogether, these philosophical and literary efforts have had little impact on prevailing modern and postmodern conceptions of human nature, which remain aggressively immanentist. The struggle to restate for contemporary culture, in a properly sophisticated manner, the most fundamental shared insight of the world's wisdom traditions—that human consciousness *participates* in the understanding, freedom, and creativity of divine transcendent being—has borne little fruit. Immanentist anthropologies are too firmly associated with civilizational progress and enlightened values to be successfully challenged on a broad front. For the majority of the intelligentsia, anthropological assumptions continue to be shaped, as they have for two centuries, by the "cultured despisers of religion" (Friedrich Schleiermacher), and even religious believers for the most part must try—sometimes desperately—to reconcile their ideas of "God" and "faith" with unconsciously absorbed immanentist images of self and world. So modern and postmodern anthropologies have eclipsed, for many, the elemental experience of consciousness as divine-human encounter. To adapt T. S. Eliot's phrase, everyone has had the experience, but many have missed the meaning.

In preceding chapters some of the reasons for the success of the immanentist models have been touched upon: the impact on modern imagination of scientific and technological achievement; a growing cultural sensitivity to historical particularity; a desire for control and predictability; a resistance to uncertainty and mystery; a linking of the notion of transcendence with oppressively totalizing systems of thought. Along the way, also, we have repeatedly noted that an effective critique of the immanentist models and the many

2. Kierkegaard, *The Concept of Anxiety,* 89; *The Sickness unto Death,* 13.

sources of resistance to transcendence requires an adequate understanding of the "differentiation" of consciousness, the historical process through which the one cosmos came to be diffracted into distinct realms of finite and transcendent meaning. Now it is time to consider the process of differentiation more carefully, to examine in some detail its permutations and perplexities. In doing so, it will become clear that the spiritual and philosophical confusions of modernity have been, to some degree, an unavoidable outcome of this differentiating process, and that consequently their solution lies, to that same degree, in learning to integrate what has been differentiated.

Differentiation

Eric Voegelin and Bernard Lonergan both present detailed accounts of the historical process of differentiating consciousness, with usefully complementary emphases. We will draw on both philosophers to guide the following discussion, which must begin by uniting, in a summarizing account, points made in preceding chapters about the nature of human consciousness.

Differentiation is a process in which the emergence of distinctions, or the actualization of potentialities, occurs within a whole that remains constant. What remains constant about human consciousness at all times is its character as a distinctive mode of participation in reality. It is that mode of participation in which a locus in reality *becomes aware of itself* as existing, as wondering about its existence, as wanting to know and learning about the order of things and structures in reality, as seeking its fulfillment, and as searching for the meaning of existence. It is, one might say, *illuminated* participation in reality. It is a site within reality where reality emerges into a questioning concern about itself, a situated consciousness drawn by awareness of its own ignorance, as well as by anxiety, curiosity, hope, trust, and love, to expand its understanding about itself, about the encompassing process in which it participates, and about the ultimate purpose or ground of reality. Because this seeking and being drawn are the essence of consciousness, Voegelin describes consciousness as a *tension,* and because it is a participation in reality, as a *participatory tension.*[3]

3. In "Equivalences of Experience," Voegelin has constructed a list of seven propositions regarding the constant structure of human existence, beginning with the "fundamental proposition" that "Man participates in the process of reality," and then identifying six "implications" and "corollaries" of this proposition with regard to the human relationship to reality and truth (see *Published Essays, 1966–1985*, 120–21).

Building on this initial description of human consciousness as a constant of participatory tension, further constants may be elaborated. A first constant has to do with *awareness of the ground of being.* Human conscious existence is always aware that it is not its own cause, not its own ground, and so there is at the heart of human concern the question about the ground. "Man," states Voegelin, "is not a self-created, autonomous being carrying the origin and meaning of his existence within himself. He is not a divine *causa sui.*" A human being is aware that his or her own essential identity and ultimate meaning will be found only through finding the ground of reality, and so an awareness of ontological dependence together with curiosity and attraction keep every human consciousness oriented as a "tension toward the ground."[4]

A second constant pertains to *awareness of participation.* Consciousness is always aware that its own reality is not something separate from either the process of reality or the ground of reality of which it is aware. "Reality . . . is not a thing confronting man, but the comprehending reality in which he himself is real by participating in it." Reality, in other words, *embraces* consciousness; consciousness is an illuminated irruption *inside* reality. Like all other participating structures, consciousness emerges from the ground of reality not as an extrusion from reality but as an individuation *within* it. "Consciousness is the experience of participation, namely, of man's participation in his ground of being."[5]

A third constant pertains to *meaning as the object of human searching.* As humans we naturally and spontaneously seek insight into (1) particulars concerning the order of reality in which we participate, including the ground of reality, and (2) the means toward our personal and communal fulfillment—with insight into (2) obviously dependent on insight into (1). Now, consciousness illuminates the reality in which it emerges through its apprehension and naming of the intelligible things, attributes, and relations that constitute the order of reality. So the human search is always a search for meanings, and not only for the meanings that constitute the given cosmos, but also for meanings of its own devising, the creative insights and constructions required for and aiming at the proper management of existence, from which arise the vast and

4. Voegelin, "Reason: The Classic Experience," in *Published Essays, 1966–1985,* 268. For a detailed theoretical exposition of conscious existence in its character as a "tension toward the ground," see Voegelin, "What Is Political Reality?" in *Anamnesis,* 345–73.

5. Voegelin, "What Is Political Reality?" in *Anamnesis,* 361, 373. See Voegelin, "Equivalences of Experience," in *Published Essays, 1966–1985,* 120.

complex worlds of social life, institutions, technology, and culture. The desire to understand the order of what is, as well as the order of what may be and what ought to be, belongs to the very structure of consciousness.

A fourth constant is *the cosmos itself.* All searching and understanding occur within the one whole of reality. As the human search has advanced, the understood structures in the order of being have multiplied, and the understood relations have become ever more complex, but the cosmos for all that does not disintegrate; the cosmos is the encompassing whole within which all meanings are understood. As distinct realms of meaning have been differentiated and related to each other, images of the one whole of reality, and conceptions of its basic structure, have indeed changed. There remains, though, the one cosmos as the constant "background," as it were, against which all such changes take place.[6]

It perhaps goes without saying that any of these constants pertaining to the essential nature of consciousness can be forgotten, ignored, or denied—that consciousness can have more or less "transparency in its self-understanding," to use a phrase of Voegelin.[7] It is only on the basis of recognizing these constants of consciousness, however, that the adventure of *differentiating* consciousness—the historical unfolding of the human potentiality for distinguishing and relating different realms of meaning in reality—can be made sense of.

Because throughout this book we have been addressing that aspect of differentiating consciousness that involves the explicit discovery of transcendent meaning, we can be relatively brief here in summarizing that differentiation and its impact, before moving on to consider both other types of differentiation and the problems of subsequent integration.

When the divine ground is recognized to be incommensurate with the finite universe, the cosmos differentiates into the two realms of immanent and transcendent being. As the cognitive source of this bifurcation, consciousness

6. In *The Ecumenic Age,* Voegelin says: "The cosmos is not a thing among others; it is the background of reality against which all existent things exist" (122). This, again, indicates why Voegelin deems critically unsound the Hindu and Buddhist conceptions of an infinitely reborn cosmos. In these traditions, he would say, consequent to the differentiation of transcendence "the cosmos" is improperly reified through identification with the immanent universe only; imaginatively sheered off from the transcendent ground, it is thus conceived as a "thing" that can be endlessly reborn. See Chapter 3 above, pp. 78–79.

7. Voegelin, "What Is Political Reality?" in *Anamnesis,* 351.

itself undergoes *the differentiation of actuating its capacity to approach, distinguish, and understand in their different characters the two realms of meaning thus illuminated.* The object of human concern remains all the while the intelligible order of reality; reality as a whole consists of intelligible meaning. The divine ground, however, is now revealed to be a realm of intelligible meaning that transcends both the conditions of space and time and direct human understanding. Transcendent being is recognized as the absolute, self-sufficient intelligibility that completes the incomplete intelligibility of the finite universe. It is the Mystery disclosed as the goal of the human Question.

It is important to remember that this differentiation *adds* nothing to reality, but only conceptually distinguishes areas of meaning *already present* in reality as apprehended by predifferentiated consciousness. A transcendent dimension that has heretofore been conceptually interfused, to some degree, with worldly or thingly reality—a dimension symbolized in terms of the mysterious powers of the gods, or a primal god, or a highest and "hidden" god—emerges into the clarity of a determinate and distinct realm of meaning "beyond" space and time. As a result of this differentiation the basic *image* of reality is altered; indeed, the conception of its basic structure undergoes a profound change. Nevertheless, "[t]he Being of the cosmos remains the Being that it was, because the Beyond was present in it even before its presence revealed itself in the act of transcendence." Likewise, in the self-apprehension of the conscious subject there is a corresponding differentiation of what was already present but undifferentiated. One's initial or rudimentary or mythopoetic apprehension of the divine ground, rooted in what Lonergan calls an elementary "experience of the mystery of love and awe," is already a response to the *presence* of transcendent meaning, but now self-understanding is raised to the explicit cognizance of one's participation in a radically transcendent mystery of "absolute intelligence and intelligibility, absolute truth and reality, absolute goodness and holiness."[8]

There are three further points to be emphasized once again about this differentiation of transcendent meaning, before leaving the topic for the last time. The first is that transcendent meaning is found nowhere but in consciousness. The insights that discover transcendence, declares Voegelin, "pertain directly only to man's consciousness of his existential tension," to

8. Voegelin, "Beginning and Beyond," in *What Is History?* 220; Lonergan, *Method in Theology,* 113, 116.

meditative or self-reflective or prayerful experiences in which it is inwardly realized that the unrestricted search for meaning must have as its ultimate goal a spaceless and timeless reality. It is therefore proclaimed, in the world's great religious and philosophical traditions, that the true ground is to be found "within," that is, in the depths of the heart or psyche or soul. "The God whom I love," says the sixteenth-century Indian mystic Kabir, "is inside." "He is the breath inside the breath."[9] This means, too, that no one can recognize the truth of the Beyond who does not succeed in performing the meditative or self-reflective or prayerful steps that lead to the differentiating insights. The differentiation of transcendence is not achieved by a more careful inspection and understanding of the physical universe. One's conception of reality will embrace and incorporate it only if one has trustingly carried through one's search for the true ground to the point where the unrestricted scope of one's questioning is met by the inward revelation of unrestricted being. This existential precondition for apprehending the truth of transcendence is underscored by Voegelin: "There is no Beyond lying around somewhere, to be or not to be included in somebody's 'system'; there is no differentiated insight concerning the Beyond and its presence in the cosmos at all, as long as there is no experience of its . . . presence in the act of meditation."[10]

The second point is that consciousness, by discovering transcendence "within" itself, discovers that it is itself not a finite "thing" like other worldly things but rather a something that, while not unqualifiedly divine, *shares in* the nature of divine transcendence. Consciousness becomes aware not only that it participates in reality, but also that it is an eminent type of participation, an immediate participation in the distinctively divine mode of being. It discovers its own nature to be unique among worldly creatures in being *coconstituted by* transcendent divine presence, a presence reaching into individual consciousness from the "unrevealed divine reality beyond its revelation" and inviting it to align itself with divine wisdom and goodness. Through discernment of the distinction between the immanent and transcendent realms of meaning, then, consciousness discerns that it is itself neither immanent

9. Voegelin, *The Ecumenic Age,* 52; Robert Bly, ed. and trans., *The Kabir Book: Forty-four of the Ecstatic Poems of Kabir,* 6, 33. For Voegelin's brief treatment of the metaphor of the "divine Within" in the context of an analysis of a passage from an Essene text, the "Apocalypse of Abraham," see *The Ecumenic Age,* 395–98.

10. Voegelin, "Beginning and Beyond," in *What Is History?* 221.

nor transcendent, but the site of their conscious interpenetration. The participatory tension of human consciousness is revealed as the *metaxy,* as the human-divine In-Between, as the ongoing "meeting between man and the Beyond of his heart."[11]

The differentiation of the transcendent realm of meaning, then, provides the basis for the first anthropologies, like those of Greek philosophy and of Upanishadic and Buddhist teachings, that delineate the nature of human being as "a synthesis of the finite and the infinite, the temporal and the eternal," to use Kierkegaard's formulation, and of human consciousness as limited participation in the limitless intelligence and creativity of divine transcendence. They make clear that the human search for meaning is itself a localized upwelling, as it were, of the divine being of thought or intelligence—that every human being, as Voegelin puts it, "is moved to his search of the ground by the divine ground of which he is in search," that the divine ground is a "moving partner" in the search for meaning. This partnership is *experienced,* of course, as a single movement of consciousness. However, within this one movement there may be distinguished the two "poles," as Voegelin calls them, of (1) the divine partner that initiates the search and serves as its ultimate goal, and (2) the human partner who questions and understands, fears and hopes, cooperates or resists cooperation, as seeker and actor.[12] No later refinements in anthropology annul this first principle of analysis, however profoundly they may explain the complexities of physical, chemical, biological, psychological, intellectual, linguistic, social, and cultural structures that constitute human being. Whatever its multitudes of conditioning elements, human nature remains preeminently defined by its distinctive mode of participation in reality: human existence is a participatory tension of consciousness in which finite cognition and transcendent presence meet and interpenetrate.

11. Voegelin, *In Search of Order,* 114; *The Ecumenic Age,* 398.

12. Voegelin, "Reason: The Classic Experience," in *Published Essays, 1966–1985,* 271; *The Ecumenic Age,* 252; "The Gospel and Culture," in *Published Essays, 1966–1985,* 183. Voegelin regularly warns of the fundamental interpretive error of "hypostatizing" the poles of the one movement or tension of consciousness, of treating them as "objects independent of the tension in which they are experienced as its poles" ("Reason: The Classic Experience," 280). For his basic explication of consciousness as a tension between "poles" of human and divine reality, or temporal and eternal being, see esp. "Eternal Being in Time," 320–30; "What Is Political Reality?" 373–81, both in *Anamnesis;* and, in the context of his most concentrated account of the Platonic-Aristotelian analysis of this structural aspect of human consciousness, "Reason: The Classic Experience," 267–83.

A third point, though it has broad ramifications for intellectual history, must be stated briefly. The discovery of transcendence is the *natural* outcome of the search for the true ground of the intelligible universe. It is the discovery, by reason, of the mysterious source of all intelligible order—a discovery prompted by the "moving partner" of divine presence in consciousness, and guided by anticipatory trust in the meaningfulness of reality. It is *reason* that follows our unrestricted desire to know to the insight that the incomplete meaning of the finite universe, if it is to be fully intelligible, must be grounded in a transcendent mystery of self-sufficient meaning. Therefore, the "faith" that cognitively affirms and stays existentially open to the mystery of transcendent being is *reasonable.* In this basic sense, then, "faith" is not antithetical to reason or to common sense. It is, rather, as Lonergan describes it, "the knowledge born of religious love," the reasonable affirmation of an ultimate coherence and goodness, and the corresponding commitment to ordering one's existence through a loving and hopeful relation to an essentially mysterious ground of reality. All notions that such faith involves a denial or crippling of reason reflect an elementary confusion about the experiences that have given rise to symbols of transcendence.[13]

13. Lonergan, *Method in Theology,* 115. The standard view that sound philosophy and science and common sense are the fruit of reason, while "faith" in transcendent being is an antirational act of belief in a reality strictly beyond human experience, reflects a gross falsification, Voegelin explains, of both the structure of human consciousness as a mutual participation of human and divine and of the Greek philosophical experiences from which the Western concept of reason first emerged. The analysis of human consciousness that unfolds in the thought of the pre-Socratics, Plato, and Aristotle reveals that the human difference—the presence of rational consciousness *(psyche noetike)*—is precisely the activity of the ordering movements of a finite intellect (nous) that *participates* in the divine intellect (Nous) that orders the cosmos. Thus, in the Greek analysis, the philosophical illumination of the structure and meaning (logos) of human consciousness is no less "revelatory," as a process initiated and guided by the divine partner in the movement of thought, than it is a "rational" process of human questioning and understanding. The interpretive occlusion, in the course of Western history, of the "revelatory" component in the Greek explication of rational consciousness—a component about which the philosophers themselves were quite clear in their writings—is blamed by Voegelin on two main factors. First, there is the ease with which imagination separates the human and divine "poles" of the interpenetrative tension of consciousness into the two unconnected "things" of a human seeker and a divine ground being sought. Second, there is the problem of what Voegelin calls the Christian "monopolizing" of the revelatory component in differentiated experiences of the divine ground ("The Gospel and Culture," in *Published Essays, 1966–1985,* 187). For Voegelin's account of the roles of faith and love in the exercise of reason, and of the rationality of faith, together with a critique of the standard dichotomy between "reason" and "revelation," see "Reason: The Classic Experience," "The Gospel and Culture," and "Immortality: Experience and Symbol," all in *Published Essays, 1966–1985;* and "Beginning and Beyond," in *What Is History?*

Thus far it has been Voegelin's treatment of the differentiating capacities of consciousness we have been tracing, a treatment that concentrates heavily, indeed almost exclusively, on the differentiation of immanent and transcendent realms of meaning, in line with Voegelin's conviction that the problem of transcendence constitutes "the decisive problem of philosophy."[14] However, in Bernard Lonergan's complementary account of the history of differentiating consciousness, two additional differentiations, and their corresponding realms of meaning, receive careful attention. Through a consideration of this feature of Lonergan's cognitional analysis, we will be able to situate our anthropological problem—the problem of giving proper due to transcendent divine presence in human consciousness—more carefully on the contemporary horizon, by appreciating the challenges that *multiple* differentiations of consciousness present to attaining a balanced understanding of self and reality in the contemporary world.

Multiple Differentiations

The discovery of the transcendent realm of meaning releases the universe of space and time into the conceptual autonomy of "immanence." However, this immanent dimension of reality, Lonergan explains, once adequately distinguished from the numinous potency and mystery of the divine ground, can itself be approached and understood in two fundamentally distinct ways. The first of these may be described as the everyday manner of relating to the world—the secular concern with personal encounters and social involvements, with solving practical tasks, with entertainment and enjoyment, and in general with shaping a successful performance in the drama of living. Lonergan calls this mode of relating to the world "common sense," and the meanings that are its concern the "realm of common sense." It is the realm of meaning to which everyday language refers, the world equally of the child, the hard-nosed businessman, the sculptor, and the marriage counselor. It is what we typically mean by the word *world*. "The realm of common sense," states Lonergan,

> is the realm of persons and things in their relations to us. It is the visible universe peopled by relatives, friends, acquaintances, fellow citizens, and

14. Emberley and Cooper, *Faith and Political Philosophy*, 34.

> the rest of humanity. We come to know it . . . by a self-correcting process of learning, in which insights gradually accumulate, coalesce, qualify and correct one another, until a point is reached where we are able to meet situations as they arise, size them up by adding a few more insights to the acquired store, and so deal with them in an appropriate fashion. Of the objects in this realm we speak in everyday language, in which words have the function . . . of completing [our focusing] on the things, of crystallizing our attitudes, expectations, intentions, of guiding all our actions.[15]

But there is still another manner of approaching the meanings that make up the immanent universe. A clue as to its difference appears at the beginning of the quotation above, in which Lonergan describes the realm of common sense as the realm of persons and things *in their relations to us.* In the exploration of the differentiated world of finite being, there arises a desire to understand things more rigorously, more systematically, than in terms of how they appear to our shifting perceptions or of how they satisfy our personal or practical needs and desires. There is in human knowing what Lonergan calls a "systematic exigence," a built-in demand of the inquiring spirit to understand what is *invariable* about things, to understand things not in terms of how they present themselves to observing subjects but in terms of what they are in themselves, in terms of their *intrinsic* properties. This is the type of concern and understanding the ancient Greeks called *theoria* (theory), and from it has arisen what we generally call science and scientific theory.[16]

The fundamental distinguishing feature of scientific or theoretical understanding is that it offers *systematic explanations* of objects in terms of "the relations constituted by their uniform interactions with one another," explanations that necessarily move beyond the imagination-based perspective of shifting points of view and commonsense descriptions. To explain things in terms of intrinsic properties and uniform interactions requires insights different from those of common sense, insights that open up a new, abstract conceptual field that constitutes a distinct realm of meaning. Anyone who has studied one of the natural sciences appreciates the difficulty involved in moving out of the commonsense realm and into the explanatory domain in the

15. Lonergan, *Method in Theology,* 81–82.

16. Ibid., 81. For an introductory account of Lonergan's analysis of the emergence of scientific understanding in the Greek world, and of its limitations in relation to the modern conception of science and theory, in the context of a general presentation of the career of differentiating consciousness, see 81–96.

pursuit of systematic knowledge of objects or processes, and of the necessity of learning a special technical language corresponding to the intelligibilities of explanatory science. Such study attends to the same world of objects, the same finite universe, as does common sense, but it approaches it from a quite different standpoint, and discloses meanings belonging to a distinct realm of understanding. "Mass, temperature, the electromagnetic field," Lonergan notes, "are not objects in the world of common sense." Their meanings *pertain* to the objects of everyday experience—because these are, after all, what scientific explanation explains—but, as technical terms, their meanings can be grasped only through comprehending their functions with related terms in often highly abstruse systems of theoretical explanation.[17]

So there is a second crucial differentiation of consciousness, arising with the development of scientific investigation and understanding, which separates the realm of theoretical meaning from the realm of common sense. Insofar as both realms of meaning concern intelligibilities of the finite universe, they are equally made ascertainable by the prior differentiation that separates the transcendent divine ground from immanent reality. Both the common-sense apprehension of the world and the scientific analysis of its structure are made possible by the conceptual discovery that the divine ground or essence consists of a transcendent realm of meaning, which renders the finite universe conceptually autonomous and frees it to be perceived "unencumbered by [cosmological] experiences and symbolizations of divine presence."[18]

This same disencumbering, as it turns out, opens up for human investigation yet another realm of meaning: the *interior* dimension of human being,

17. Ibid., 82, 258.

18. Voegelin, *The Ecumenic Age,* 301. Voegelin explains that science, as we understand the term, arose in the West, and specifically out of the Greek differentiation of transcendence, because the Greek differentiating experiences focused on the illumination of divine being as Intelligence (Nous), and correspondingly approached the world as constituted primarily by intelligibility, or form, inviting its investigation as a system of stable structures and dependable relations and regular events. "Cognitively structured reality . . . is correlative to the theophany of the Nous . . . . No science as the systematic exploration of structure in reality is possible, unless the world is intelligible; and the world is intelligible in relation to a psyche that has become luminous for the order of reality through the revelation of the one, divine ground of all being as the Nous" (301). Thus, Greek *noesis,* or rational-critical thought, "was the first to lay open the autonomous structure of the world for scientific investigation" ("What Is Political Reality?" in *Anamnesis,* 376).

the investigating human subject, whose operations of questioning and understanding, discerning and judging, bring to light all meanings whatsoever. As we have seen, the discovery of transcendence forces attention upon human consciousness, prompting the development of the first philosophical anthropologies, the first explications of the structures and operations of that mode of participating in reality that is at once a localized cognitive process and a sharing in transcendent divine presence. The classical Greek and Buddhist psychologies are already enormously intricate in their analysis of the operations of human consciousness. During the subsequent two millennia, of course, this realm of interiority, as Lonergan calls it, has been ever more profoundly and thoroughly explored. In the West, one can trace a line of development from Platonic-Aristotelian foundations through Augustinian self-inspection, Scholastic detailing of mental powers and acts, the modern "turn to the subject" associated with Descartes, Kant's synthesis of empiricist and rationalist epistemologies, the Hegelian analysis of the subject and Kierkegaardian exposition of the self, phenomenological and existentialist clarifications of conscious intentionality and Being-in-the-World, and the twentieth-century contributions of experimental and depth psychology. Lonergan's own examination of human consciousness, whose elements are laid out in his two principal works, *Insight* and *Method in Theology*, is perhaps the most broadly explanatory systematic analysis of the realm of interiority to date.

Thus, we have a further differentiation of consciousness to take into account, that which emerges when the inquiring human subject turns its attention upon itself and succeeds—through the labor of what Lonergan calls (as did Kierkegaard) "self-appropriation"—in discerning and explaining its own conscious activities as a field of intelligible structures, as an interior realm of meaning distinct both from the outer realms of common sense and theory and from the realm of transcendence.[19] So it is that "[i]n fully differentiated consciousness," Lonergan explains,

19. Lonergan notes that due to its systematic and explanatory character, the articulated appropriation of one's own interiority resembles theory. He points out, though, that the process of self-appropriation is unique in that it "is a heightening of intentional consciousness, an attending not merely to objects but also to the intending subject and his acts. And as this heightened consciousness constitutes the evidence for one's account of knowledge, such an account by the proximity of the evidence differs from all other expression" (*Method in Theology*, 83). It is one thing to explain the biological structure of a dog or the physical properties of atomic particles;

> there are four realms of meaning. There is the realm of common sense with its meanings expressed in everyday or ordinary language. There is the realm of theory where language is technical [and] simply objective in reference. . . . There is the realm of interiority [which speaks] of the subject and his operations [and] rests upon a self-appropriation that has verified in personal experience the operator, the operations, and the processes [of conscious intentionality]. Finally, there is the realm of transcendence in which the subject is related to divinity in the language of prayer and of prayerful silence.[20]

Historically, knowledge in all four realms develops. Common sense becomes more competent, more efficient in its devising of institutions, more inventive in its technologies, richer in its cultural and artistic achievements. Theory, proceeding in the West from its first phase in classical science through its sophistication and explosive expansion by means of the modern scientific method, becomes ever more powerful and refined in its explanations. Understanding of interiority deepens and broadens as indicated above. And insights into the realm of transcendent mystery advance, too, through the achievements of theology as well as through increasing clarity about the mystical experiences that ground the world's major religions. However, this ongoing advance of knowledge along many fronts hardly makes the general structure of reality more readily accessible and assimilable. On the contrary, the relentless expansion of increasingly specialized knowledge of structures in reality and the concomitant flow of human practical and cultural invention, combined with the difficulty of carefully distinguishing between the realms of meaning and of appreciating, coordinating, and integrating their respective insights—all of it the product of what Voegelin calls our "omnidimensional" desire to know—have rendered reality almost unmanageably complex and the drama of existence intensely confusing.[21]

---

it is another to explain the structural properties and procedures of the knowing subject whose operations produce sciences of biology and physics, as well as commonsense knowledge, and insight into the fact of transcendent being.

20. Ibid., 257. Lonergan later in the text indicates that a further division of realms of meaning can be helpful when analyzing the various domains of human inquiry and accomplishment; at one point he specifies a "realm of scholarship" and a "realm of art," noting that "[a]ny realm becomes differentiated from the others when it develops its own language, its own distinct mode of apprehension, and its own cultural, social, or professional group speaking in that fashion and apprehending in that manner." Still, common sense, theory, interiority, and transcendence constitute what he calls "the four basic realms of meaning" (272).

21. Voegelin, *The Ecumenic Age*, 301.

Integration

Such is a summary account of the multiple differentiations of consciousness that may be drawn from Voegelin's and Lonergan's writings. In light of this account, the principal contemporary challenge to achieving an adequately sophisticated and balanced understanding of what it means to be human may be formulated as follows.

As the multiple differentiations of consciousness have unfolded historically, the cultural legacy of insights into the order of reality has become ever more complex and its language ever more specialized, while still each person's understanding of reality has no option but to "begin primitively," as Kierkegaard puts it, in the primordial wonder and undifferentiated consciousness of childhood. This means that every person has the task of catching up to the historical stage of differentiated consciousness that he or she inhabits. *And only someone who has undergone the tutelage of first surmising, then suffering confusion about, and finally to some extent appropriating the differentiating insights that separate and relate the various realms of meaning is in a position to appreciate their various languages and truth claims.* The soundness of any contemporary interpretation of the human place in reality as a whole, then, will correspond more or less directly to the achieved degree of successfully differentiated, and consequently integrated, consciousness in the interpreter.

The next task is to delineate the range of problems this poses for a contemporary appreciation of transcendent divine presence in human consciousness. To do this, let us first briefly describe the impact of the process of differentiating consciousness on the experience and symbolization of transcendence. Then, we will consider a few of the problems that follow from insufficient familiarity with the various realms of meaning and the uncritical blending of their various languages.

In early cosmological societies, the understanding of reality is undifferentiated, or "compact," as Voegelin puts it. The realms of theory and interiority are not yet known, and the realm of transcendence, while surmised, is not yet distinguished precisely *as* transcendence. The mystery of divine being remains in some measure bound to spatiotemporal imagination. One could say that timeless meaning is perceived and responded to, but only through the prism of the descriptive understanding that belongs to common sense. So, Lonergan explains, in undifferentiated consciousness "the second and third realms [theory and interiority] do not exist, while the first and fourth [common sense and transcendence] interpenetrate." As a result, cosmological religion appears to us "rudimentary," because it uses commonsense procedures and language "indiscriminately" in its representation and interpretation of divine being.[22]

With the differentiation of transcendence in cultures East and West a clear distinction emerges between the realm known by common sense and the realm of divine transcendence. This, it must be restated, constitutes the first and elemental differentiation of consciousness, basic to the extraordinary social and philosophical developments of the so-called Axial Period of human history. For most human beings from then until the present, it has remained the only differentiation of any real significance in the search for self-understanding and fulfillment—the realms of theory and interiority being, relatively speaking, matters of specialized concern and education. "[I]n the history of mankind both in the East and the Christian West," Lonergan states, "the predominant differentiation of consciousness has set in opposition and in mutual enrichment the realms of common sense and of transcendence."[23]

This "enriching opposition" has brought forth a host of language symbols to signify the divine ground that is radically other than the world. The majority of these symbols come from everyday undifferentiated language, but in these cases the original meaning of the symbol has come to be used in a special, discriminating way for the purpose of disclosing the realm of meaning that transcends the world. For example, in China, the everyday word *Tao*, "the way," has become a symbol representing the transcendent principle that grounds and guides reality. In Western cultures the word *God*, derived from cosmological symbolizations of divine being as "the gods" and reflecting the personalistic character of experiences of unrestricted loving and being loved, has come to stand for the transcendent divine essence that, properly speaking, defies representation. To these examples could be added a long list of familiar terms and phrases referring to the realm of transcendent meaning: *heaven, the other shore, the next world*, and so on. Symbols of

22. Lonergan, *Method in Theology*, 84, 257. "In the earliest stage [of meaning], expression results from insight into sensible presentations and representations. There easily is pointed out the spatial but not the temporal, the specific but not the generic, the external but not the internal. . . . So it is by associating religious experience with its outward occasion that the experience becomes expressed and thereby something determinate and distinct for human consciousness" (108).

23. Ibid., 266.

transcendence fashioned from commonsense language—always, of course, subject to misinterpretation—have provided the basic lexicon for those who have achieved the elemental differentiation of consciousness.

When the realms of theory and interiority come to be recognized and explored, each of them, as well, enriches and complicates the understanding and symbolization of transcendence. Theory, as the systematic explanation of intrinsic properties and uniform relations, not only is applicable to the structures within immanent reality but can also be applied to the order of reality as a whole, systematically explaining that order in terms of the relational structure between transcendent and immanent being, the properties belonging to each of them, and the regularities governing their interactions. In this manner there arises formal theology, with its "technical unfolding" of religion, and along with it the inevitable tension between the evocative, metaphorical symbols used in everyday ritual and prayer and the dry, explanatory symbols of formal theology—between "the old commonsense apprehension instinct with feeling and the new theoretical apprehension devoid of feeling and bristling with definitions and theorems. So the God of Abraham, Isaac, and Jacob is set against the God of the philosophers and theologians."[24] Or, the gleeful worship of Krishna is set against the systematic discourses of the Upanishads.

The disclosure and clarification of the realm of interiority, too, produces its distinctive approach to the realm of transcendence. Here transcendent meaning is considered in terms of the procedures of human consciousness—the cognitional operations of questioning, longing, imagining, remembering, understanding, judging, loving. Thus, it is found, as with Augustine, that the human experience of time presupposes the experience of an eternal present; or it is recognized, as with Descartes, that the affirmation of one's own conscious existence presupposes some understanding of the divine perfection without which one could not conceive of one's own imperfect or participatory being; or it is revealed, as with Kierkegaard, that all ethical striving presupposes the eternal validity of moral meaning. In each of these cases transcendent meaning is approached in terms of the operations of human consciousness, with the meaningfulness of the language pertaining to transcendence dependent upon the insights that accompany self-appropriation.

24. Ibid., 114–15.

So each of the differentiations brings new subtlety and variety to the appreciation and expression of transcendent meaning. The elemental differentiation produces symbols for transcendence drawn from ordinary or commonsense language, like the spatial metaphor of *the Beyond.* The terms *transcendence* and *immanence,* by contrast, derive from theory, from the systematic explanation of the structure of reality as a whole, and have no sensory or imaginal referents; like terms of physical science such as *mass* and *force,* they do not refer to things, but rather are explanatory terms whose meanings are defined implicitly by their relation to each other—their function is "exegetic, not descriptive."[25] When the analysis of interiority reveals *questioning* to be the dynamic principle of human consciousness, and this questioning to be unrestricted in scope, the mystery of transcendent being may come to be defined as the ultimate *to-be-known* and *to-be-loved* of our conscious intentionality, in union with which we would find our natural fulfillment. Finally, the realm of transcendence may be approached directly through the "mystical mode" of apprehension, with its discipline of withdrawal from world and language, in which experiences of "all-absorbing self-surrender" leave as symbolic residue only such terms as *the ineffable* or *the silence.*[26] Each of these forms of expression has its proper place in the understanding and symbolization of transcendence; each complements and helps to illuminate the others.

To consciousness that is fully, or adequately, differentiated, these various styles of reference to transcendence are neither confusing nor off-putting. They are recognized as merely belonging to different modes of exploring the intelligible structures in reality, a reality that is still the one cosmos of human experience, despite its conceptual division into distinct realms of meaning. Such a consciousness understands, first of all, the legitimacy of symbols of transcendence, because it has meditatively reenacted the elemental differentiation; second, it is tolerant of the many languages—everyday, poetic, psychological, theological—that refer to transcendent meaning, and tolerant also of

25. Voegelin, "Beginning and Beyond," in *What Is History?* 185. In theoretically differentiated consciousness, Lonergan notes, "objects are apprehended . . . in their verifiable relations to one another. Hence, basic terms are defined implicitly by their relations to one another, and these relations in turn are established by an appeal to experience" (*Method in Theology,* 274). The experiences appealed to in establishing the relation between *transcendence* and *immanence* are those involved in the meditative steps that lead to the inward revelation of unrestricted being.

26. Lonergan, *Method in Theology,* 109–10, 273; Voegelin, "What Is Political Reality?" in *Anamnesis,* 397.

the mystic's insistence that all symbols of transcendence are a burden and an illusion. The tutelage of differentiation has allowed it to recognize its own "polymorphism," to use one of Lonergan's terms: to recognize its own capacity to uncover meaning in a variety of fundamentally different modes. So it is able to make sense of a world that presents it with the global varieties of religion, with the truth claims of science and the products of technology, with the revelations of psychological and philosophical analysis, and with the compelling insights of its own common sense, by having learned to distinguish and understand the separate realms of meaning and to relate the separate realms to one another. This is the unity of *integrated* consciousness—not to be confused, Lonergan notes, with the homogeneity of undifferentiated consciousness, with its indiscriminate use of common sense for religion, explanation, and self-knowledge. It is the unity of a consciousness that appreciates the validity of each realm of meaning, and that can relate to each other the otherwise fragmented languages and insights produced by the multiple differentiations of human understanding.[27]

However, such integrated consciousness is, needless to say, a rare achievement. In the contemporary world the predominant human condition is that of inchoately or incompletely differentiated consciousness, where language symbols deriving from the differentiations of the realms of transcendence, theory, and interiority blend uncritically with the perceptions and language of common sense. Most people, that is, operate comfortably in the realm of common sense and have an awareness of the other realms of meaning, but "their apprehension of these [other] realms is rudimentary and their expression vague." Add to this the fact that, dazzled as we are in contemporary life by the explanatory power of modern science, it is the differentiation between the realms of common sense and theory whose impact holds the most fascination for us, whether or not we understand the procedures and languages of scientific thought. To complicate matters, the modern Enlightenment-based assaults on religion and mystery and the aggressive postmodernist rejection of transcendence, combined with the impact of modern science on our imaginations, have for many rendered almost incomprehensible the first elemental

27. Lonergan, *Insight,* 410; *Method in Theology,* 84. Lonergan's treatment of the differentiations of consciousness and the four basic realms of meaning in *Method in Theology* considers only one aspect of the "polymorphism" of human consciousness. For an introduction to his account of the mind's polymorphism and its implications, see *Insight,* 204–12, 410–12, 451–52, 712–13.

differentiation between world and divine ground, the experiences and insights that historically released the world into the conceptual autonomy that both common sense and science take for granted. Finally, there are many among the culturally influential who have achieved only what Lonergan calls "singly differentiated consciousness": they are familiar with the procedures and specialized languages of one of the realms of meaning besides common sense—that of science, or of interiority, or of religion—but are only vaguely conversant with the other realms.[28] The result of all this is that our culture is, inevitably, plagued by problems involving fundamental misinterpretations of reality deriving from an inability to adequately appreciate and relate to each other the various realms of meaning disclosed by the multiple differentiations of consciousness.

Briefly, let us consider two sets of such problems, both of which bear on the difficulty of attaining a balanced understanding of divine presence in human consciousness. A first set of problems concerns the granting to one realm of meaning unique possession of valid truth claims and sole authority in the determination of what is real. For instance, when *common sense* assumes its own omnicompetence, the objects proper to the other realms are judged to be real only to the extent that they conform to the sensory, affective, or pragmatic criteria that form the basis of commonsense judgments. The realm of transcendence then vanishes, or is reduced to the external occasions and social uses of religion. Or, when genuine truth is considered the exclusive property of *science* or *theory*, transcendence is either dismissed as an illusion, by scientistic immanentism, or reduced to the doctrines of formal theology—while the insights of common sense are slighted, and the realm of interiority is either reduced to an object of psychological science or ignored altogether. Or, when fascination with the creative role of consciousness in the disclosure of meaning leads to the conviction that meaning resides exclusively in the operations of *interiority*, transcendence is often reduced to a mere "ideal" or invention of human thought.[29] Or finally, the realm of *transcendence*, too,

28. Lonergan, *Method in Theology*, 272, 273.

29. This exaltation of interiority can also, it should be noted, result in the human subject becoming radically *identified* with the transcendence of the divine Absolute Subject, as in German idealism. This view has the virtue of recognizing that human consciousness is an immediate participation in divine transcendent being, but it runs the danger—and Hegel did not unequivocally succeed in avoiding it, according to Kierkegaard, Voegelin, and other critics—of downplaying and at times losing sight of the fact that human subjectivity is not simply identical

as we have pointed out in earlier discussions of imbalanced consciousness, can be allowed to usurp all truth and all being, placing the world known by common sense and theory, along with the typically overlooked realm of interiority, under the index of irrelevance, illusion, or evil. In each of these cases, a defensive or obsessive attachment to one realm of meaning has rendered the legacy of the differentiated understanding of reality incoherent and a balanced understanding of transcendence impossible.

A second set of problems concerns the misinterpretations of transcendence that follow from uncritically blending the languages and ideas belonging to different realms of meaning, due primarily to insufficient familiarity with the differences between the methods and the objects peculiar to each realm. For example, it is typical for the descriptive imagery of common sense to impinge uncritically on the world of theoretical thought—for people to think of *mass* and *voltage* and *subatomic structure* as objects in the world of sense perception, not properly understanding that, in the world of theory, "things are conceived and known, not in their relation to our sensory apparatus . . . but in the relations constituted by their uniform interactions with one another." Thus, in much popular understanding, the *language* of theoretical explanation—an essentially abstract language of implicitly defined, nonimaginable terms and relations—is uncritically associated with the palpable, imaginable world of commonsense description, and so the realm of theoretical concern is not only essentially misconceived but also narrowed to the physical, external world.[30] In this way the precise theoretical distinction between *transcendence* and *immanence* is rejected as unverifiable by common sense, the realm of transcendence is considered outside the range of valid theoretical investigation, and the transcendence-immanence distinction is dismissed as irrelevant to any systematic explanation of reality.

Again, commonsense understanding can uncritically mix with and distort insights into transcendent meaning, as when it is assumed that language

with divine being, but merely *participates,* in a limited and perspectival way, in the knowledge, freedom, and creativity of the divine ground.

30. Ibid., 258. Theory or science, Lonergan repeatedly emphasizes, provides explanations of things in themselves, and "no thing itself, no thing as explained, can be imagined. . . . Once one enters upon the way of explanation by relating things to one another, one has stepped out of the path that yields valid representative images" (*Insight,* 275). Of course, the success and prestige of the physical sciences, and the establishment of their procedures as the model of all "scientific" knowing, have also contributed greatly to the view that systematic explanation pertains only to "the data of sense," to the external universe.

symbols pertaining to experiences of transcendence—such as God, nirvana, heaven, immortality, and so on—function just as do everyday descriptions of things or places or events. This is the perennial mistake of literalists and religious fundamentalists the world over. It consists of mistaking images whose purpose is *heuristic*—images meant to be no more than guiding clues to the understanding of realities as yet substantively unknown, and, in the case of transcendence, never fully knowable from the human perspective—for *representative* images, descriptive images that directly portray things. This error gives rise to the quite understandable assertion on the part of the atheist and the skeptic that such "things" and "places" and "events" do not exist, from which it is an easy, if unwarranted, step to the assertion that transcendent meaning is altogether illusory.

All such problems arise from the fact that as the different realms of meaning have historically emerged and undergone development, it has become ever more difficult to maintain a balanced appreciation of each and to work out their relations with each other. To do so in contemporary life requires, first, some awareness of the historical occasions and refinements of each of the differentiations; second, an ability to tolerate the complexities and ambiguities arising from the existence of multiple worlds of meaning; third, a readiness to find in the cognitional operations and procedures of one's own interiority the sources of valid understanding in each of the realms; and finally, openness to the fact that one's own existence is *participation* in the one cosmos whose mysterious ground, throughout all advances in understanding, remains the core of one's being and deepest identity. These are unavoidable requirements for the contemporary integration of differentiated consciousness, as well as for any philosophical or intellectual recovery of a conception of human nature that realistically and satisfyingly explains our native orientation to, and many languages regarding, transcendent meaning.

To appreciate how difficult such a recovery can prove to be even when many of the clues are in place, it will be illustrative, finally, to look at a central chapter in Ernest Becker's *Denial of Death* (1973), the masterwork of one of the most discerning and original social scientists of the twentieth century.

The Dilemma of Ernest Becker

Ernest Becker was a cultural anthropologist who took seriously the idea that his field, as a social science, should be able to offer a comprehensive theory of human culture, providing broad and verifiable explanations of individual behavior and social life. He understood that human culture is a consequence of the human search for meaning, and that basic functions of culture include defining what our human situation in reality is and what meaningful and dignified living consists of—what we are, and what the right way of doing things is. But in *The Denial of Death* and subsequent works, he offered a startling new approach to understanding how culture actually fulfills these functions, and what society requires of individuals if they would contribute to cultural meaning and stability. And in providing this new approach to cultural anthropology, he explicitly relied—in an act of philosophical scholarship both rare and courageous in his social scientific tradition—on Kierkegaard's anthropology of human existence as "a union of opposites," as a synthesis of the finite and the infinite.

Stated with stark brevity, Becker's central and most original thesis as presented in *The Denial of Death* is as follows. As animals to whom self-consciousness has been given, we humans are aware that we will die, and this awareness produces in us a basic anxiety, indeed a fundamental terror, about our vulnerability, the violent ways of nature, and the inevitability of death. Therefore, we devise all sorts of strategies for suppressing awareness of our mortality. This denial of death, says Becker, is *one of the basic functions of culture.* How does culture manage this? First, by explaining human existence to be part of an enduringly meaningful universe, thus giving each of us a sense that our individual lives are significant and valuable; and second, crucially, by controlling our basic anxiety through the devising of "death-denying hero systems," or "immortality projects," that enable us to believe and feel that, through our participation in them, our lives transcend mortal perishing. In the summarizing words of Sam Keen, from his foreword to the 1997 edition of *The Denial of Death:* "We achieve ersatz immortality by sacrificing ourselves to conquer an empire, to build a temple, to write a book, to establish a family, to accumulate a fortune, to further progress and prosperity, to create an information-society and global free market." Through participating in "culturally standardized hero systems" that assure us that our selves or our tasks are of imperishable value, we feel immortal, and render our terror of death unconscious.[31]

31. Becker, *The Denial of Death,* xiii; Becker, *Escape from Evil,* xvii. *Escape from Evil* was Becker's final work, posthumously published.

Unfortunately, Becker explains, our projects of immortalizing heroism tend to inflate one specific worldview, or group, or institution—*this* religion, *this* nation, *this* type of government—into the only vehicle of human connection with imperishable meaning. Thus, when human beings encounter alternate belief systems or worldviews, they are experienced as *threats*—first because each argues for an ultimate truth at least somewhat different from one's own, and second because the very fact of a plurality of belief systems or worldviews indirectly reveals that one's own "project" is merely a local and arbitrary construct, a "vital lie" of culture and character, built for protection against the terrifying realities of mortality.[32]

Because of this we are led, according to Becker, to try to defuse the threat that "otherness" poses to our own immortalizing hero systems, and we pursue this in various ways. We may attempt to convert others to our own beliefs. We may seek to accommodate other points of view, by looking for and finding aspects of them that seem compatible with our own. A cruder, but common, strategy is to denigrate others who do not share our belief systems, belittling and dehumanizing the "others." Then, as a most thorough solution, we can wage war, attempting to vanquish or even annihilate those whose differences threaten to expose the artificial character of our own "system" for transcending death. Through humiliating, damaging, and defeating the enemy; through mass deportations; through ethnic cleansing and genocide, we can at once eliminate threats to our heroic self-esteem and prove that it is we who are living and fighting in the service of everlasting truth. This, Becker argues, must be understood as the principal source of human violence and war: the inability to tolerate people significantly different from ourselves because to do so would betray the arbitrariness and falsehood of our own death-denying immortality systems, take away our psychological protection against our basic terror, and force us to face our true situation as self-conscious creatures who know that we have to die.[33]

32. In "Human Character as a Vital Lie," chap. 4 in *The Denial of Death,* Becker discusses how, beginning in childhood, each of us must protect himself or herself from feelings of helplessness and solitude by inventing "lies of character" that allow us to feel secure, protected, powerful, and in control of life and death. Therefore, each person, at least originally, has no choice but to style his or her character as a "vital lie"—"vital" because "it is a *necessary* and basic dishonesty about oneself and one's whole situation" (55).

33. The analysis of death denial as a perennial source of violence and evil is developed most fully in *Escape from Evil* (1976), which Becker described as a "companion volume to *The Denial*

In *The Denial of Death,* Becker developed this thesis and its implications for psychoanalysis, addressing ideas of Freud and other humanistic psychologists, especially the (in his view) underappreciated Otto Rank. The critical power and sweep of its central arguments were quickly and widely acknowledged; the book became a best-seller and won the 1974 Pulitzer Prize for general nonfiction. Becker had obviously uncovered one of the hidden mainsprings of psychological and cultural life, and shaped a powerful new tool both for ideological critique and for analyzing and redefining psychological "health."

Where does Kierkegaard fit into this analysis? In chapter 5, titled "The Psychoanalyst Kierkegaard," Becker enthusiastically presents elements of Kierkegaard's "psychological expositions" in order to deepen and clarify his own arguments, asserting an essential congruence between Kierkegaard's understanding of human nature and that offered in *The Denial of Death.* Throughout the chapter he pays tribute to Kierkegaard's genius, calling him a "master analyst of the human situation," a psychologist of "uncanny brilliance" engaged in an "unbelievably subtle" existential analysis that has given us "some of the best empirical analyses of the human condition ever fashioned by man's mind." Present-day psychiatry, he claims, "lags far behind" Kierkegaard in its theories of human existence. One reason for this is that Kierkegaard's analysis exploits to the utmost "the basic insight of psychology for all times": that a human being is a "union of opposites, of self-consciousness and of physical body"; that this conjoining of self-consciousness with a body subject to death and decay constitutes a paradox; and that "this paradox is the really constant thing about man in all periods of history and society." Kierkegaard understands, says Becker, that being a "spiritual," that is, self-conscious, animal—a godlike being, who nevertheless decays and dies—produces in us a fundamental anxiety, or dread, induced by our powerlessness to overcome the ambiguity of our ontological situation. Most impressively, Becker says, in Kierkegaard's two great works of psychological exposition, *The Concept of*

---

of Death" (xvii). Here Becker identifies the embrace of death-denial ideologies and the urge to achieve a heroic self-image as the "root causes of human evil," incessantly feeding as they do *"man's hunger for righteous self-expansion and perpetuation"* (xvii, 64, 135). My synopsis of Becker's main thesis in *The Denial of Death* is indebted to a lecture by Professor Sheldon Solomon of Skidmore College presented in 1994 at the University of Washington, sponsored by the Ernest Becker Foundation.

Anxiety and *The Sickness unto Death,* he has analyzed in "a broad and incredibly rich portrait of types of human failure" variants of the two elementary ways that we flee from the truth about our situation and its attendant anxiety. These are: (1) our denial of the responsibilities of self-conscious freedom, through immersion in bodily experience or in the givens of society, and (2) our denial of our "animal limitations," through soaring into fantasies of unlimited possibility, including the fantasy of preservation from death and destruction.[34]

Kierkegaard's analysis of the many variants of these two basic types of flight from ontological anxiety, Becker states, enables us to understand how widespread is human denial of the human condition. Kierkegaard shows us how the fatalist, the determinist, the social conformist, the happy consumer, the hedonist, the dreamer or fantasist, the worshiper of technology—even the schizophrenic and the clinical depressive—can all be understood as living "vital lies" of denial with regard to human existence in its given structure as an uneasy conjunction of body and spirit (or, as Kierkegaard puts it, "of finitude and infinitude"). Each of these types tries to escape the anxiety of the human ontological situation by fleeing either creatureliness (body) or self-conscious freedom (spirit). The dreamer and the technology worshiper defy their creaturely dependence on accidents, evil, and decay. The conformist and the happy consumer dissolve their freedoms into the "social hero-systems" into which they were born. The determinist and the fatalist deny, respectively, the fact and the meaning of freedom. The hedonist, through living for the immediacy of sensations, simultaneously flees spiritual responsibility and tries to take control over the meaning of existence.[35] Each can be seen to be trying to escape the anxiety of being that union of opposites, a "spiritual animal"—either by blotting out self-conscious freedom or by denying creatureliness.

Kierkegaard has thus provided the anthropological basis, explains Becker, for recognizing how central to the human psyche are both experiences of basic anxiety and psychological defenses against it, *and therefore for an appreciation by cultural anthropology of both the origin and ubiquity of death-denying hero systems.* In providing this, he continues, Kierkegaard has given us something even more valuable, the "golden fruit of all his tortuous labors": he has shown what authentic existence—existence *without* cultural heroism and the vital

34. Becker, *The Denial of Death,* 67–70, 75, 85–86.
35. Ibid., 76, 82, 84.

lies of character—would look like.[36] Becker approvingly describes, at the end of his chapter "The Psychoanalyst Kierkegaard," this true "health," this authentic existence that would face into its basic anxiety, accept the paradox of its being, and accept the knowledge of death.

The authentic person, Becker states, is the one who opens up to and embraces his or her true human situation—which means, most important, breaking away from the "programmed cultural heroics" designed to protect against awareness of mortality, and fully acknowledging creatureliness and the fragility of existence. Authenticity, writes Becker, requires letting awareness of mortality penetrate consciousness to the point where one's habitual sense of self, as constituted and sustained by all the fragility-and-death-denying emotional character armor built up since childhood, is "destroyed, brought down to nothing." In this psychological process, a person honestly and courageously accepts the nothingness implicit in all finite being, abandons all dependence on personal, cultural, and worldly assurances of enduring meaning, assurances equally empty. And in this extremity of honesty and courage, a transformation occurs. By dying to all "finite being," the self begins to be able "to see beyond it," and learns "to relate itself to infinitude, to absolute transcendence, to the Ultimate Power of Creation which made finite creatures." The self discovers in the dark night of its abandonment of reliance on finitude that there is, after all, a legitimate focus of its search for enduring meaning: one can, in hope and courage, affirm that "one's very creatureliness has some meaning to a Creator," to a transcendent ground that guarantees one's personal significance within "an eternal and infinite scheme of things." But this affirmation is *faith*. Faith is that opening and reaching out to infinitude, to absolute transcendence, whereby one links one's "secret inner self" to "the very ground of creation." This, states Becker, is the culmination of Kierkegaard's anthropological analysis and his ultimate message, with which Becker here concurs: human authenticity, with its full emotional acceptance of mortality, is based upon and impossible without that religious faith through which "the invisible mystery" at the heart of a creature "attains cosmic significance by affirming its connection with the invisible mystery at the heart of creation."[37]

36. Ibid., 86.
37. Ibid., 87, 89–91.

In his approval of Kierkegaard's account of genuine religious faith and its role in authentic human living, Becker appears here to have fully embraced Kierkegaard's anthropology, which affirms precisely that human existence is a union of the finite and the infinite, of time and eternity. If a human being is capable of affirming the connection between his or her own "invisible mystery" and "the invisible mystery at the heart of creation," then human consciousness is necessarily both immanent and transcendent.

Kierkegaard himself is eloquently detailed on the matter. "A human being," he explains,

> is a synthesis of the infinite and the finite, of the temporal and the eternal, of freedom and necessity. . . . The self is the conscious synthesis of infinitude and finitude that [in self-consciousness] relates itself to itself, whose task is to become itself, which can be done only through the relationship to God. To become oneself is to become concrete. But to become concrete is neither to become finite nor to become infinite, for that which is to become concrete is indeed a synthesis. . . . [From this may be derived] the formula for faith: in relating itself to itself and in willing to be itself, the self rests transparently in the power [God] that established it.[38]

A self can, Kierkegaard states, through willing to be itself, "rest transparently in God" because human consciousness is the site where eternal being enters time. Each "moment" of conscious experience, of self-presence, is "that ambiguity in which time and eternity touch each other"; human temporality is that flow of conscious presence "whereby time constantly intersects eternity and eternity constantly pervades time." Therefore, human beings experience anxiety (angst): anxiety proclaims our concern over the possible uses of our freedom in the task of bringing our fragile, sexed, mortal lives into attunement with the eternal ground of our being.[39] This is an anthropology that serves as a sharp rebuke, and a therapeutic antidote, to modern immanentist anthropologies, and through his analysis and embrace of Kierkegaard Becker appears to be in a position to usefully exploit it in his own social science. He seems ready to recover a conception of human nature that accounts for our native orientation to transcendent meaning by affirming—along with

38. Kierkegaard, *The Sickness unto Death,* 13, 29–30, 49.

39. Kierkegaard, *The Concept of Anxiety,* 89; on human temporality as the intersecting of time and eternity, see 85–93.

Jaspers, Scheler, Marcel, Levinas, Lonergan, and Voegelin—that human existence is life in the In-Between of immanence and transcendence.

In fact, though, we find neither the articulation nor the development of such an anthropology either in subsequent chapters of *The Denial of Death* or in its successor and companion volume, *Escape from Evil,* Becker's final work. Kierkegaard's ontology of human existence is nowhere to be found in their often brilliant discussions of psychology, religion, culture, and the human sources of violence and evil, which instead consistently portray human beings, in typical modernist fashion, as *purely immanent animals* who just happen to have the productive and ennobling, but also tragic and self-torturing, appurtenance of self-consciousness.

This divergence from Kierkegaard may be seen even in the chapter "The Psychoanalyst Kierkegaard," where some of Becker's conclusions about the import of Kierkegaard's analysis clearly deviate from those drawn by the philosopher himself. For instance, at one point Becker states that, in Kierkegaard's analysis of anxiety, "the final terror of self-consciousness is the knowledge of one's own death." In another place, he indicates that, for Kierkegaard, the "prison" of inauthentic character is "built to deny one thing and one thing alone: one's creatureliness. The creatureliness is the terror."[40] Neither of these assertions accurately portrays Kierkegaard's own understanding.

For Kierkegaard, the basic anxiety of consciousness is not over the fact that one is finite and mortal. It is a response to the fact that one is finite *and* transcends finitude—that one participates in time as a fragile, sexed, and mortal creature *and* participates in the eternal, nonfinite being that transcends mortality. Human inauthenticity, the "sickness unto death" with which we are all infected, is not simply the result of shrinking from mortality, but of our despair over the task of accepting and reconciling *both* dimensions of our nature, the temporal and the eternal. The basic anxiety that belongs to the "sickness unto death" is not simply the terror of annihilation and its indignity, but anxiety that wells up from the recognition that we are responsible both for facing up to our creatureliness *and* to the claims of the eternal upon us, claims that transcend the transitory domain of physical death.[41] Becker

40. Becker, *The Denial of Death,* 70, 87.

41. On Kierkegaard's use of the concept of the "sickness unto death" and his identification of it as "despair"—and in particular the despair that knows an "even greater danger" (18) than death—see *The Sickness unto Death,* 17–21.

misconstrues Kierkegaard by overstressing one side of his account of the origins of anxiety: the threat of meaninglessness posed by death. Kierkegaard himself emphasizes that an equal, *if not greater,* source of anxiety and despair is the threat of mismanaged participation in eternal being.

For Kierkegaard, then, a human being is truly a "union of opposites," a uniting of animal being with the "immortalizing presence" that makes of that very being a paradox. For Becker, on the contrary, a human being is not really a *synthesis* of temporal and eternal, finite and infinite, but merely a creature that happens to be "self-conscious"—a creature burdened with a secondary or ancillary capacity to have *ideas* or *thoughts,* including thoughts of mortality and timelessness. Despite his justified admiration for and use of Kierkegaard's analyses of existential failure, which offer profound support for Becker's insight into the extent to which the denial of death—as one pervasive form of the denial of the human condition—shapes human life and culture, Becker does not really take advantage of Kierkegaard's anthropological exposition. To do so would require a radical break with the immanentist subject of modern social science, for whom transcendent being can be only a mental invention or projection—and this break Becker is not able or willing to engage in.[42] Thus, his embrace of Kierkegaard in *The Denial of Death* involves Becker in a sort of philosophical confusion, or dilemma, that he is unable to resolve. He recognizes Kierkegaard's genius as a "master analyst of the human situation" whose insights both reveal the origins and extent of death denial and explain what it means to live a life *without* such denial. He cannot, however, incorporate either Kierkegaard's actual anthropology or his explication of the authentic life of faith into his own psychological and cultural critique, because immanentist assumptions about human nature and human knowing prevent the Kierkegaardian insights from taking hold.[43]

42. See, for example, *The Denial of Death,* 167–68, 172. Becker's reliance on immanentist models of human being and thinking is seen clearly in a sentence from *Escape from Evil:* "As soon as you have symbols you have artificial self-transcendence via culture" (4). The revealing word is *artificial.* Becker's anthropological and epistemological model does not allow for *genuine* self-transcendence, where consciousness and the physical world could alike be understood as "natural" due to their joint emergence from and participation in a transcendent ground of being.

43. Kierkegaard's human ontology is, in fact, more complex than Becker seems to appreciate, despite an explanatory footnote in *The Denial of Death* on Kierkegaard's use of the term *self* (76). When Kierkegaard describes a human being as "a synthesis of the infinite and the finite" and of "the temporal and the eternal," he goes on to explain that this relation between elements (or their combined totality) does not yet make a "self." A self is constituted, Kierkegaard says,

Becker's dilemma is perfectly represented in his approach to the notion of *immortality.* He shares with Kierkegaard a passionate, derisive criticism of those who are certain of their personal immortality, as if eternal being were their possession, and who often bolster that sense of certitude and possession through the denigration and victimization of others. The idea of immortality is seen by both thinkers as a perennial source of self-delusion, smug egotism, false heroics, and injustice. For all this, though, the symbol *immortality* clearly has, for Kierkegaard, an authentic and justifiable meaning and function. It is one of the symbols we use to make sense of our experiences of eternal and nonfinite being, to stand for the questions and hopes and images that arise from our mysterious participation in transcendence.[44] However, in Becker's *Denial of Death* and *Escape from Evil,* notions of immortality are always linked to inauthentic and self-deluded human yearnings to escape mortality. While Becker acknowledges that human beings subscribe to what he calls "immortality ideologies" because of a love of and longing for fuller life, for him any thoughts of imperishable meaning are always in part a "reflex of the death-anxiety," so that the notion of immortality is always, for him, both a promise and a lie.[45] To be true to his own insights into authentic existence

---

only through this relation "relating itself to itself"—that is, through acts of this given synthesis engaging in conscious self-relation, acts that establish what he calls a "positive third" element, namely, the "self" proper, beyond the two original terms of the synthesis. It is precisely the "self" constituted through these acts of self-relation that Kierkegaard calls "spirit" (*The Sickness unto Death,* 13). Thus, it is incorrect to state, as Becker does, that for Kierkegaard a human self is a mixture (or totality) of the "animal" and the "spiritual," as if for Kierkegaard these terms correspond respectively to "creature" and "self-consciousness," or to "physical body" and "symbolic self" (*The Denial of Death,* 76 n). Further, there is the matter of Kierkegaard's careful use of pseudonymous authors in his philosophical writings (including *The Concept of Anxiety* and *The Sickness unto Death*) for the purpose of distinguishing, to various degrees, the respective "viewpoints" of these texts from his own—a matter that raises interpretive questions that I have chosen, like Becker, to leave unaddressed for the purposes of a brief discussion, but that should always at least be noted.

44. For a philosophical analysis of the symbol *immortality* that discusses its origins in cosmological imagination, its authentic functions, and the confusions of meaning entailed in doctrinal and dogmatic propositions regarding "the immortality of the soul," see Voegelin, "Immortality: Experience and Symbol," in *Published Essays, 1966–1985.*

45. Becker, *The Denial of Death,* 152–53. This is stated with passionate force in *Escape from Evil:* "Each person nourishes his immortality in the ideology of self-perpetuation to which he gives his allegiance; this gives his life the only abiding significance it can have. . . . History, then, can be understood as the succession of ideologies that console for death. . . . If it is no longer the clan that represents the collective immortality pool, then it is the state, the nation, the revolutionary cell, the corporation, the scientific society, one's own race. . . . From which we can conclude that man is an animal who has to live in a lie in order to live at all" (64, 119, 122).

in "The Psychoanalyst Kierkegaard," Becker would have to acknowledge legitimate and salutary—as well as self-delusory and destructive—functions of the symbol *immortality.* Correspondingly, he would have to incorporate into his work a careful distinction between, on the one hand, the false heroics of inauthentic religious faith, which seeks primarily self-righteous certitude and self-inflation, and, on the other hand, the genuine heroics of authentic faith, which accepts the human condition as it is and stands open to the risks and mysteries of participation in transcendent meaning—the faith exemplified by Zen masters, Socrates, Gandhi, and Martin Luther King Jr. But these distinctions are not developed, and Becker's cultural anthropology—with its bold embrace of ideas that challenges the narrow conventions of contemporary social science—leaves human beings still only groping for transcendence, rather than struggling with the mystery of its presence.[46]

Becker's dilemma is that of a scientist who knows that the data he has isolated are of profound importance, but who can only interpret them in terms of a familiar but faulty theoretical paradigm. The data pertain to the desire to invest human life with imperishable meaning. Relying as he does on the faulty theoretical model of the modern, immanentist subject—who does not *participate* in eternal reality but merely has ideas about it—Becker interprets this concern as signifying *primarily* a denial of mortality. However, what our concern with imperishable meaning signifies *primarily* is awareness of existing in-between finite being and transcendent divine presence. Becker is not wrong to insist that the human fascination with transcending death is an important key to establishing a new and profound cultural anthropology. But it does not unlock for him the anthropological theory our age needs: one that breaks completely with the immanentist model of consciousness and history, and reestablishes at the core of psychological and social science the fundamental insight that human existence participates in the understanding, freedom, and creativity of divine transcendent being. Becker had amassed many of the clues—especially in Kierkegaard's psychological expositions—that would have allowed him to make this breakthrough. Why were they not sufficient? What would have enabled him to do so?

Our account of differentiating consciousness indicates at least part of the answer. The history and significance of human grappling with transcendent

46. For a discussion of Becker's misinterpretation of Kierkegaard congruent with my own, see Charles K. Bellinger, *The Genealogy of Violence: Reflections on Creation, Freedom, and Evil,* 39–41.

meaning cannot be understood without a clear grasp of (1) the primary experience of the cosmos, in which the whole of reality including its transcendent ground is experienced as an undifferentiated oneness, and (2) the elementary differentiating process wherein meditative acts lead to the conceptual separation of immanent and transcendent realms. As with most contemporary intellectuals, in Becker there is no theoretical acknowledgment of the primary, predifferentiated experience of the cosmos; no meditative reenactment of the experiences of religious and philosophical genius through which the transcendent realm of meaning was first conceptually distinguished and the mystery of our participation in it clarified; no critical apprehension that the realms of science and human interiority become accessible only *because of* the prior differentiation between divine transcendence and a conceptually autonomous immanent universe; and consequently, no solution to the anthropological dilemmas of our age, which require a theory of human consciousness that explicitly recognizes that transcendent meaning is *a given presence in consciousness*—that our longing for transcendence is not an act of desperation, as Becker proclaims, but rather the natural longing to clarify what we already experience.

A psychology or cultural anthropology (or any other science, or philosophy) that truly addresses the needs of our times requires above all a critical appreciation of the differentiating process, without which science cannot understand what it itself is: the uncovering of one of the realms of meaning—the realm of systematic explanations of things, of their intrinsic properties and uniform interactions—by a human consciousness whose questioning is created and drawn by the ground of being, the divine partner whose presence both permeates the finite world and illuminates that very consciousness with the revelation of divine transcendence.

CONCLUSION
The Drama of Universal Humanity

> If every man does not participate essentially in the absolute, then the whole game's up.
>
> —Søren Kierkegaard, *The Concept of Anxiety*

EFFORTS TO ignore or deny transcendent reality are, in the long run, futile. Anthropologies that fail to take into account the experience of divine presence in human consciousness will never be able to provide convincing explanations of the deepest human experiences and motives, nor penetrate to the root of pathologies that derive from the loss of the balance of consciousness in between immanent and transcendent meaning. And philosophies of history that fail to base themselves on the truth that all of history unfolds within the encompassing context of a divinely transcendent meaning will remain incapable of explaining the all-important historical transition from cosmological to differentiated consciousness; of accurately diagnosing deformations of historical meaning such as apocalyptism (religious or secular); or, for that matter, of accounting for the emergence of historical consciousness itself. Immanentist anthropologies and philosophies of history are finally self-defeating, because they do not explain enough. The truth of transcendence will reassert itself, because it overwhelmingly informs the historical data, and because it is continually available in conscious experience in the "meeting between man and the Beyond of his heart."[1]

As disconcerting as it may be, then, for those incredulous toward religious "metanarrative" and mystery, the fact is that all of the great world religions are founded on, and nourished by, an elemental truth. This truth is that human existence is grounded in transcendent being. And this, in turn, means

1. Voegelin, *The Ecumenic Age*, 398.

that history is (in Eric Voegelin's words) "not a merely human but a divine-human process," and that "[m]eaning in history is constituted through man's response to the immortalizing movement of the divine . . . in his soul."[2]

Deconstruction or rebuttal of religious vision, narrative, or faith *as such*, then, is a misdirection of energies in the contemporary response to the problem of transcendence. The real task at hand is: (1) to clarify the shared experiential bases of the religious and philosophical traditions that honor transcendent being, recognizing that each has arisen in personal, ethnic, and cultural contexts providing distinctive means of symbolizing and explaining divine-human encounter; (2) to work toward critical discernment of what is authentic and inauthentic, coherent and incoherent, normative and aberrant, within each tradition—distinguishing that which promotes the balance of consciousness from that which undermines it, that which sustains the cultural fact of cosmopolis from that which erodes it; and (3) through this process, to bring the various traditions into fruitful communion with each other, so that the equivalences, complementarities, and resolvable divergences among their truths may be revealed, and their degrading attitudes and doctrines repudiated.[3]

This brief description of the contemporary critical task concerning the problem of transcendence condemns religious exclusivism on principle. Genuine experiences of the one divine ground of being and differentiated insights into divine transcendence are not the privilege of one people or tradition. No one of the world's great religions, no single set of symbolizations of transcendence, holds a monopoly of insight into authentic divine-human encounter. In each of them the human Question has sought and found the Mystery that is its source and its deepest identity.

This is not to suggest, however, that the world's major religious and wisdom traditions are of equal sophistication or penetration or clarity in their expositions of the divine ground, in their anthropologies and cosmologies, or in their insights into historical meaning. As we have seen, the various traditions evidence a range of thoroughness and intensity with regard to the differentiation of transcendence. And, of particular importance to note, the

2. Ibid., 374–75.

3. For Lonergan's account of the ongoing task of critical analysis of the authentic and inauthentic in religious traditions, see "Religion" and "Dialectic," chaps. 4 and 10 in *Method in Theology,* 101–24, 235–66.

cultural spheres of the different religious traditions have not proved equally productive of, or receptive to, the further differentiations of the realms of science and of interiority; the working out of the relationships of the four basic realms of meaning to one another; or the development of cultural outlooks and institutional structures and policies informed by these critical accomplishments. Finally, to be sure, each major tradition carries its peculiar tendencies of oversight and bias, which enormously complicates the task of their appreciation, assessment, refinement, comparison, and harmonization. Still, the task is unavoidable, unless one is prepared to deny the very notion of a common humanity.

For it is every person's participation in the one flux of divine presence that unites human beings in the common enterprise that we call "history." There could be no common enterprise, no drama of universal humanity, without human participation in a dimension of meaning that transcends all biological, geographical, linguistic, and cultural particularities. Only universal participation in timeless reality binds the meaning of each person's life to the meaning of all. This is why—as the historical record shows—it was only the explicit recognition of transcendent being that first made it possible to conceive of a genuinely universal human drama. The idea of a God who is "a light to all the nations" appeared only with the Hebrew prophetic clarifications of transcendent divinity, and philosophical notions of *universal* standards of justice and reason arose only in the wake of the Greek revelation of a transcendent Nous. It was quite precisely, as Voegelin states, during the first millennium B.C.E. that a "scattering of societies, belonging to the same biological type . . . [was] discovered to be one mankind with one history, by virtue of participation in the same flux of divine presence." Only because of this participation may we speak intelligibly of *universal history*, of the mystical contemporaneity and solidarity of all peoples of all times and places.[4]

Only our recognition of this fact of participation can ensure that we remain sensitive both to the open-endedness of history and to the mystery of its ultimate meaning. The "stop history" movements, both religious and secular, that pressure us with images of the end of history or with claims to knowledge of history's final goal, are betrayals both of the complexity of the multiple lines of meaning in history and of the Mystery that transcends and embraces history. Only by remembering that history is "not a merely human but a

4. Voegelin, *The Ecumenic Age*, 377.

divine-human process"—that the field of human decision and action itself is, in Thomas Mann's words, a "God-invention"—can we preserve a conception of history maximally open to all human struggle and aspiration, to universal human dignity.[5]

The aspects of the writings of Eric Voegelin and Bernard Lonergan that have been our focus are potent contributions to the philosophical clarification of these issues. As acts of intellectual recovery of transcendence, of catching up to our historical stage of differentiated consciousness, and of "resistance to the distortion and destruction of humanity committed by the 'stop-history' Systems" of modernity, they are profoundly responsive and responsible both to contemporary political and existential traumas and to the conditions and challenges of postmodernity.[6] It remains true, of course, that philosophical explanation belongs to the cultural superstructure. Its complexities of thought and abstruse language severely limit its short-term appeal and impact. It is therefore no answer to the need, at the everyday level of spontaneous human living, for evocative symbols and ambient visions of the Whole that satisfyingly orient people in relation to the ultimacies and mysteries of the universal human drama. So we are led to ask: where, in our time of broken images and devitalized myths, are such symbols and visions to be found?

Perhaps, after all, the prospect is not so desolate. We enjoy a vast historical legacy of symbols, myths, rituals, and visions that protect the truths of transcendence and encourage dedication to universal human dignity, a legacy that is increasingly accessible in its global variety. In this situation, it is not so much that new symbols and visions are needed—although new artistic evocations of the divine-human In-Between are a permanent requirement—as that the wealth of symbols and visions already available to us needs to be retrieved, or rescued. Rescued from what? Above all, from their having been treated as self-contained truths—as grimly authoritative *information,* certain and complete, in relation to which we are invited only to bow and acquiesce. The fact is ignored that all symbols and creeds pertaining to transcendence exist only as the articulated responses to *living questions,* and are meaningful only if in some measure they illuminate or provide answers to

5. The phrase appears in the concluding sentence of Mann's tetralogy, *Joseph and His Brothers;* Mann, *Joseph the Provider,* 608.

6. Voegelin, *The Ecumenic Age,* 410.

one's own questions; they symbolize *experiences,* and are meaningful only to the degree that they can be found to resonate with *one's own experiences.* It is forgetfulness of this fact, more than any other single factor, that alienates us from the traditional symbols, that stales and deadens the teachings of prophets, philosophers, sages, and saints. The symbols and visions in the Gospels, in Plato's myths, in the Bhagavad-Gita, in the writings of Meister Eckhart and Shankara, in the Psalms and the Lotus Sutra, in the *Tao Te Ching* and *The Cloud of Unknowing,* in the poetry of Rūmī and Ryokan and Rilke—quickened by the testimonies in music, painting, architecture, sculpture, theater, dance, and film—may still provide crucial existential orientation to one who penetrates to the experiences of loving openness to transcendence that engendered them. One must only enter into a living dialogue with them, approaching them neither as artifacts from an irrelevant past nor as arsenals of answers in the perennial wars between competing doctrines or dogmas, but as illuminations of truths about our human situation that have arisen from the In-Between tension of consciousness, that is, from the initiating movement of the divine partner meeting the exceptionally open and creative human response.

The key to being able to take advantage of this legacy of illuminative insights is therefore a certain choice of attitude toward our cultural heritage itself. First, one must reject, along with the ideologies of immanentism, the stance toward history that they tend to promote and to provoke, where the human past is seen primarily as a long passage through blindness and folly from which we have only recently begun to emerge, and our cultural heritage felt to be an imposition of authority from which we must struggle to liberate ourselves. A realistic and humble openness toward the historical past, then, may foster appreciation of our wealth of historical symbols that testify to a loving readiness to follow unrestricted questioning as far as the inward revelation of transcendent truth—the revelation in the light of which we can recognize our essential solidarity with every participant in the drama of universal humanity. It is a choice of attitude wonderfully expressed in comments written in 1920—just about the time Eliot was composing "The Waste Land"—by the Russian poet Vyacheslav Ivanov to his friend, the historian M. O. Gershenzon:

> The state of mind that now torments you, your exasperated intolerance of the cultural heritage you feel weighing upon you, stems essentially from the

fact that you experience culture, not as a living repertory of gifts, but as a subtle mechanism of multiple compulsions. And this is not surprising, culture having indeed sought to become a system of compulsions. For my part I see it as a ladder of Eros, a hierarchy of acts of veneration. So many are the things and persons I am moved to venerate, beginning with man and his tools and his labors and his insulted dignity and ending with the lowliest bit of mineral, that I find it sweet to go down in this sea—*naufragar mi è dolce in questo mare*—, to drown in God.[7]

7. V. I. Ivanov and M. O. Gershenzon, *Correspondence across a Room*, 7.

Bibliography

Auden, W. H. *Secondary Worlds.* New York: Random House, 1968.

Baynes, Kenneth, James Bohman, and Thomas McCarthy, eds. *After Philosophy: End or Transformation?* Cambridge: MIT Press, 1987.

Becker, Ernest. *The Denial of Death.* New York: Free Press Paperbacks, 1997.

———. *Escape from Evil.* New York: Free Press, 1976.

Beckett, Samuel. *Endgame.* New York: Grove Press, 1958.

———. *Waiting for Godot.* New York: Grove Press, 1954.

Bellinger, Charles K. *The Genealogy of Violence: Reflections on Creation, Freedom, and Evil.* New York: Oxford University Press, 2001.

Bly, Robert, ed. and trans. *The Kabir Book: Forty-four of the Ecstatic Poems of Kabir.* Seventies Book ed. Boston: Beacon Press, 1977.

Borges, Jorge Luis. *This Craft of Verse.* Ed. Calin-Andrei Mihailescu. Cambridge: Harvard University Press, 2000.

Borgmann, Albert. *Crossing the Postmodern Divide.* Chicago: University of Chicago Press, 1992.

Bornstein, George, ed. *Ezra Pound among the Poets.* Chicago: University of Chicago Press, 1985.

Campbell, Joseph, ed. *The Mystic Vision: Papers from the Eranos Yearbooks.* Bollingen Series 30, no. 6. Princeton: Princeton University Press, 1968.

Camus, Albert. "Create Dangerously." In *Resistance, Rebellion, and Death,* trans. Justin O'Brien, 249–72. New York: Alfred A. Knopf, 1961.

Caputo, John D. "Being and the Mystery of the Person." In *The Universe as Journey: Conversations with W. Norris Clarke, S.J.,* ed. Gerald A. McCool, 93–113. New York: Fordham University Press, 1988.

Chan, Wing-Tsit, trans. and ed. *A Source Book in Chinese Philosophy.* Princeton: Princeton University Press, 1969.

Cohn, Norman. *Cosmos, Chaos, and the World to Come: The Ancient Roots of Apocalyptic Faith.* New Haven: Yale University Press, 1993.

Davenport, Guy. "Ezra Pound, 1885–1972." In *The Geography of the Imagination: Forty Essays by Guy Davenport,* 169–76. San Francisco: North Point Press, 1981.

———. "The Pound Vortex." In *The Geography of the Imagination: Forty Essays by Guy Davenport,* 165–68. San Francisco: North Point Press, 1981.

Davie, Donald. *Ezra Pound.* New York: Viking Press, 1976.

———. *Ezra Pound: Poet as Sculptor.* New York: Oxford University Press, 1964.

De Bary, Wm. Theodore. *East Asian Civilizations: A Dialogue in Five Stages.* Cambridge: Harvard University Press, 1988.

Derrida, Jacques. *Writing and Difference.* Trans. Alan Bass. Chicago: University of Chicago Press, 1978.

Descartes, René. *Meditations on First Philosophy* and *Discourse on Method.* Trans. Donald A. Cress. Indianapolis: Hackett Publishing, 1983.

Diogenes Laertius. *Lives of Eminent Philosophers.* Trans. R. D. Hicks. Vol. 2. Loeb Classical Library. New York: G. P. Putnam's Sons, 1925.

Dodds, E. R. *Pagan and Christian in an Age of Anxiety: Some Aspects of Religious Experience from Marcus Aurelius to Constantine.* New York: W. W. Norton, 1970.

Donoghue, Denis. *The Arts without Mystery.* Boston: Little, Brown, 1983.

Doran, Robert M. *Theology and the Dialectics of History.* Toronto: University of Toronto Press, 1990.

Easwaran, Eknath, trans. and ed. *The Upanishads.* Tomales, Calif.: Nilgiri Press, 1992.

Eliade, Mircea. *The Myth of the Eternal Return; or, Cosmos and History.* Trans. Willard R. Trask. Bollingen Series 46. Princeton: Princeton University Press, 1974.

———. *No Souvenirs: Journal, 1957–1969.* Trans. Fred H. Johnson Jr. New York: Harper and Row, 1977.

———. *The Sacred and the Profane: The Nature of Religions.* Trans. Willard R. Trask. New York: Harcourt, Brace, and World, 1959.

———, ed. *From Primitives to Zen: A Thematic Sourcebook of the History of Religions.* New York: Harper and Row, 1967.

Eliade, Mircea, and Joseph M. Kitagawa, eds. *The History of Religions: Essays in Methodology.* Chicago: University of Chicago Press, 1950.

Eliot, T. S. *Four Quartets.* In *The Complete Poems and Plays, 1909–1950,* 115–45. New York: Harcourt, Brace, and World, 1962.

Emberley, Peter, and Barry Cooper, eds. and trans. *Faith and Political Philosophy: The Correspondence between Leo Strauss and Eric Voegelin, 1934–1964.* University Park: Pennsylvania State University Press, 1993.

Espey, John J. *Ezra Pound's "Mauberley": A Study in Composition.* Berkeley and Los Angeles: University of California Press, 1955.

Feder, Lillian. "Pound and Ovid." In *Ezra Pound among the Poets,* ed. George Bornstein, 13–34. Chicago: University of Chicago Press, 1985.

Franz, Michael. "Brothers under the Skin: Voegelin on the Common Experiential Wellsprings of Spiritual Order and Disorder." In *The Politics of the Soul: Eric Voegelin on Religious Experience,* ed. Glenn Hughes, 139–61. Lanham, Md.: Rowman and Littlefield, 1999.

———. *Eric Voegelin and the Politics of Spiritual Revolt: The Roots of Modern Ideology.* Baton Rouge: Louisiana State University Press, 1992.

Hall, Donald. *Their Ancient Glittering Eyes: Remembering Poets and More Poets.* New York: Ticknor and Fields, 1992.

Hass, Robert. *Twentieth Century Pleasures: Prose on Poetry.* New York: Ecco Press, 1984.

Heidegger, Martin. *Being and Time.* Trans. John Macquarrie and Edward Robinson. New York: Harper and Row, 1962.

Heiler, Friedrich. "The History of Religions as a Preparation for the Cooperation of Religions." In *The History of Religions: Essays in Methodology,* ed. Mircea Eliade and Joseph M. Kitagawa, 132–60. Chicago: University of Chicago Press, 1950.

Hughes, Glenn. "Balanced and Imbalanced Consciousness." In *The Politics of the Soul: Eric Voegelin on Religious Experience,* ed. Glenn Hughes, 163–83. Lanham, Md.: Rowman and Littlefield, 1999.

———. *Mystery and Myth in the Philosophy of Eric Voegelin.* Columbia: University of Missouri Press, 1993.

Hughes, Glenn, Stephen A. McKnight, and Geoffrey L. Price, eds. *Politics, Order, and History: Essays on the Work of Eric Voegelin.* Sheffield, England: Sheffield Academic Press, 2001.

Hughes, Robert. *Nothing If Not Critical: Selected Essays on Art and Artists.* New York: Alfred A. Knopf, 1990.

Hyde, Lewis. *The Gift: Imagination and the Erotic Life of Property.* New York: Vintage Books, 1983.

Ivanov, V. I., and M. O. Gershenzon. *Correspondence across a Room.* Trans. Lisa Sergio. Marlboro, Vt.: Marlboro Press, 1984.

Jacobsen, Thorkild. *The Sumerian King List.* Chicago: University of Chicago Press, 1966.

Jaspers, Karl. *The Origin and Goal of History.* Trans. Michael Bullock. London: Routledge and Kegan Paul, 1953.

———. *Philosophy.* Trans. E. B. Ashton. 3 vols. Chicago: University of Chicago Press, 1969–1971.

The Jerusalem Bible. Garden City, N.Y.: Doubleday, 1966.

Jonas, Hans. *The Gnostic Religion: The Message of the Alien God and the Beginnings of Christianity.* 2d ed. Boston: Beacon Press, 1963.

Kaufmann, Walter, ed. and trans. *The Portable Nietzsche.* New York: Viking Press, 1968.

Kearns, George. *Guide to Ezra Pound's "Selected Cantos."* New Brunswick: Rutgers University Press, 1980.

Kenner, Hugh. *The Poetry of Ezra Pound.* Lincoln: University of Nebraska Press, 1985.

———. *The Pound Era.* Berkeley and Los Angeles: University of California Press, 1974.

Kierkegaard, Søren. *The Concept of Anxiety.* Ed. and trans. Reidar Thomte in collaboration with Albert B. Anderson. Princeton: Princeton University Press, 1980.

———. *Concluding Unscientific Postscript.* Trans. David F. Swenson. Princeton: Princeton University Press, 1941.

———. *The Sickness unto Death.* Ed. and trans. Howard V. Hong and Edna H. Hong. Princeton: Princeton University Press, 1983.

Levinas, Emmanuel. *Basic Philosophical Writings.* Ed. Adriaan T. Peperzak, Simon Critchley, and Robert Bernasconi. Various translators. Bloomington: Indiana University Press, 1996.

———. *Ethics and Infinity: Conversations with Philippe Nemo.* Trans. Richard A. Cohen. Pittsburgh: Duquesne University Press, 1985.

Levy, David J. *Political Order: Philosophical Anthropology, Modernity, and the Challenge of Ideology.* Baton Rouge: Louisiana State University Press, 1987.

Lewis, Franklin D. *Rumi—Past and Present, East and West: The Life, Teachings, and Poetry of Jalâl al-Din Rumi.* Oxford: Oneworld Publications, 2000.

Lipsey, Roger. *An Art of Our Own: The Spiritual in Twentieth-Century Art.* Boston: Shambhala Publications, 1989.

Lonergan, Bernard J. F. *Collection.* Vol. 4 of *The Collected Works of Bernard Lonergan,* ed. Frederick E. Crowe and Robert M. Doran. Toronto: University of Toronto Press, 1988.

———. *Insight: A Study of Human Understanding.* Vol. 3 of *The Collected Works of Bernard Lonergan,* ed. Frederick E. Crowe and Robert M. Doran. Toronto: University of Toronto Press, 1992.

———. *Method in Theology.* New York: Herder and Herder, 1972.

———. *A Second Collection.* Ed. William F. J. Ryan, S.J., and Bernard J. Tyrrell, S.J. Philadelphia: Westminster Press, 1974.

———. *Topics in Education.* Vol. 10 of *The Collected Works of Bernard Lonergan,* ed. Robert M. Doran and Frederick E. Crowe. Toronto: University of Toronto Press, 1993.

———. *Understanding and Being.* Vol. 5 of *The Collected Works of Bernard Lonergan,* ed. Elizabeth A. Morelli and Mark D. Morelli. Toronto: University of Toronto Press, 1990.

Löwith, Karl. *Meaning in History.* Chicago: University of Chicago Press, 1964.

Lyotard, Jean-François. "The Postmodern Condition." In *After Philosophy: End or Transformation?* ed. Kenneth Baynes, James Bohman, and Thomas McCarthy, 73–94. Cambridge: MIT Press, 1987.

———. *The Postmodern Condition: A Report on Knowledge.* Trans. Geoff Bennington and Brian Massumi. Theory and History of Literature, vol. 10. Minneapolis: University of Minnesota Press, 1984.

Mann, Thomas. *Joseph the Provider.* Trans. H. T. Lowe-Porter. New York: Alfred A. Knopf, 1944.

Marcel, Gabriel. *The Mystery of Being.* 2 vols. Vol. 1 trans. G. S. Fraser. Vol. 2 trans. René Hague. Gateway ed. Chicago: Henry Regnery, 1960.

Marcus, Greil. *The Dustbin of History.* London: Picador, 1966.

Marx, Karl, and Friedrich Engels. *The German Ideology.* Ed. C. J. Arthur. Trans. W. Lough, C. Dutt, and C. P. Magill, with revisions by C. J. Arthur. New York: International Publishers, 1970.

McCool, Gerald A., ed. *The Universe as Journey: Conversations with W. Norris Clarke, S.J.* New York: Fordham University Press, 1988.

Mitchell, Stephen, trans. *Tao Te Ching.* New York: Harper and Row, 1988.

Montgomery, Marion. "Ezra Pound: The Quest for Paradise." In *The Men I Have Chosen for Fathers: Literary and Philosophical Passages,* 62–102. Columbia: University of Missouri Press, 1990.

Musil, Robert. *The Man without Qualities.* Trans. Eithne Wilkins and Ernst Kaiser. Vol. 2. Picador ed. London: Pan Books, 1979.

Nassar, Eugene Paul. *The Cantos of Ezra Pound: The Lyric Mode.* Baltimore: Johns Hopkins University Press, 1976.

Nikhilananda, Swami, ed. and trans. *The Upanishads.* Abridged ed. Torchbook Series. New York: Harper and Row, 1964.

Nussbaum, Martha C. *Cultivating Humanity: A Classical Defense of Reform in Liberal Education.* Cambridge: Harvard University Press, 1997.

Otto, Rudolf. *The Idea of the Holy.* Trans. John W. Harvey. 2d ed. London: Oxford University Press, 1950.

Philo. *Works.* Trans. F. H. Colson and G. H. Whitaker. Vol. 1. Loeb Classical Library. London: William Heinemann, 1949.

Pieper, Josef. "The Philosophical Act." In *Leisure: The Basis of Culture,* trans. Alexander Dru, 87–169. New York: Pantheon Books, 1952.

Plato. *Gorgias.* Trans. W. D. Woodhead. In *The Collected Dialogues of Plato,* ed. Edith Hamilton and Huntington Cairns, 229–307. Princeton: Princeton University Press, 1973.

———. *The Republic of Plato.* Trans. Allan Bloom. New York: Basic Books, 1968.

———. *Symposium.* Trans. Michael Joyce. In *The Collected Dialogues of Plato,* ed. Edith Hamilton and Huntington Cairns, 526–74. Princeton: Princeton University Press, 1973.

Pound, Ezra. *The Cantos of Ezra Pound.* New York: New Directions, 1972.

———. *Guide to Kulchur.* New York: New Directions, 1970.

———. "Interview: Ezra Pound." In *Their Ancient Glittering Eyes: Remembering Poets and More Poets,* by Donald Hall, 316–35. New York: Ticknor and Fields, 1992.

———. "Patria Mia." In *Selected Prose, 1909–1965,* ed. William Cookson, 99–141. New York: New Directions, 1973.

———. "Prolegomena." In *Selected Prose, 1909–1965,* ed. William Cookson, 216. New York: New Directions, 1973.

———. "A Visiting Card." In *Selected Prose, 1909–1965,* ed. William Cookson, 306–35. New York: New Directions, 1973.

Price, Geoffrey L. "Recovery from Metastatic Consciousness: Voegelin and Jeremiah." In *Politics, Order, and History: Essays on the Work of Eric Voegelin,* ed. Glenn Hughes, Stephen A. McKnight, and Geoffrey L. Price, 185–207. Sheffield, England: Sheffield Academic Press, 2001.

Quispel, Gilles. "Gnostic Man: The Doctrine of Basilides." In *The Mystic Vision: Papers from the Eranos Yearbooks,* ed. Joseph Campbell, 210–46. Bollingen Series 30, no. 6. Princeton: Princeton University Press, 1968.

Rilke, Rainer Maria. *Duino Elegies.* Trans. J. B. Leishman and Stephen Spender. New York: W. W. Norton, 1963.

———. *The Selected Poetry of Rainer Maria Rilke.* Ed. and trans. Stephen Mitchell. New York: Vintage Books, 1984.

Rorty, Richard. *Contingency, Irony, and Solidarity.* Cambridge: Cambridge University Press, 1989.

Rosenblum, Robert. *Modern Painting and the Northern Romantic Tradition: Friedrich to Rothko.* New York: Harper and Row, 1983.

Sartre, Jean-Paul. *The Words.* Trans. Bernard Frechtman. New York: George Braziller, 1964.

Scheler, Max. *Man's Place in Nature.* Trans. Hans Meyerhoff. Boston: Beacon Press, 1961.

Steiner, George. *Real Presences.* Chicago: University of Chicago Press, 1989.

Tillich, Paul. *Dynamics of Faith.* New York: Harper and Row, 1958.

Voegelin, Eric. *Anamnesis.* Ed. and trans. Gerhart Niemeyer. Notre Dame: University of Notre Dame Press, 1978.

———. *Anamnesis: Zur Theorie der Geschichte und Politik.* Munich: R. Piper, 1966.

———. *Anamnesis: On the Theory of History and Politics.* Vol. 6 of *The Collected Works of Eric Voegelin,* ed. David Walsh, trans. M. J. Hanak, based upon the abbreviated version originally trans. Gerhart Niemeyer. Columbia: University of Missouri Press, 2002.

———. *Conversations with Eric Voegelin.* Ed. R. Eric O'Connor. Thomas More Institute Papers/76. Montreal: Perry Printing, 1980.

———. *The Ecumenic Age.* Vol. 4 of *Order and History.* Vol. 17 of *The Collected Works of Eric Voegelin,* ed. Michael Franz. Columbia: University of Missouri Press, 2000.

———. *In Search of Order.* Vol. 5 of *Order and History.* Vol. 18 of *The Collected Works of Eric Voegelin,* ed. Ellis Sandoz. Columbia: University of Missouri Press, 2000.

———. *Israel and Revelation.* Vol. 1 of *Order and History.* Vol. 14 of *The Collected Works of Eric Voegelin,* ed. Maurice P. Hogan. Columbia: University of Missouri Press, 2001.

———. "Letters to Leo Strauss." In *Faith and Political Philosophy: The Correspondence between Leo Strauss and Eric Voegelin, 1934–1964,* ed. and trans. Peter Emberley and Barry Cooper. University Park: Pennsylvania State University Press, 1993.

———. *Modernity without Restraint: The Political Religions; The New Science of Politics; and Science, Politics, and Gnosticism.* Vol. 5 of *The Collected Works of Eric Voegelin,* ed. Manfred Henningsen. Columbia: University of Missouri Press, 1999.

———. *Plato and Aristotle.* Vol. 3 of *Order and History.* Vol. 16 of *The Collected Works of Eric Voegelin,* ed. Dante Germino. Columbia: University of Missouri Press, 1999.

———. *Published Essays, 1966–1985.* Vol. 12 of *The Collected Works of Eric Voegelin,* ed. Ellis Sandoz. Baton Rouge: Louisiana State University Press, 1990.

———. *Revolution and the New Science.* Vol. 6 of *History of Political Ideas.* Vol. 24 of *The Collected Works of Eric Voegelin,* ed. Barry Cooper. Columbia: University of Missouri Press, 1999.

———. *What Is History? And Other Late Unpublished Writings.* Vol. 28 of *The Collected Works of Eric Voegelin,* ed. Thomas A. Hollweck and Paul Caringella. Baton Rouge: Louisiana State University Press, 1990.

———. *The World of the Polis.* Vol. 2 of *Order and History.* Vol. 15 of *The Collected Works of Eric Voegelin,* ed. Athanasios Moulakis. Columbia: University of Missouri Press, 2000.

Walsh, David. *Guarded by Mystery: Meaning in a Postmodern Age.* Washington, D.C.: Catholic University Press of America, 1999.

Watson, Burton. *Chinese Lyricism: Shih Poetry from the Second to the Twelfth Century.* New York: Columbia University Press, 1971.

Webb, Eugene. *The Dark Dove: The Sacred and Secular in Modern Literature.* Seattle: University of Washington Press, 1975.

Wenders, Wim. *Emotion Pictures: Reflections on the Cinema.* Trans. Sean Whiteside in association with Michael Hofmann. London: Faber and Faber, 1989.

———. *The Logic of Images: Essays and Conversations.* Trans. Michael Hofmann. London: Faber and Faber, 1992.

Yeats, William Butler. *The Collected Poems of W. B. Yeats.* Ed. Richard J. Finneran. Rev. 2d ed. New York: Simon and Schuster, 1996.

Zaehner, R. C. *Hinduism.* Galaxy Book ed. New York: Oxford University Press, 1966.

———. *Mysticism Sacred and Profane.* Oxford: Oxford University Press, 1961.

Zimmer, Heinrich. *Myths and Symbols in Indian Art and Civilization.* Ed. Joseph Campbell. Bollingen Series 6. New York: Pantheon Books, 1946.

Index

Permissions

A NUMBER of chapters in this book were developed from essays that have previously appeared elsewhere. The final section of the Introduction and Chapter 1, "The Problem of Transcendence," have been expanded from "The Drama of Living, and Lonergan's Retrieval of Transcendence," which first appeared in *Lonergan Workshop, Volume 10: The Legacy of Lonergan,* ed. Fred Lawrence (1994); and Chapter 5, "Cosmopolis, Culture, and Art," was adapted from "Images, Art, and Cosmopolis," in *Lonergan Workshop, Volume 11: Language of the Heart: Lonergan, Images, and Feelings,* ed. Fred Lawrence (1995). Both appear here by gracious permission of the editor. Chapter 2, "The Terror of History," appeared in an earlier version as "Reflections on the Terror of History," in *Jesus Crucified and Risen: Essays in Spirituality and Theology in Honor of Dom Sebastian Moore,* ed. William P. Loewe and Vernon J. Gregson (Collegeville, Minn.: Liturgical Press, 1998); it is reprinted here by permission of the publisher. Chapters 3 and 4, "History and Transcendence" and "Deformations of History," are together an expanded version of "The Line That Runs from Time into Eternity: Transcendence and History in *The Ecumenic Age,*" which first appeared in the *Political Science Reviewer* 27 (1998), and is reprinted here with kind permission of the journal. Chapter 6, "Ezra Pound and the Balance of Consciousness," first appeared in an earlier, somewhat different version as "Eric Voegelin, Ezra Pound, and the Balance of Consciousness," in the *Modern Schoolman* 75:1 (November 1997); it is reprinted here with the permission of the journal.

Permission to cite material from the works of Bernard Lonergan has been graciously granted by the Trustees of the Lonergan Estate.

Permission to quote at length from a number of works of Eric Voegelin has been granted by the University of Missouri Press, including: *The Collected Works of Eric Voegelin, Volume 6, Anamnesis: On the Theory of History and Politics,* ed. David Walsh (2002); *The Collected Works of Eric Voegelin, Volume 12, Published Essays, 1966–1985,* ed. Ellis Sandoz (1990); *The Collected Works of Eric Voegelin, Volume 14, Order and History, Volume I, Israel and Revelation,* ed. Maurice P. Hogan (2001); *The Collected Works of Eric Voegelin, Volume 17, Order and History, Volume IV, The Ecumenic Age,* ed. Michael Franz (2000); *The Collected Works of Eric Voegelin, Volume 18, Order and History, Volume V, In Search of Order,* ed. Ellis Sandoz (2000); and *The Collected Works of Eric Voegelin, Volume 28, What Is History? And Other Late Unpublished Writings,* ed. Thomas A. Hollweck and Paul Caringella (1990).

Excerpts from Cantos 3, 13, 51, 53, 54, 74, 81, 91, 99, 110, 116, and 117 by Ezra Pound, from *The Cantos of Ezra Pound,* copyright © 1934, 1937, 1940, 1948, 1956, 1959, 1962, 1963, 1966, and 1968 by Ezra Pound, are used by permission of New Directions Publishing Corporation.

Excerpts from "Burnt Norton" from *Four Quartets,* by T. S. Eliot, copyright 1936 by Harcourt, Inc., and renewed 1964 by T. S. Eliot, reprinted by permission of the publisher and Faber & Faber, Ltd., London, UK. Excerpt from "The Dry Salvages," in *Four Quartets,* copyright 1941 by T. S. Eliot and renewed 1969 by Esme Valerie Eliot, reprinted by permission of Harcourt, Inc., and Faber & Faber, Ltd., London, UK. Excerpt from "Little Gidding," in *Four Quartets,* copyright 1942 by T. S. Eliot and renewed 1970 by Esme Valerie Eliot, reprinted by permission of Harcourt, Inc., and Faber & Faber, Ltd., London, UK.

"Politics," by W. B. Yeats, from *The Collected Works of W. B. Yeats, Volume 1, The Poems, Revised,* ed. Richard J. Finneran, is reprinted with the permission of Scribner, an imprint of Simon and Schuster Adult Publishing Group, copyright © 1940 by Georgie Yeats; copyright renewed © 1968 by Bertha Georgie Yeats, Michael Butler Yeats, and Anne Yeats; and by permission of A. P. Watt Ltd. on behalf of Michael B. Yeats.

Excerpts from *Waiting for Godot* and *Endgame,* by Samuel Beckett, are used by permission of Grove Press.

"Elegy 9," from *The Selected Poetry of Rainer Maria Rilke,* by Rainer Maria Rilke, trans. Stephen Mitchell, copyright © 1982 by Stephen Mitchell, is used by permission of Random House, Inc.

Excerpts from *The Kabir Book,* trans. Robert Bly, are used by permission of Beacon Press.

Excerpts from the *Masnavi* of Rumi, trans. Franklin D. Lewis, in *Rumi—Past and Present, East and West: The Life, Teachings, and Poetry of Jalâl al-Din Rumi,* by Franklin D. Lewis, copyright © 2000 by Franklin D. Lewis, are used by permission of the author and Oneworld Publications, Oxford.

Lines from pages 1 and 25 [16 ll.] from *Tao Te Ching by Lao Tzu, A New English Version, with Foreword and Notes,* by Stephen Mitchell, trans. copyright © 1988 by Stephen Mitchell, reprinted by permission of HarperCollins Publishers Inc. and Macmillan, London, UK.

Glenn Hughes is Professor Emeritus of Philosophy at St. Mary's University in San Antonio, Texas. He is the author of *A More Beautiful Question: The Spiritual in Poetry and Art*, published by the University of Missouri Press, and the editor of three volumes, including *The Voegelin Reader* (co-edited with Charles R. Embry).